MEDIA AND COMMUNICATIONS IN THE THIRD WORLD

Media and Communications in the Third World

Edited by

ZAHID HUSSAIN
VANITA RAY

In Association with

ACADEMY OF THIRD WORLD STUDIES
NEW DELHI

KANISHKA PUBLISHERS, DISTRIBUTORS
NEW DELHI-110 002

KANISHKA PUBLISHERS, DISTRIBUTORS
4697/5-21 A, Ansari Road, Daryaganj
New Delhi-110 002
Phones : 2327 0497, 2328 8285
Fax : 011-2328 8285
E-mail : kanishka_publishing@yahoo.co.in

Media and Communications in the Third World

First Published–2000

Edition–2007

PRINTED IN INDIA

Published by Madan Sachdeva for Kanishka Publishers, Distributors, 4697/5-21A, Ansari Road, Daryaganj, New Delhi-110 002, Typeset by Sunshine Graphics, Delhi, and Printed at Nice Printing Press, Delhi.

Preface

The present volume is a follow-up of the discussions held in a Seminar titled *"Media and Communications in the Third World"* organized by the Academy of Third World Studies, Jamia Millia Islamia. Papers presented at the Seminar have been revised and edited in the perspective of the unprecedented impact of globalisation and the revolutionary advances in information and communications technologies of the last two decades that have set the trends for the new Millennium. The articles address the significant and far-reaching impact of these developments, particularly in the developing countries of the Third World, a large majority of which remain outside the realms of the progress and benefits that devolve from it.

Thanks are due to all the contributors for their wholehearted cooperation in this venture and to all colleagues in the Academy for their help in organising the Seminar. I particularly acknowledge the unstinted help, encouragement and assistance of Prof. Z.H. Zaidi, the Director of the Academy.

VANITA RAY

Contents

SECTION III
Religion, State and Media

SECTION IV
Social Impact of Media

Introduction

—*Vanita Ray*

In the era of fast globalisation the rapidly changing field of information, communications and technology, which is the dominant theme in the intellectual and political discourse of the last several decades, is one of the most outstanding developments of the past century. It has radically altered the politico-economic scenario. National territorial frontiers hold little relevance in many spheres, which have affected peoples and societies the world over. But it is the Third World societies that have undergone extensive and widespread changes arising from the growth and expansion of the modern communications systems—the production, distribution and management of technologies, and cultural resources ranging from books, journals, films and television programmes. These means were originally developed not as mere vehicles of mass communication but also in relation to specific national markets and processes of capitalist accumulation and centralisation. The emergence of satellite broadcasting and the growth of transborder data flows had indeed opened to these societies the avenues for increasing information and communication opportunities. But the reliance on the technological sophistication of the Western industrial world and their data banks and information technology hardware does tend to globally reproduce the old colonial patterns of dependence and domination in the economic, political and cultural senses. Several writers support this hypothesis.[1] Besides, since the development of the Press, the radio and the electronic media in these parts of the world was essentially geared to the political and economic policies of colonialism, the expansion of capitalism, the organization of economically productive activities on a global scale and the extension of its information and communication structures, Third World underdeveloped countries had no option than to depend on their technologically more advanced former metropoles and other Western industrialised countries. Third World countries in the post-independence phase also had more urgent developmental priorities on their hands and were anyhow in no position to engage in any competitive communications development or advanced technology. Resultantly, they soon became as on writer states, the users of the "end products of technology,"[2] the receivers of the world views of others. And this is the running theme through the entire length and breadth of the Third World extending from Asia, through Africa and Latin America resulting in widespread dependence—political, economic and cultural.

The Western countries, on the other hand, through what they term as "free flow of information" have managed to politically, economically and culturally penetrate and subordinate Third World countries' values and also bring them within the purview of the global capitalist economy. The overall result is not only a communications hegemony but also a cultural imperialism by the Western industrialised world. Media imperialism, according to Boyd Barrett, the first to formulate the media imperialism thesis, is "a process whereby the ownership, structure, distribution or content of the media in any one country are singly or together subject to substantial pressure from the media interests of any other country or countries without proportionate reciprocation of influence by the country so affected."[3] It is thus either a product of expanding influence as part of a deliberate commercial or political strategy or else disseminated unintentionally and without clear direction such as during the period of European colonialism in Asia and Africa. Countries such as the United States, Britain, France, Germany and now increasingly Japan, that have developed sophisticated modes of mass communication, not only account for the bulk of the information software (television films, records compact discs, audio cassettes, books, magazines, newspapers, video and educational materials) but also control advertising through the multinational corporations. These countries and their agencies exercise unchallenged dominance in scientific and technological research as well as music and entertainment packages—most of which are beyond the means of the dependent societies, their levels of economic development hardly enabling indigenous production because of the prohibitive costs. These societies thus rely on information from the more advanced countries. This in fact has been the bane of information and communications expansion and extension in the Third World often resulting in subverting and destroying the local code of ethics and values in favour of those of the dominant industrialised economies.

Cultural-ideological domination through media and mass communication also implies for its victims economic dependence and underdevelopment. In this sphere, the role of the ruling elite in the developing world has been crucial. Safeguarding their own privileged position and status in the State and society they have gone all along with the international mainstream media to promote and propagate the myths and images that emerge from the capitalist world. At the same time their own social issues and problems are substantially tempered by the intellectual and ideological frameworks and perceptions set in place by the industrialised world centres. In this way the developing countries' ruling classes have remained under the hegemonic control of the industrial-capitalist world which in turn ensures that the Third World ruling elite continue to rule the region to ensure their own global hegemony.

Scope of the Study

The present volume is an attempt to examine in greater detail/ depth the foregoing and related issues regarding the new information and communications technologies—especially its impact on Third World State and society. The task undoubtedly is difficult since the new information and communications technologies are integrated into unified and interconnected networks which have radically altered society and its life patterns. But contributors to the volume have ably come upto the task; they look at the extent of media and communications development in the Third World and have analyzed its bearing and repercussions on these societies. The extent of media development in the Third World is the theme of Section I. Section II analyzes the issue of freedom of information and of political control. Media and communications' impact on religion and State is covered in Section III, while Section IV looks at the social implications. The final Section V reviews the global impact and ramifications.

Section I

Section I traces the extent and range of media development in the Third World—the emerging trends of the twenty-first century, including media manipulation, developments and their implications in the countries of East Asia and Africa, and finally a review of the Arab attempts of journalism. In the first article, J.S. Yadava dwells on the trends for the 21st Century in the perspective of the revolutionary changes ushered in by the new communications technologies of the recent decades. He discusses the implications of the "Information Superhighways" which would produce a fundamental shift in life patterns, transforming everything from work to education, to culture or even the government of the day. These emerging directions, Yadava believes, would infact usher in a whole new brave world in the very immediate future and the most important development of twenty-first century.

A note of caution is sounded in the second article by Pradeep Mathur. He warns of increasing media manipulation by the scientifically more advanced industrial Western countries—the main source of news and information. The quantitative and qualitative imbalances of news and information flows between the developed and the poor countries, he explains to the nature of the historical relationship between the two since the colonial period. Overall, the communications resources are improperly distributed and advanced communications technologies are mostly in the hands of the developed world. The need of the hour for the Third World countries, especially India, is to make concerted efforts to become players rather than remain on the sidelines as mere spectators.

Articles 3 and 4 in this Section trace the reach and spread of media and communications in regional context. While Shri Prakash discusses the issue of media development in East Asia, and Vanita Ray analyzes its impact on society and development in Africa. With the help of empirical data both writers have analyzed the trends of growth and its ramifications in the respective regions.

Shri Prakash controverts the "global generalizations about society's encounters with media and *vice versa*." In East Asia, he says, the media forms a part of a larger system and functions within identifiable civilizational economic and political structures in different countries. In the single party Communist ruled states of China and Vietnam, or even those having elite consensus—Korea and Japan—media is a one way street without enough room for innovation, criticism, diversification and internationalisation. In other countries such as Taiwan, Japan and South Korea, where there is privatisation and multi-ownership of mass media, there is scope for diversification and space to grow and expand. But there is very little transborber interaction as also limited inward traffic from outside—the region remaining outside the scope of globalisational impacts.

Vanita Ray evaluates the impact of media and communications development on the African continent assessing its crucial bearing on society, culture and politico-national developments. In the perspective of communications and its network growth, she examines the impact of access of international information and of western media imperialism that has created its own distinct repercussions between the haves and the havenots. However, it is the broad transformation across board of society and social relations that is the most important having its own positive and negative implications. The distinctive features that emerge from Ray's study are that media and communications development have a far ranging and diverse impact on African countries both in respect of the availability of the number of receivers and the systems of networking, development of human capital and the widening of its horizons and the overall impact on the politico-economic developmental status of these countries. Secondly, the imbalances in media development and diffusion of its products, as also the nature of African society, having widely differing levels of economic growth, has enabled a techno-economic and socio-cultural hegemony of the West on the continent. But the principal point that emerges is that notwithstanding the earlier economic hegemony which affected every sector of the media and communications networks, it is the socio-cultural hegemonic control and sociological upheavals it has wrought on society which are dramatic and which threaten the processes of development.

The fifth paper in the section, by Asad Rizvi, reviews the Arab attempts at journalism—attempts that evolved and developed its own distinct version that made it a permanent feature of its social, political and cultural reality. Rizvi's paper identifies and examines the basic characteristics and factors through its evolution—factors that shaped its unique nature that reflects its complex history, the history of an institution struggling to assimilate in a society reluctant to relinquish its traditional conventions.

Section II

Freedom of information and repercussions of political control is the theme addressed in this Section. Four papers examine the issue in their own respective analysis. Prof. Moegiadi speaks of UNESCO's commitment to the free flow of information. Dwelling on the role of the media in the fast changing global scenario, Moegiadi emphasizes the need for freedom of expression, the promotion of an independent and pluralistic media, educational and cultural freedom and the need for the preservation of media diversity as a prerequisite to the advancement of societies.

Ajit Bhattacharjea in a Keynote Paper, devoted to the theme of the volume, critically analyses in depth the role of the media in this age of globalization and global market forces. He stresses the need for media freedom but emphasizes social responsibility and the promotion of a culture of self regulation as a prerequisite to this freedom.

The viccissitudes that confront media freedom in Pakistan and how these are reflected in the socio-political conditions of peoples under most authoritarian and civil military regimes is the focus of Sushant Sareen's paper. He reviews the country's media developments in historical perspective and compares it with those of other developing countries. Sareen concludes that despite the travails and tribulations confronting the print media in Pakistan, it has retained its dynamism and vibrancy.

Chapter 9 by S. Prasad reviews the evolution of censorship and the growth of the media as an instrument of power. He has based his hypothesis on episodes from the Emergency.

Section III

This Section carries five papers; four essays collectively discuss the nature of media in the perspective of religious influences on society. The fifth theoretically evaluates the nature of the Indian State and media and communications development.

The first paper by Upendra Vajpeyi, discusses the multi-dimensional nature of both media and religion. Even while their objectives and functions are independent of each other, he believes, they do converge at several points. He analyzes the different dimensions of this alliance and is critical of media's role in fomenting social disorder, laying emphasis on the need to study its collusion with religion's repulsive fervour.

In the following two papers by Subir Ghosh and Shohini Ghosh, the focus is the communal polarization of media in the nineties. Subir Ghosh looks at media's role in the post-Ayodhya scenario in the backdrop of India's rich and composite culture exemplified by its music, arts, architecture, literature and even religion. In such a situation when communalism is not a religious but a political phenomenon, Subir Ghosh underscores the need for a balanced and discretionary evaluation of all inflammable incidents and for objective reporting. In a similar vein, Shohini Ghosh analyzes media's role in communalizing art and culture with reference to the writings and the Hindu Right's role against artist Hussain's work. In this context, Sohini has analyzed in-depth several writings and incidents that were deliberate and intended to deride the artist's work. Given such a scenario, she suggests the need for intervention by the secular and democratic polity to silence the claims of majoritarian privileges.

Religion and the film media is the subject matter of Khan Afridi's paper. He discusses the impact of old traditions and religious sentiments on the Indian psyche and the role of the film media in projecting the evaluation of the secular character of the nation.

The nature of the Indian State and the role of media and communications in the present globalized context is evaluated by S.N. Malakar. He traces the historicity of the changes in the State structure and the media within the context of its socio-political linkages. And it is through these latter linkages, he concludes, that the State and media have managed to sideline the country's masses from the real issues of society and relevant social developments.

Section IV

The impact of media and communications on Third World society and its peoples—an area where its effects have been most significant—is the theme of this Section. All five contributions analyze one or the other aspect, be it of the electronic media, that on education or health issues.

Regina Mulay Parakh makes a comparative analysis of the development of the electronic media in the region of South Asia, giving a new dimension to the possibility for exchange of ideas and information. She also analyzes its role in the building of a "third culture"—the creation of a mass culture—in the region resulting in significant value changes.

In Chapter 16 Rajeev Bhatnagar analyzes the same theme of the impact of the electronic media on society. He reflects on the content of the modern day Indian television programmes and expresses his disapproval at the abundance of sex, violence, vulgar dreams, vulgar literature etc., that is regularly aired. This offensive onslaught on

India's rich cultural heritage for that of the West, he warns, has already had its impact making man a slave to it.

The last article in the Section by Wajahat Alam, also examines the specific nature of media impact on Indian society. The author questions the role of the print media in the hands of the capitalists; it lacks a solid democratic foundation and has failed to reflect the socio-economic realities of society. It instead has political leanings and is close to the government. Given such a scenario, Alam calls for an alternative media policy which would safeguard it from Western domination and help it acquire an independent identity.

Media and communications' usefulness to education is highlighted by Mohd. Miyan. He presents the exciting possibilities of developing media and telecommunications capacity to deliver education in a variety of new ways. Telecommunications has taken education beyond the realms of the classroom, the skills of specialised educators can now be made available to millions and small communities and remote areas far from the sophisticated centres of learning can also now have access to excellent education. These educational technology developments, say Mohd. Miyan, would certainly enable in the future a more meaningful fusion between accumulated human knowledge and wisdom.

Finally, Anjali Gandhi and Niti Malhotra deliberate the seriousness of HIV/AIDS as an important health and social problem. The authors highlight media's—radio, television and the Press—significant role in making people aware of the seriousness of the disease, but it is always, they maintain, with an eye to sensationalize by emphasizing the rare and the bizarre ways that HIV can be transmitted. Nevertheless, media's role in bringing the issue to public attention is noteworthy and must be lauded.

Section V

The subject of discussion of this final Section is appropriately that of the global impact and implications of media and communications. Biswajit Das analyzes the global impact of media in the Third World in its diverse contexts. He addresses problems of integration and rationalisation of the communications sector through the process of globalisation of India. This is undertaken by an analysis at two distinct levels—firstly looking at India's problems within the larger perspective of the Third World and secondly by reviewing the internal difficulties that confront the country as a result of globalisation.

The second paper in this Section, by Moinuddin and Beg, evaluates the growth of telecommunications infrastructures and its impact on the Indian economy. The authors present projections for the period 1996-2000 to upgrade the rural networks and harness new communications technologies that would enable a better quality of life for its people.

The final paper is a critical study of media and the environment. Sabiha Alam discusses the role of the media on environment concerns by moving from the realms of scientific and academic discourse to public policy issues. She highlights the anomalies of environment development issues *via-a-vis* the media, the role of the media in international negotiations and the emergence of environmental journalism in India.

Overall, contributors have comprehensively analyzed the issue of media and communications development in the Third World reflecting on the various implications and ramifications. Several perspectives emerge—the most notable being the need to evolve an integrated balance between the more advanced technologies and indigenous traditional systems of information and communications. The need for a more vibrant media in the Third World, insulated from its historically rooted structural dependence on the advanced industrial countries of the G-8, remains underscored through the entire volume. The present communications order, replicating the over-arching global hierarchy of power and authority, is neither conducive to universal justice within the existing global order, nor its transition towards it. As an appendage of power and domination within the inequitable global order, Third World media remains its potent instrument. The liberation of this media from the structure of global oppression remains underscored through this volume as contributing towards global justice and Third World liberation.

References

1. Juan Rada (1981): "The Microelectronic Revolution: Implications for the Third World," *Development Dialogue*, Vol. 2, 41-67; Raphael Kaplinsky (1982): "Trade in Technology—Who, What, Where and When?" Paper presented at International Workshop on Facilitating Indigenous Technological Capability, University of Edinburgh and Cees Hamelink (1983), *Cultural Autonomy in Global Communications*, New York, Longmans.
2. Cees Hamelink (1983): *Cultural Autonomy in Global Communications*, New York, Longmans, p. 18.
3. Oliver Boyd-Barrett (1977): "Media Imperialism: Towards an International Framework for the Analysis of Media System" in James Curran, Michael Gurevitch and Janet Woolacott (Eds.), *Mass Communication and Society*, London, Edward Arnold, Chapter 5.

Section I

Extent of Media Development in Third World

1

Mass Communications: Trends in Twenty-first Century

*J.S. Yadava**

> Radio waves never respect frontiers, and from an altitude of 36,000 kilometres, national boundaries become singularly inconspicuous. The world of the future will be an open world.
>
> *Arthur C. Clarke*

Winds of change now sweeping across much of the world are paving the way for an open world environment. Today, the advances that man has made in the area of communication technologies is so fundamentally transforming organized human life that many social scientists speak of the dawn of a new era—the *Information Age*.

With the twenty-first century knocking at our door, media has assumed significance which it had never witnessed before. Starting as an institutionalized approach to generate awareness and inform the masses, media has become instrumental in governing our lives. Rather than a form of cultural expression, it has a culture of its own. It was supposed to report on the way of life of people, it has now become a way of life itself. Moreover, it is one of the most important industries of our time.

* Dr. Yadava is Director, Indian Institute of Mass Communication, New Delhi.

Many societies are already changing from being advanced industrial societies to 'information societies' in which computer, technologies, their networks and other enhanced forms of interpersonal and institutional communication are a major force. Some of the Western countries have already entered into the information age. In the United States alone information activities engage more than 46 per cent work force earning over 553 per cent of labour income.

The giants of American communications are in the process of building a vast web of electronic networks "information super high ways" of fibre optics and computer networks which will deliver an abundance of services to offices and homes—video images, phone calls, enormous amount of data on various required fields by the user/customer. They promise to change the way people work and live.

The vision of a communications abundance has been possible because of sharp decline in costs. According to one estimate, the cost of microprocessors is falling by 22 per cent, computer memories' cost is down by 40 per cent and that of communication equipment by 11 per cent per annum. By the year 2000, may be even earlier, the cost of a computerized home system should be about the same as that of an automobile today, thus coming within the reach of the common man in the developed countries. The protagonists of the new communication technologies have been promising a revolution of abundance and diversity of information for all.

When we examine the characteristics of the new communication technologies one notes that they have already changed the information environment today. As a matter of fact, most of the so-called new communication technologies have been with us for the last couple of decades. What is relatively new is the convergence and integration of these technologies. Another feature of the present day situation in communications is the scale of operations which the microprocessors and the 'chips' have not only made possible but economical too. The results of these two processes, convergence and scale, are revolutionary.

The convergence of emerging telecommunication technologies and computers is transforming business operations, broadcasting, telephone systems and human interactions in general. We are on the threshold of having a high-resolution two-way video and personal computers tied to networks so that sitting at home or in office, one can receive and send information from and to anywhere in the world, and engage in a two-way video conversation across the world.

As the world shifts to a service-oriented economy, vast amounts of money, goods and services are being circulated as well. In the last few years breakthrough in satellite and high-speed computing have given leading users an overwhelming economic advantage over those who have not kept pace. Thus, the stakes in new communication technologies are high and of global dimension. Although for the foreseeable future, the responsibility, if not power, to plan and decide about communications will continue to rest with the nation-states, already many of the operations are beyond them. The result is enormous expansion and significance of multinational corporations. Through multinationals and other trade channels the advanced Western countries are pushing hard the new communication technologies in the Third World countries to maintain their economic and political interests. The 'push' is sustained by the 'pull' force for the 'latest' and the 'best' on the part of the ruling elites in the Third World countries.

Thus, in brief, there have been revolutionary changes in technologies of mass communications both challenging and providing opportunities. The new fervour for modernisation and progress through adoption of the latest communication technologies enhances the capabilities of communication at various levels, both within and outside the organization. Technologies increase the efficiency in terms of speed, spread and also in terms of books and appearances. With latest mass communication technologies you are able to multiply your messages fast enough and also reach the intended audiences quickly or even instantly. You may also produce attractive information/communication packages. But enhancement of capabilities is not necessarily an assurance for effective communication.

With this broad spectrum of changes that have taken place in communication technologies serving as a backdrop, I would focus my discussion here on one of the most important development *i.e.* "Information Superhighways" that have been formed in the closing years of the twentieth century and are likely to have enormous implications in the twenty-first century as well.

Information Superhighways

"Information Superhighways" is the new conversational buzz word. Its content and meaning is often illusive. Nonetheless it is frequently used in discussions about recent developments in communication technologies.

Different people mean different things when they speak of information superhighways. It is like the story of an elephant and the five blind men, each one looking at it from his own limited perspective. Be that as it may, there is an enormous interest and debate in recent years on the subject, especially since the American Vice-President, Al Gore made it a major policy issue of the US Administration.

A communications revolution is underway. A new "National Information Infrastructure" is rapidly moving into place—it will carry video, audio and information into offices and homes across the United States. Its emergence will produce a fundamental shift in American life, transforming everything from work to education, to government, to culture. The information superhighways or National Information Infrastructure will help stimulate US economy and help the latter maintain a competitive edge over other countries.

With digitalization and fibre optics, hitherto separate technologies and services are merging and integrating into one large interactive communications system offering consumer services, 500 channels of interactive television and the electronic marvel of cyberspace and virtual reality. Technologically speaking, all these are now within easy reach. Consequently, traditional boundaries between different communication/media related industries are becoming blurred. A struggle is on for survival and operating space between different media industries as well as among companies controlling and operating these industries and services. Earlier US regulations provided for monopoly operating rights in a particular area for assured access to its services in the given area to all citizens. The regulations laid out that if a company provides one service, say telephone, it cannot enter into another communication service, say television or newspaper industry. With the technological integration of communications industries and services the present restrictive regulations are being changed allowing merger and take over. Now telephone companies can provide other communication services also, say television, cable services and *vice versa*.

Although the Clinton Administration is committed to the National Information Infrastructure, the Administration sees the government role as confined to nurturing technologies through appropriate legislation and incentives leaving the actual creation and operation of the electronic highway to the private sector.

The biggest corporate merger in history of Bell Atlantic, serving 18 million customers and 8 lakh cellular phones, with TCI No. 1 Cable Company, with franchise in many states serving 13 million subscribers and having a powerful stake in television programming, through its ownership of Liberty Media and also partly owning Turner Broadcasting, took place in October, 1993. It is reflective of the emerging scenario of mega media conglomerates. The combined firm is worth more than the gross national products of most nations. Such a corporate giant capable of marshalling the enormous resources needed to build the electronic superhighway are pitching in for their share of pie in the promised era of abundance and prosperity both for the consumers and their shareholders.

In addition to Bell Atlantic and TCI, corporate giants like Time Warner, Paramount, Bell, South and Pacific Telesis, to mention just a few, are committing billions of dollars to today's telecommunication gold rush. This race to stake out tollbooths on the new electronic superhighway has many similarities with the California Gold Rush of 1849.

The multi-billion dollar rush to build the interactive electronic superhighway is prompted by dreams of the financial bonanza to come from home delivery of movie on demand, electronic shopping, video games, push button financial transactions and unlimited personal access to all kinds of data and information. But test results of the pilot projects in Cerritos, California and Columbus, Ohio, were not very encouraging raising doubts that even if the interactive electronic highway is in place would American people use it to the extent making the whole project economically viable. Even so, the unexpected runaway success of Internet is an example of unintended but favourable consequences. The computer network linking defence establishments is not by free market enterprise but was established by the Pentagon spending Federal taxpayers money. Ordinary civilians 'discovered' Internet and started using it by connecting their phone, modem and personal computers, transmitting and sharing all sorts of information—personal, scientific, political and from data banks.

Internet is now a huge electronic superhighway regularly travelled by a virtual community of millions of diverse enthusiasts throughout the nation and the world.

In brief, the information superhighway, the buzz word whose meaning is elusive, invokes a variety of images and promises a whole new brave world not in a distant future but within 5 to 10 years or even earlier. Certainly it will be a major force in the twenty-first century. In someways it is already there. It is essentially a network of networks operating and providing a variety of services.

Telephone, cable, broadcasting, newspapers, magazines, data banks, department stores, libraries and laboratories are all getting integrated through computers, fibre optics, digitalization, phone and television. Like highways in the United States (national-state)—the extensive road infrastructure in place—enables citizens to move to any place and anytime not dependent upon the public transport system and not restricted to time schedules, the electronic superhighway would enable citizens to have access to anything and everything of their choice—movies, games, books, news, bank accounts, travel agents, shopping, data bank, friends, relatives, peer-groups and interest groups—and at a time of their choice without stirring out of the comfort of their homes with just a flick of a button of their remote control and computer keyboard. Not only that, voice activated signals may do away with all this trouble of pushing buttons. But like the roads one has to pay tolls as and when you are using the electronic highway for any service.

Even while it is difficult to visualize the precise nature of the unfolding communications scenario, it is certain that it is being put in place and that it would fundamentally transform American life—the way people live and work and in turn perhaps the 'life world over.' Unparalleled and unlimited human connectivity without stirring out of homes will radically transform intellectual, cultural, economic and political life. It will help in saving on transport and real estate. But what will happen to the superb highway system and the skyscraper office buildings? What implications home bound living and working will have on the already fragile family life? Would it lead to greater participation in political debate and decision-making process as is being projected? Citizens would be able to convey their views on any political agenda or legislation electronically to their representatives and hence necessitate the on-going political campaign all the time. In a way the citizen would take the power to make legislation into his or her own hands. They would not need to wait till election time to express views and show preference on any aspect of public life.

Already there is widespread controversy about legislations redefining the rule and norms governing the different aspects of information superhighways. Concerns are being expressed that the Information Superhighway, if left completely to market forces, will by-pass the poor and minorities. So the public good and making access to all affordable needs is to be ensured by the Federal Government through appropriate legislative safeguards. Whatever may be the precise pattern of the emerging information superhighway, it will provide the US enormous competitive edge in international economic and political relations. Developing countries like India need to take urgent steps to anticipate its full implications and use the inevitable emergence and availability of technologies for its benefits and to address some of its major problems of illiteracy, poverty and health service in our own economic, social and cultural context. Technologies do promise workable and affordable solutions to our problems.

Conclusion

Global television is likely to facilitate greater decentralization and participatory democratic functioning in India. Further, if accepted as a challenge in the right spirit, it would stimulate greater creativity for better and more relevant television production and programming contributing to cultural resurgence and giving a boost to economic activities. The growing importance of satellite based electronic media which is making global television an increasing reality today, needs to be properly appreciated as it opens up enormous new vistas for marketing goods and services regionally and globally. India certainly can emerge soon as a major player in global television and hence also as an economic market place. Similarly the information superhighway, or in common parlance Internet, etc., would come handy in greater spread in terms of reach and access of a variety of relevant and useful information to different regions, sections and segments of Indian society, thereby ushering in a communications revolution and the dawn of an information age which hopefully will demolish the present hierarchy of social structure leading to a more egalitarian society.

2

Media Manipulation and Third World: The Indian Perspective

*Pradeep Mathur**

The new information technology has made the whole communication process easy and economical. It has also opened floodgates of knowledge for all through devices like the *Internet*. Since the technology is freely available to the developing countries, they are getting an exposure to new ways as never before. However, this ready access to new information technology has not changed the basic fact that the developed countries of the world control, direct and manage the flood of information and manipulate media for their strategic and commercial interests to the detriment of the developing world.

This paper attempts to study this phenomenon in the context of the struggle by the Developing Countries, particularly India, to fight poverty and economic imbalance and to give themselves a new information order that would reverse the one-sided flow of information. The battle is tough, the developing countries have to fight with their backs against the wall.

* Dr. Mathur is a senior Faculty member of the Indian Institute of Mass Communication, New Delhi.

We live in an information age which is witnessing an explosion of knowledge, brought about by the new technology based essentially on satellite communications, optical fibre transmission and computer calculations. Known as the information technology, it has obliterated the boundaries of sovereign states and made the world a global village—a concept that was fancied by communication scientists about a quarter century ago. Information technology has made our lives far more organised and comfortable. No doubt this technology is also of great advantage to the developing countries of the Third World. However, they are not players, but only viewers in the global game of media manipulation that is being played by the developed countries through the new technology. Therefore, there is need to know how media is manipulated to their disadvantage by the developed world.

Before we go into studying this question, there is need to have a look at the background of the situation which made this world a grossly imbalanced world. The realisation about this came after the end of the Second World War (1939-1946) which also saw the end of the era of colonialism.

Even 50 years after the international efforts for reconstruction of the former colonies, the Third World remains poor and backward. Imbalances are still great in this region. Countries in the Gulf, Horn of Africa, Latin America, sub-Saharan Africa and South Asia continue to be steeped in poverty. The last 25 years have seen a steady decline in the growth of Third World countries' trade. From a meagre 1.5 per cent in 1980, it reached zero per cent in 1981, meaning thereby that the nations of the Third World made practically no contribution to world trade. On the other hand, the private capital flows to the Third World have been increasing steadily which means that the nations here are being forced to depend more and more on commercial loans which carry a high rate of interest. The interest rate rose from 40 per cent in 1970 to 65 per cent in 1980 and to 75 per cent in 1998. There is little doubt that the MNCs are making deep inroads in the economies of the developing countries leading them to a virtual state of pauperisation.

Some of the striking facts of the world economy in relation to the Third World are obvious from the following four news-items which have been randomly picked up from an American news weekly.

They pertain to the non G-7 world.

- On this day of August 4, Polish farmers blocked 250 roads and several transit points to protest extremely low grain prices, the *Berliner Zeitung* reported. Grain prices have been going down in the Central European Free Trade Zone (CEFTA), which includes Poland. Most farmers had to finance their harvests by taking loans, expecting to repay the same from the proceeds. They would be bankrupt if they cannot sell their crops.
- The grain harvest in Russia, "under the best circumstances," will be 67 million tons, compared to 88.5 million tons last year, Agriculture Minister Viktor Semyonov reported to the state Duma (Parliament) in early August, 1998.
- Israeli unemployment rose to 9.3 per cent in May, up from 8.4 per cent in January. Growth has dropped from a high of 9.5 per cent during the height of the peace process in 1994, to 1.5 per cent this year. Unemployment is the number one issue on the minds of most Israelis, the daily *Ha'aretz* reported.
- Pakistan's Finance Minister, Sartaj Aziz, told the *Wall Street Journal*, issue dated 6 August, that the International Monetary Fund has "enough casualties on their hands. They don't want another. If we get $ 3 billion, that's what we pay back out anyway—we will get no net benefit. And unless we get resources, we can't pay."
- There is a direct link between information and trade which does not look apparent. Information about a product, event, social group or country creates an image in the minds of the informed. Constant exposure to positive information will create a good image which will favourably condition the mind of the receiver of information. This will also influence his economic behaviour. This interaction of information, image and economic behaviour generates a process that can be explained by the following principle of three I's.

The striking thing about this principle is that the three angles of the triangle play a fully complementary role in the process. Income or resources generated by a good image help promote technological upgradation of the information infrastructure or system that helps in building a good image that in turn helps in promoting trade (income). The transfer of information also has a direct relationship with development. A country tends to develop faster if its information network is firmly saddled to project the resources/avenues which can earn foreign exchange. This point can be illustrated by citing the case of China whose state controlled media highlighted the areas which can be exploited for earning foreign exchange. "Right to information" as a fundamental right has thus been envisaged in the Constitution of many countries and in India, too, this legislation has gotten underway.

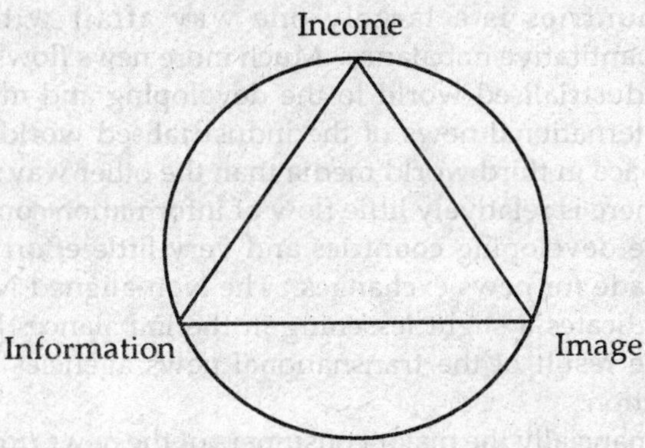

Development is the removal of poverty, the lessening of disparities between regions and classes, the building up of the technological infrastructure, modernisation of society through shedding feudalism, tribalism and superstition and the gradual achievement of economic self-reliance. Information on issues related to any of the above areas need to be transmitted for development. For an effective transmission, technological tools are required. These tools are, however, in the hands of those rich and affluent countries which have grabbed most of the available resources to become masters of the world.

There is need to understand some basic facts about the news and information scenario in the world. These are:

- The control of the international flow of news is essentially in the hands of four transnational communication enterprises with headquarters and policy control in three countries of the highly industrialised world, specifically the United States, United Kingdom and France. These are the Associated Press (AP), the United Press International (UPI), Reuters and the *Agence France Press* (AFP).

- There is a clear qualitative imbalance in the flow of news that is processed by the international news agencies. A high proportion of the news being about events or activities in the essentially Western world and consequently less about other countries particularly the developing countries.
- The flow of news between the developed and developing countries is a largely one way affair with a high quantitative imbalance. Much more news flows from the industrialised world to the developing and much more international news of the industrialised world occupies space in third world media than the other way around.
- There is relatively little flow of information coming from the developing countries and very little effort has been made for news exchanges. The Non-aligned News Pool indicates a slight lessening in the imbalances but is not the result of the transnational news agencies and their action.
- Financially the major consumers of the news provided by the agencies are in the Western countries and hence the content of their news is designed for the Western market audiences.
- There is an awareness that to some degree the home country government, private business interests and politics influence the way international news is gathered, processed and distributed.
- There are many critics, who stress the commercial or market nature of the international news agencies and they contend that this influences the news flow in ways that are detrimental not only to the Third World countries but to all countries.
- Aside from the quantitative imbalances in the international flow of news, interesting concerns are expressed over the qualitative content of the news. This includes the

importance in coverage of certain subjects that are of essential interest to the developed world but of little interest or even damaging to much of the rest of the world. It also includes the absence of news of interest from Third World countries to other Third World countries and positive news items on economic and social development matters.

The emergence of the Non-aligned Movement in an institutional form at the First Summit Conference at Belgrade, 1960 was an attempt to checkmate the big powers which had monopolised information and were regulating its flow. NAM opposed this information system wherein the developed countries, belonging to the two power blocs, were at the transmitting end while the Third World was at the receiving. It attempted to evolve an information system wherein the demands and aspirations of the Third World countries could be properly projected. The Fourth Non-Aligned Summit at Algiers in 1973, first mooted the idea of a new international information order which would correct the information flows imbalance. The concept was further elaborated at the Conference of Foreign Ministers of Non-aligned Countries in Lima in 1975, and in a Symposium of Non-aligned countries on Information in Tunis 1976, NAM reiterated the point that the information flow in the world displayed a disequilibrium and called for a decentralisation of information. Finally, a breakthrough was made the same year when the Fifth Non-aligned Summit in Colombo decided to set up a Non-aligned News Agency Pool to regulate and enhance flow of information among Non-aligned countries.

The Non-aligned News Agency Pool proved a successful venture since it ensured smooth flow of information among NAM countries. However, with the coming to an end of the Cold War NAM suffered a setback and the News Agency Pool followed suit. During subsequent years, the gradually weakened position of USSR disturbed the balance of power in the world consequently leading to the weakening of the NAM and the NAM News Agency Pool.

The disintegration of USSR in 1991 converted the bipolar world into a unipolar one, US now became the only master. While NAM was making efforts to evolve an information network for the benefit of Third World countries, organisations like the UN

General Assembly and UNESCO were instrumental in developing a broad-based information system known as the New World Information and Communications Order (NWICO). It was again in the same year, when the NAM News Agency Pool was formed, that the NWICO came into existence following the Declaration on the Contribution of Mass Media at the Nairobi Conference.

The Nairobi Conference also led to the setting up of the International Commission for the study of communication problems by the UNESCO Director General Mac Bride. The Mac Bride Commission in its report titled *Many Voices, One World* made eighty-two recommendations pertaining to different areas of communication development. Following this, the UNESCO General Conference approved comprehensive guidelines for NWICO in 1980.

Though efforts have been made under the banner of the NWICO to remove imbalances in the flow of information at the international level, Third World countries continue to receive inadequate and improper information. It is an accepted fact that 80 per cent of information flows from the developed countries to the developing constitute news of political crises, natural calamities and other distress stories. Communication resources are improperly distributed in the developing and the developed countries, and advanced communication technologies are mostly in the hands of the developed countries.

Conclusion

A country can insulate itself from the technological advances in the world only at its own peril. Neither can the technological advances be rolled back. The developing countries also cannot wish away the fact that the G-7 countries have made a head-start in the use of new technology which they naturally exploit to further their interest. What then should the developing countries do in this situation? Or to be precise what should India do?

The first thing is to go for this new technology in a big way. This is necessary to get into a position of controlling the information system and the media. But this has to be taken up as a subject of high priority and national concern. The important thing is that the developing world, especially big countries like India, should be players and not mere spectators in the global information scenario. They have to be in the position of software exporters and not mere importers. Only this will reverse the one sided flow and give them a chance to improve their image.

To come to the position of a player calls for concerted efforts in which all creative, intellectual and material sources of a society will have to be deployed. The United States is the most advanced country of the world and the biggest exporter of armaments and sophisticated technology. Yet 40 per cent of its total earnings are from software exports or the culture industry as it is called. India being extremely rich in culture, it could do much better in this field. The economically exploited countries of the developing world do not seem to be understanding their basic economics well. Often India's economic interests get compromised because of our inability to understand the intricacies of international trade. This shortcoming has to be removed to obtain an even playing field with the developed world. But the main need of the hour is the inculcation of a scientific temperament among the people of our country. It is only the scientific temper of the masses that will give them the creativity to be leaders and not followers in the field of technology and its offshoots which control modern day life.

3

Media Development and Communications in East Asia: Limits of the Globalization Process

*Shri Prakash**

It is difficult to think of the progressive spread of old media, print media, radio, television, films, new media—video cassettes, compact discs, World Wide Web (internet) on personal computers—and Communications—telephones, ordinary, mobile, cellular, satellite uplinking, digital technology, fibre optic cables—without at the same time considering their impact on a country's domestic economic development, cultural perceptions and practices and social as well as political behaviour. While it is valid to make global generalizations about society's encounters with Media and *vice versa* these become meaningful only in the context of ground level situations created by the simultaneous actions of a multitude of factors, which include state regulation, cultural discreteness and distinction, separate nationalisms, linguistic affinities and religious groupism. These are the features that militate against any simple-minded theory about Media development imposing homogenous uniformities on unwilling populations. Government control, elite consensus and public regulation all play a role in building alignments between Media and business, state and society. In East Asia, as elsewhere, the

* Dr. Shri Prakash is Professor in the Academy of Third World Studies, Jamia Millia Islamia, New Delhi.

Media forms a part of a larger system and functions within identifiable civilizational, economic and political structures which it helps to sustain, mould and perhaps change at the same time. Its ability to perform any one of these three functions to a larger or lesser degree is dependent on the specific situation in separate countries relating to the resources at the disposal of the Media and the freedom enjoyed by it to function according to recognized professional standards.

At a fundamental level the development and depth of Media in any country by now forms an integral part of the very criteria by which to assess development even while media growth is a direct result of the strength of the development process itself. **Table 3.1** shows clearly that the availability of daily newspapers and access to televisions are on an average five to nine times greater in the developed countries than is the case in the developing countries.

Table 3.1
Numbers of Daily Newspapers and Televisions
(per 100 people—in selected countries)

	Daily Newspapers		*Televisions*	
	1992	*1994*	*1992*	*1994*
Avg. for Industrial Country	29	27	53	50
Avg. for Developing Countries	1	4	6	14
USA	24	23	82	78
Japan	58	58	61	62
China	1	2	3	23
India	3	3	4	6
South Korea	41	40	21	32
Vietnam	1	1	4	2
Malaysia	12	14	15	23
Singapore	34	36	38	38

Human Development Report, 1995, pp. 158-59, 1997, pp. 164-65.

The hardware of Media and Communications by itself only ensures basic social development like improved literacy levels, greater spread effect of information and news, wider preference for sports and entertainment and not the least of a greater familiarization with one's national or group culture even while interacting with foreign, mainly American or European media productions and products. An expansion of the number of choices available in different spheres of life and society is thus an unexceptionable result of media development. To the extent this actually happens and the Media can function freely, it exerts a pressure for greater democratization within any system. To the extent that the Media and Communications system in any country is tightly controlled either by the government as in one party Communist ruled states or even by elite consensus as in South Korea and Japan, Media is a one way street with not enough room for innovation, criticism, diversification and internationalization. Considered in terms of these criteria the Media in East Asia is very much a part of the nation state-society continuum existing within direct or indirect limits and controls to a much greater degree than is the case in South Asia generally and India particularly. In terms of the spread and depth of the Media and Communications system there can be no doubt that the East Asian region is characterized by a highly uneven development of infrastructural facilities. On the one hand Japan has the highest availability of newspapers per 100 persons in the World, almost twice that of USA. In the matter of access to television also, Japan ranks higher than the global average for the industrial countries although lower than that for USA (cf. Table 3.1). South Korea ranks next to Japan, not being very far behind. However, China and Vietnam are in a different category being much lower down the order. Even in 1994, China had just two newspapers per 100 persons; Vietnam had one. This was less than that for India. However, in the matter of the number of televisions, China in 1994 had 23 per 100 persons, while Vietnam had 2 and India had 6 per 100 persons.

As regards films, which are another important part of the Media broadly defined, it is India which leads when comparisons are made between East and South Asia. As one study of the Asian film industry has noted "India's prolific film output is in the range of 750 to 800 features a year which exceeds that of any country in the world. Studios in Bombay, Bangalore, Bhubaneshwar, Calcutta, Hyderabad, Mysore and Trivandrum contribute to that total in the 16 officially recognized languages as well as others." 63 per cent of the total films are produced in the 4 major languages of southern India *viz.* Telugu, Tamil, Malayalam and Kannada. However, the Hindi language films which make up about 20 per cent of the total production and are known for their commercial formulas have captured the all-India market, while regional language films remain confined to their own linguistic communities and geographic areas.[1]

Compared to the size, diversity and freedom enjoyed by films in India, which in recent times has been recognized as a full-fledged industry, countries in East Asia represent various levels of development. In China for sometime, especially during the years of the Cultural Revolution (1966-76) only eight films were released and these were primarily operas adopted for political ends. Since the mid-1970s film production in China has gradually but steadily increased until the annual production of feature films now ranges from 125 to 150. Most of these films are made in the 16 studios officially permitted to produce commercial works.[2] In Japan, the number of feature films dwindled in the early 1980s, since then the figure has stabilized at around 297/298. The Japanese case clearly shows the adverse impact of the video cassettes, television growth on the revenues of the film industry. The distribution profits for 1988 in the Japanese cinema industry was 325 billion yen (0.32 billion US Dollars). This is a dismal statistic when compared with video cassette sales of more than 3 trillion yen (US $ 2.4 billion). The number of movie theatres have shrunk by some 40 to 50 a year leaving the cinema industry with something like 2000 theatres. This represents a two-thirds reduction since the peak year of 1958 when the average Japanese saw at least one movie a month. Now it is fewer than one a year.[3] A similar phenomenon is to be seen in Taiwan. From the highs of well over 200 a year in the 1960s and 1970s the figure has shrunk to considerably fewer than the 99 recorded in 1985. Even a big producer such as the Kuomintang controlled Central Motion Picture Corporation, which averaged 16 films a year through 1986, finished only 3 short and 2 feature length films by the end of 1988.[4]

While government controlled or regulated Media are a common part of the information set up in most countries, the different situations can be categorised in relation to the degree of freedom of ownership and operation which is granted to private companies. There can be no denying the fact that the extent of media development as well as diversification is greater in those countries where the private sector has greater space to grow and expand. A comparative analysis of China and Vietnam with Taiwan, Japan, South Korea and India underscores this point in relation to Asia.

Multi-ownership of mass media prevails in Taiwan. For example, radio stations are owned either by private enterprises, Kuomintang or government agencies. The Kuomintang stations make up the largest radio network and there are 28 privately owned broadcast companies with 59 medium wave transmitters. The television industry which developed after the radio ownership pattern includes large investments by private companies. Not one television station is entirely owned by government, Kuomintang or a private citizen. The Taiwan Provincial Government invested 49 per cent of Taiwan Television Enterprise's capital, 11 per cent was invested by local private sources and 40 per cent came from Japanese private firms. Similarly, in the case of the other big television company in Taiwan, the China Television Company having 50 per cent of the capital, 28 per cent came from a financing group formed by 28 private radio companies and 22 per cent came from a group of private citizens who had applied for a TV station license. Despite their dependence on public agencies for financing, all three TV stations in Taiwan are technically defined as "private," operating entirely on sales of advertising time.[5]

By comparison, China which is a much bigger country than Taiwan has an underdeveloped Media for domestic users but a huge service for overseas listeners. Made up of 21 provinces, 5 autonomous regions and two special municipalities (Beijing and Shanghai), China has a land area of 9.56 million square kilometres; the largest in Asia. In 1994 it had a population of 1208.3 million the largest in the world. At least ten cities have populations of 2 million or more, the largest being Beijing (the capital) with eight million and Shanghai with 6 millions. Yet, the national media apparatus are located in these two key cities alone.[6] As Table 3.1 shows, compared to South Korea, certainly to Taiwan and Singapore, China lags considerably behind in Media development. One of the reasons certainly is the fact that the burden of Media development in China is borne entirely by the government. Media is seen as a tool of class struggle and must assume such militant roles as "collective propagandist," "collective agitator" and "collective organizer." The broadcasting system is completely under the control of the Department of Propaganda of the Communist Party Central Committee. A diagrammatic depiction of the line of control of party and government over Media show how little autonomy these have in reality.

Figure 3.1: Organisational Chart of Chinese Broadcasting

Key: Policy Controls ------------------------------------

Administrative Controls ----------------------

The Propaganda Department operates through Propaganda Divisions in every regional, provincial and local branch of the Communist Party and governmental agencies in charge of cultural and educational affairs. The Broadcasting Administration Bureau carries out party policies channelled through the State Council. This dual system of supervision operates all the way from the National Central People's Broadcasting Station in Beijing to provincial stations in each capital, to municipal stations servicing the cities and to local stations in country communes, factories and mines. Radio receiving networks are run by the People's Liberation Army. Circulation of news is encouraged through collective listening and posters. To overcome the problems of insufficient radio facilities and limited number of radio receivers in the 1950s, the Chinese developed "radio-receiver networks." These consisted of two parts. First of all a Central Government Law of April, 1950 ordered government agencies at county and municipal levels, People's Liberation Army Units and all organizations, factories and schools to appoint broadcasting monitors. The duties of monitors were to listen and take down news, political instructions and other important items; to organize collective listening sessions and to circulate the news in the form of small newspapers, *tatzepao*. As part of this monitoring system, the Chinese Communists developed "wired broadcasting networks" patterned after the Soviet Union radio diffusion exchange system. Wired broadcasting loudspeakers are installed everywhere—in village squares, school playgrounds, market places, rice paddies, factories, mines, communal mess halls, dormitories, households and even on treetops and telephone poles, for the political and cultural education of the peasants, the dissemination of advanced experiences in agricultural production and the advancement of cultural life in rural areas.[7] In 1973 about 50 per cent of television sets were in Party and government offices, workers clubs and commune halls. Although more sets are now with private viewers, government still strictly controls the content and number of television programmes and films.

As recently as 1996 several changes were made in the government policy towards films, film making and television programmes. At the end of March 1996, a conference took place in Changsha where Ding Guangen, Director of the Central Propaganda Department, reaffirmed the importance of film as an educational and ideological tool. Directors were advised that in the future "special attention should be given to incorporating the ideology of the Party into artistic creation."[8]

In July 1997, new regulations governing the film and television industry were introduced. They include clear rules which studios and film makers have to observe. Many things which hitherto could be carried out in a semi-legal atmosphere are now no longer possible. For example, a person can now only become a director if he has studied directing at the Film Academy whereas in the past people such as Zhang Yimou proved that it was possible to move from cinematography into directing. Independent film making is illegal so that it has become more difficult for studios to turn a blind eye and let independents use their facilities. Also Sino-foreign co-productions are subject to complicated rules. As reported in the Hong Kong film magazine *City Entertainment*—For Chinese films produced by companies within the PRC, the director has to be a PRC resident and most other personnel should also be residents. In all other cases (when subject matter or role require this) people from abroad may be contracted but only with the approval of the Film Bureau. A lot of films—6 out of 8—made by the Beijing Film Studios were rejected and 4 had to be revised, 2 being shelved. Films which were rewritten were on simple themes like *Baba* (Father), *Mi* (Rice) and *Wuchao* (Dance Craze). Private investors are now increasingly reluctant to finance film projects.[9]

The greater impetus to the development of the Media in situations of private and government ownership in quantitative as well as qualitative terms can be seen in South Korea. In 1970 of the 46 radio stations in South Korea, 17 were owned by the Government and 29 by private parties. South Korean television has a much larger share of US produced programmes being dubbed and screened. It is not that government does not prohibit criticism of a political or policy nature in South Korea, Taiwan and Japan. However such regulation is done by broad-based public bodies and not by a one party regime. That is why it has been possible for Media in non-Communist states to show news about dissident social and political movements and play a greater role in promoting such change, as well as constructing an elite consensus. Greater autonomy for the Media enables it to play a larger role in promoting economic and social development.

It is notable that in East Asia the introduction and expansion of new technologies, satellite communications, video recording, personal computers, cellular phones—have not promoted transborder television or broadcasting unlike in Europe. Each country, specially Taiwan, China and Japan have large establishments broadcasting in overseas languages but the inward traffic from outside the country is very limited. One of the major reasons is that the bulk of the audience functions in their national language and unlike in South Asia, English is not a major link language, nor Hindi, or Urdu. A second cause for lack of interaction, what to say of integration between the Media of East Asian countries, is the diversity of political perceptions, systems and those of economic structures as well. This is in sharp contrast with Europe where there has been a concrete approach towards the adoption of an 'Open Skies' policy which was set out in the European Community's Green Paper on satellite communications.[10] Thus, for example, in Japan seven broadcasting and communication satellites are used with more than 100 transponders but these are all for domestic services in Japanese. English language programmes have poor reception value. The uplinking with foreign cable TV is three times more expensive than domestic TV fees. At the regional level too there has been a very poor response to effect a stepping up of exchanges between news agencies. In 1981 some 23 national news agencies of the region, all members of the Organization of Asia-Pacific News Agencies (OANA), set up the Asia-Pacific News Network (ANN) to provide for a daily exchange of news and features among themselves, a venture that was designed to increase the flow of information within the region. Yet sadly enough, the output of the Network remains poor and so does its usage.[11]

Introduction of satellite technologies with the potential of regional/global telecasting has not yet produced enough interactive influences. The limits to the globalization of the Media in East Asia are provided by the self-sustaining discreteness of local cultures. A comparative study of Chinese values in the *Xinhua Press* releases during the 1950s and 1990s showed that these had become more important in the construction of news.[12] Globalization of capital flows through Foreign Direct Investments and large scale expansion of trade has not meant a faceless or arbitrary homogenization of cultures much less an Americanization of cultures in East Asia. Countries have absorbed technological progress and new consumer goods and services without losing their self-identity. Mainland China which now has 382 newspapers, with a combined circulation of more than 70 million, takes its leading stories mainly from the *People's Daily* founded in 1948 and which is the official paper of the Chinese Communist Party's Central Politburo publishing about 5 million copies.[13]

One of the distinctive features of Media in East Asia has been its use in reinforcing school and college education especially in the rural areas. For example, systematic efforts have been made in Taiwan to supplement school instruction with electronic Media. Educational Radio with an island-wide service of instructional programmes has existed since 1950. Broadcasting eight hours daily, the station offers courses on both the high school and college levels in languages, history, geography and government.[14] Educational television in China started in March 1960 with the inauguration of the Peking Television College. College level courses were made available in factories, mines and in villages. In North Korea, government fully controls all Media but has also used it to universalize the programme to provide ten year compulsory higher education. In Japan, television has expanded at a rapid pace. A Tokyo resident, for example, has a selection of eight TV channels—one educational, three NHK, public sector and five commercial and ten radio services. In other large cities the situation is the same as in Tokyo. A rural resident, for instance in Aomorei prefecture at the northern end of Honshu, can select from four TV channels and five radio programmes with broadcasting hours as long as those in Tokyo.[15] Educational TV and expansion of Media to the rural areas has brought about greater social and economic equality.

Notes

1 John A. Lent, *The Asian Film Industry* (Christopher Helm, London, 1990), pp. 230-31.
2 *Ibid.*, p. 12.
3 *Ibid.*, p. 46.
4 *Ibid.*, p. 66.
5 Sydney W. Head and John A. Lent (Ed.), *Broadcasting in Asia and the Pacific* (Temple University Press, Philadelphia, 1978), p. 17.
6 *Ibid.*, pp. 22-23.
7 *Ibid.*, pp. 27-28.
8 Anne Sytske Keyser, *China Information*, Vol. XI, No. 4, Spring 1997, p. 117
9 *Ibid.*, p. 118.
10 O.P. Khushu, "Satellite Communications in Asia: An Overview," *Media Asia*, Vol. 20, No. 1, 1993, p. 6.
11 S.M. Ali, "Asian Journalism in the 1990s," *Communicator* (IIMC, New Delhi), Vol. XXV, No. 2, June 1990, p. 8.
12 Charles Elliott, "Towards the Construction of Asian Values: A Study of Chinese Values in *Xinhua* Press Releases," *Media Asia*, Vol. 20, No. 1, 1993, p. 12.
13 J.C. Merrill, *Global Journal*, 1983, London Inc., p. 124.
14 Sydney W. Head, *op. cit.*, p. 20.
15 *Ibid.*, p. 61.

4

Media and Communications Development: Socio-Political Implications in Africa

*Vanita Ray**

The power and the role of media and communications in the World today is immense and this fact cannot but be stressed when one discusses the issue of its development. Information and communication and its dissemination through the print and electronic media, which has increased by leaps and bounds over the last decade, has come to be a sophisticated weapon that plays an extensive and all encompassing role influencing the socio-cultural, politico-economic and developmental processes. This period described as the *Information Age*[1] replaces the earlier two Western civilizational phases—agrarian and industrial—and marks a break with the past as it opens a new era of economic, social and cultural developments. For the first time in the history of humanity global exchanges of capital are formed of non-material transfers of ideas and images which make up the new economy, an economy directed by science and its new perceptions of knowledge. Distances are no longer of great consequence space having lost its articulations and boundaries as a result of the spectacular development of information technologies and creation of planetary

*Dr. Ray is Reader at the Academy of Third World Studies, Jamia Millia Islamia, New Delhi.

networks, all of which have ushered in a new revolution that can shuttle vast amounts of information the world over in minutes and seconds. The entire process has given rise to a number of challenges which not only bring great hopes but also attendant risks.

This unprecedented development that created whole new societies in cyberspace, when science and technology have given way to greater economic interdependence and cultural interaction, has enabled the heretofore excluded/isolated populations of the developing countries to have an easy access to information and knowledge. It is in these parts of the Third World that its impact has been the most impressive and devastating. While it has helped to liberate peoples from ignorance demonstrating that knowledge is power, it has also considerably subverted and destroyed traditional cultural identities and imposed values of the dominant economies. For example, even in today's satellite age, a large section of the written Press and most television and radio networks depend on the four Western news agencies—the Associated Press and the United Press of the United States, Reuters of UK and the *Agence France Press of France*—that play a key role in disseminating information world-wide 24 hours a day. They together disseminate more than 80 per cent of the international information utilized by the print and the electronic media. Besides, through the use of sophisticated technologies such as overcrowding of radio spectrums, geo-stationary orbits and regulation and non-regulation of direct broadcast satellites the West not only controls but also manipulates world-wide information and news networks. As one writer has said, by any reckoning the big four Western news agencies are "the heart" and "major arteries" of that global system. They hold it together and drive it providing at least half and probably three quarters of the information that flows through it.[2] Control by the global information and telecommunications conglomerates has quickened the pace of industrialisation of cultures and put an end to the freedom of information and pluralism. This has been further facilitated by the fierce competition of the globalisation of markets in which only the powerful survive. Consequently these information conglomerates not only threaten the cultural products of the smaller markets but also increase the risks of their impoverishment. At the same time, ownership, control and direction in most Third World countries of the various organs of information and communication by the State, has not only made its development contingent to the State's national policies and levels of development but has also naturally been responsible for its use as a tool of power and control. As a result it has dramatically increased the plight and frustrations of underdevelopment in the Third World as groups and classes of people remain deprived while others are more privileged. This is a major challenge that confronts most countries—either they surrender their specific identities and cultural values to the forces of globalization or assert a collective response for "a free flow of information."

It is in this backdrop that an attempt is made here to trace the development of media and communications and to examine the impact of access to global information and communications on the African continent assessing its crucial bearing on society, culture and politico-national developments. The present paper will address issues of media imperialism by the Western states analysing its socio-cultural, political and developmental implications and distinct disparities in knowledge and information at the state level between the haves and the havenots.

THE AFRICAN SCENARIO

Development of the media and communications infrastructure has remained painfully slow on the African continent, almost contingent to and one that reflects its less developed status; of the 38 least developed countries in the world, 28 are in Africa. This state of underdevelopment of media and communications can to some extent be explained to the continent having been a late starter in the adoption of modern techniques; even as recently as the pre-colonial phase of African history there was no equivalent of the modern institutions of mass communication. Society had then depended on the "oramedia" such as the folk media network which was grounded in an "indigenous culture produced and consumed by members of a group."[3] However, notwithstanding this late start, the state of information and communications development is indeed deplorable. It does not even today meet UNESCO's 1961 prescribed targets[4] to measure the sufficiency or insufficiency of mass communications for developing countries. The Organization's, "immediate target" was that every country should aim to provide for every 100 of its inhabitants ten copies of daily newspapers, five radio receivers, two cinema seats and two television sets. In fact if UNESCO's minimum standards were achieved, it would mean that one out of every two families would have a daily newspaper, one out of every four families a radio receiver and a television set and one cinema seat for every ten families. This is still a far cry and two-thirds of the world's people still fall below these standards.

TELECOM Infrastructure Development Neglected

Telecommunications, whose development would enable quick and increased news flow between and within countries, has received surprisingly little attention and African countries have the world's fewest telephone lines per unit of population. Even as recently as a decade ago internal micro-wave and telex systems connected only the principal cities leaving vast rural areas with few outside contacts. Besides, telephone calls between countries on the continent and outside were routed through London and Paris, the former colonial country's metropole. The scenario has now changed, but even while the per capita availability of telephones has increased (1.5 telephone lines per 100 people)[5] their numbers still continue to be woefully inadequate and the telephone is still a luxury in the developing countries. According to 1996 figures, the number of telephone lines per 1000 inhabitants on the African continent ranged between 1-11. The only exceptions to this general rule were the affluent countries of North Africa—Algeria had 44 lines; Tunisia 64 and Morocco 45; in Southern Africa—South Africa had 100 lines and Namibia 54, while Gabon had 32 lines.[6] All other countries on the continent had been unable to merit more than .03 per cent of their GDP towards communications network development. This, even while development of the telecommunications sector was not only important for mass communications but also for networking interpersonal communications channels, both of which are an important key to social and economic growth.[7]

The Diverse State of the Print Media

The print media scenario in Africa is more encouraging. The state of the Press in most countries on the continent is relatively better than before, even while as a means of mass communication of news its reach is small and restricted when compared to radio broadcasts and television transmissions. The print media is essentially a legacy of the European colonialists who had started editions of metropolitan newspapers to cater to the needs of its own bureaucracy and the educated African elite. This modern print media form was the strongest in the former British colonies where in places as far apart as India, Singapore and Zambia, editions of the metropolitan newspapers such as the *Mirror* and the *Times* were started by journalists who extended imperial influences, that continued long after. In fact, Western domination and control of communications is unmistakable in the print media of the continent. The latter has over the years been totally dependent for all current national and international news and information on the Big Four Western news agencies that provide at the least half and more than three fourths of it every day. Their services are thus vital for all major and small dailies, powerful television networks, down to radio broadcasts. But most of this news disseminated gives little attention to Third World problems of poverty, illiteracy and disease. And very often the coverage is not only uninformed and superficial but sets out facts in a manner as would be favourable to their own interests and of the transnational system.

Mustafa Masmoudi, a leading innovator of a new global communications order that called for the need to harness communications for political development, set out in graphic details the Western domination of communication in the Third World. The existing global news and information systems, he stated, was characterised by several flaws:

> A flagrant quantitative imbalance between North and South...created by the disparity between the volume of news and information emanating from the developed world and intended for the developing countries and the volume of flow in the opposite direction...resulting in a veritable *de facto* monopoly on the part of the developed countries.
>
> A *de facto* hegemony and the will to dominate...evident in the marked indifference of the media in the developed countries particularly in the West, to the problems, concerns and aspirations of the developing countries.... They are exercised above all through the control of the information flow, wrested and wielded by the transnational agencies operating without let or hindrance in most developing countries and based in turn on the control of technology, illustrated by the communication system, satellites, which are wholly dominated by the major international consortia....

> By transmitting to the developing countries only news processed by them, that is, news which they have filtered, cut and distorted, the transnational media impose their own way of seeing the world upon the developing countries....Moreover, [they often] present these communities—when indeed they do show interest in them—in the most infavourable light, stressing crises, strikes, street demonstrations, putsches, etc., or even holding them upto ridicule....
>
> The present day information system enshrines a form of political, economic and cultural colonialism which is reflected in the often tendentious interpretation of news concerning the developing countries. This consists in highlighting events whose significance, in certain cases, is limited or even non-existent; in collecting isolated facts and presenting them as a "whole"; in setting out facts in such a way that the conclusion to be drawn from them is necessarily favourable to the interests of the transnational system; in amplifying small scale events so as to arouse justified fears; in keeping silent on situations unfavourable to the interests of the countries of origin of these media....
>
> Likewise, information is distorted by reference to moral, cultural or political values peculiar to certain states, in defiance of the values and concerns of other nations. The criteria governing selection are consciously or unconsciously based on the political and economic interests of the transnational system and of the countries in which this system is established.... Even important news may be deliberately neglected by the major media in favour of other information of interest only to public opinion in the country to which the media in question belong. Such news is transmitted to the client countries and is indeed practically imposed on them despite the fact that readers and listeners in these countries have no interest therein....[8]

This trend became quite notable in the immediate post-independence period of the sixties and the seventies; the State now owned and controlled the Press through proxy of the African educated elite. They, with their links with the erstwhile colonial masters, were generally not averse to relying on the Western news conglomerates. This was also the period of slow development of the print media. As reported by delegates at a Paris Conference on "*Development of Information Media in Africa*" in 1962, in seven African countries there was no daily Press except roneo typed bulletins put out by the Government Information Services, while in 15 countries there was no daily newspaper of any kind.[9] UNESCO in 1961 estimated Africa's total number of daily newspapers to be 220, compared to Asia's 1270, South America's 750, North America's 2200, Europe's 2980, USSR's 460 and Oceania's 110.[10] These figures when compared with the number of daily newspapers per 100 in the different parts of the world (see Table 4.1), indicate that Africa then had one-sixth of the world's average newspaper circulation and one-twentieth as many dailies per 100 as the peoples of North America.

Table 4.1
Number of Daily Newspapers, Radio Receivers, Cinema Seats and Television Sets Per 100 Persons in Regions of the World

	Copies of Newspapers	*Radio Receivers*	*Cinema Seats*	*Television Sets*
The World	9.8	13.2	2.3	3.8
Africa	1.2	2.3	0.6	0.07
North America	25.0	73.0	5.5	23.4
South America	8.0	11.0	3.4	2.0
Asia	4.0	2.1	0.6	0.6
Europe	23.0	21.8	5.4	7.4
Oceania	29.0	20.6	7.7	8.8
USSR	18.1	20.5	5.6	3.0
Three mostly underdeveloped regions (with two-thirds of the World's people)	3.8	2.7	0.8	0.6
Four mostly developed regions (with one-third of the World's people)	22.7	35.8	5.5	10.7

Source: *UNESCO World Communications Report 1964* (Paris 1964).
—Quoted in Wilbur Schramm: *Mass Media and National Development—The Role of Information in the Developing Countries* (Stanford, California 1964).

Nevertheless, whatever the growth in the African print media, it must be appreciated as the continent started from scratch; it had till very recently the least developed traditional Press system. Not until the colonial period did it have any developed modern mass media or press network, but also it worked against tremendous odds such as poor telecommunications facilities, slow and poor communication between cities, towns and the large rural areas and limited circulation of newspapers because of low literacy levels and poor purchasing power of peoples. But despite these heavy odds Africa is one part of the developing world that has undertaken several experiments, using mass media for purposes of national integration, for developmental objectives and even for personal promotion. Illustrating the latter point first, Kenyan President Daniel Arap Moi, presenting himself as a symbol of new nationalism, used the media to promote his executive position. A Presidential Press Unit was set up at the Voice of Kenya and used daily for "protocol news"—the ceremonial comings and goings of public officials, airport arrival and departure ceremonies, conferences, banquets, toasts and high sounding communiques. A lead story about the President and what he was doing for the country.was a daily occurrence. The story was beamed on both the television and radio networks and the two newspapers in the capital city Nairobi were also expected to carry it. In other countries newspapers were used to support and popularise socio-economic developmental projects relating to literacy, health information, education and developmental links between villages and the central government. Even while these papers were only mimeographed sheets that appeared irregularly they served a useful purpose in educating the rural population. Another interesting experiment was carried out by a Dutch Developmental Agency in Kenya. A fully equipped mobile van was provided in the villages and residents were expected to train their own people as editors and reporters who could then produce their own newspaper.

These efforts notwithstanding, the overall print media scenario degenerated considerably in the seventies and the numbers of newspapers in circulation on the continent came down dramatically. According to one estimate the numbers declined by half from 1960 to the end of the seventies and six Black African countries had no newspaper at all.[11] Another writer counted only 156 dailies in 1977 against the earlier 1964 estimate of 220.[12] Media growth thus was nowhere near that in other parts of the developing world and Africa in the eighties remained the most newspaper poor region in the Third World, way below the UNESCO prescribed yardstick of 100 copies per 1000. Meanwhile, Asia and Latin

America had moved ahead. Asia, for example, leads in the number of dailies, total circulation is large and has increased considerably over the last decade, even while being offset by the large population. Countries such as China, Japan, Hong Kong, India, Indonesia and Malaysia have relatively large numbers of newspapers and large total circulation when compared with Africa. Japan and Hong Kong head the list; they have circulations of 576 and 719 dailies per 1000 peoples respectively. Korea follows second, having a circulation of 404 dailies while Malaysia has 124 and both India and Indonesia have a little over 20 dailies per 1000 each.[13] Even in Latin America—Argentina, Brazil and Colombia—all in stages of development not too far ahead of the African countries, the institution of the Press and news circulation is well advanced. There are a large number of dailies, large total circulations as also high per capita dispersion ratios being 138, 45 and 64 per 1000 respectively.[14] These circulation figures are way above those of the African continent and the glaring disparities between the two regions speaks for the state of underdevelopment itself. It must however be noted that the state of the Press in Africa differs widely from one country to another varying in relation to the different political, cultural and economic contexts inherent in every state. The only very significant and common denominator in all of them is the continuing official control.

The state of underdevelopment on the continent has continued even in the recent phase of the nineties' decade and this is reflected in the very slow growth of the print media and its circulation. As recently as 1994, four sub-Saharan African countries had no daily newspaper; these were the least developed regions of Burkina Faso, Chad, Rwanda and Mauritania. In 9 other countries—Angola, Botswana, Gabon, Ghana, Kenya, Liberia, Nigeria, Swaziland and Zimbabwe—circulation was to the order of 10 newspapers per 1000 inhabitants. Only in the more developed region of Southern Africa—in Namibia and South Africa—the circulation figures are somewhat more impressive—10 and 30 per 1000 respectively.[15]

The Independent private Press that emerged on the continent on the wave of the liberalisation/democratisation processes has fared no better because of the same cultural, educational and economic factors of underdevelopment and the tight controls by the political regime in power. In 1997, there were approximately 100 private newspapers published regularly over the whole continent. While some such as *La Gazette du Golfe* in Benin, *Sud Hebdo* in Senegal or *Le Messager* in Cameroon have been popular and successful, others in Mali, one of the least developed countries on the continent, have had to confront several difficulties. Its four national dailies for the country's 10 million inhabitants have been continually bogged down by problems of illiteracy, poor readership, low purchasing power, a distribution network restricted to towns and cities, limited advertisement revenues, not to mention the increasing and prohibitive costs of paper allocated by Government monopolies. This latter has in fact proved to be a major hurdle to the development of the Independent Press in Africa; in certain cases it has even been used as a weapon by the State to throttle the dissemination of opposition views. Because of these problems, the Independent Press in Africa has failed to take off.

Phenomenal Growth of the Radio Network

The continent has nevertheless witnessed a phenomenal growth of radio and radio broadcasting networks far outpacing the development of telecommunications infrastructures and the extent and the reach of the print media. From modest beginnings in the 1950's of one receiver on an average per 100 persons, the radio has had the maximum growth in the last twenty years acquiring wide sweep and popularity. The radio is the oldest means of communication; not only is it cheap but also easily accessible to audiences both in the urban and the rural areas. "No village seems so remote," says a writer in his survey of communications and rural development, "that radio at least does not reach it."[16] Daniel Lerner and Wilbur Schramm, eminent researchers who pioneered studies of the rise and role of communications as a multiplier of knowledge and opinion formation in traditional societies, visualized the radio as a powerful medium that could be used for national development and growth. Lerner, a MIT sociologist, was one of the first to suggest this in his study[17] that observed the rupture of history as a result of clashes between tradition and modernity in seven countries that formed an arc around the Eastern Mediterranean. The radio, he noted, had totally changed centuries of isolation in the Middle East and enabled its peoples to get a glimpse of what their future could be. The model of development that he proposed on the basis of his study relied heavily on mass media which would help multiply and speed change. Mass media, he suggested, could be utilised for a wide range of developmental objectives ranging from birth control and sanitation to education, the adoption of new agricultural practices and to change centuries old social patterns.

Similarly, Wilbur Schramm in a 1964 UNESCO publication[18] that focused on the human expression of underdevelopment in Asia and Africa; reiterated the role of mass media for rapid economic and social change. This Schramm believed could be done by integrating communication into the broader context of national policy and thereby speed change. "We must remember," he said,

> "the full power of mass communication has never been used, in any developing country, to push economic and social development forward....The really exciting question [now is] how much could we increase the present rate of development, how much could we smooth out the difficulties...how much further could we make our resources go, how much more could we contribute to the growth of informed, participating citizens in the new nations, if we were to put the resources of modern communication skilfully and fully behind economic and social development?"[19]

For both Lerner and Schramm mass media really meant the radio, for it was then the traditional means of communication in the developing countries. They predicted that it was the perfect medium for multiplying developmental effort; what one agent could do in a single village, the radio and later television could do in a hundred or a thousand villages simultaneously. It is not surprising then that its potential as an instrument for the dissemination of information of all types—political, developmental or social—has been fully exploited by most Third World countries.

Given its immense potential, radio and radio broadcasting has received considerable attention and evolved innovatively in Africa. In the initial post-independence period most governments emphasized the need for numbers and wide dissemination of broadcasts. Radio networking in that period increased by leaps and bounds. From the 1965, 9.4 million radios, their numbers went upto 40 million in 1980 and four years later, it jumped to 60 millions. The African continent had arrived at the UNESCO stipulated minimum of 50 radios per 1000 by 1970; a decade later the number of radios per 1000 had doubled.[20] The number of radios increased much faster than the population; from 34 per 1000 people in 1965 to 100 radios per 1000 in 1980 and 129 per thousand in 1984. By 1994, 15 countries in sub-Saharan Africa—Mauritania, Senegal, Gambia, Sierra Leone, Liberia, Ivory Coast, Ghana, Nigeria, Cameroon, Gabon, Congo Republic, Ethiopia, Uganda, Namibia and Botswana—had between 100-200 radio receivers per 1000 persons; 13—Mali, Niger, Burkina Faso, Guinea, Central African Republic, Zaire, Angola, Zambia, Sudan, Kenya, Tanzania, Mozambique and Zimbabwe—had fewer than 100 receivers per 1000 persons; while South Africa and Malawi had more than 200 receivers per 1000 persons.[21]

African countries have recently started public service Community Radio Networks to encourage and facilitate developmental activity based on the concept of listener participation at all socio-economic levels within the community. The Community Radio Network is widespread throughout the continent and has developed at a fast pace following liberalisation and democratisation. West Africa was the first region to start community radio systems in the rural areas. By 1995 there were more than a 100 local rural public service or private radio stations.[22] Burkina Faso and Mali have the largest number of such community radio stations—10 and 21 respectively—in the rural areas as against the commercial radio stations in the urban centres. In Burkina Faso the network has been performing useful functions promoting health campaigns, women's conferences and providing education and training to small farmers. Mali's larger Community Radio Network has been playing an active part in local development planning and education while enhancing community participation through group discussions. Mali has also started the first All Women's Radio Station that has been working in collaboration with women's associations.[23] Ghana, Guinea and Guinea Bissau also started similar rural radio experiments to help inform and educate the community on health and hygiene issues.[24]

Commercial broadcast services also developed during this period. West Africa has the largest number of these networks both specialized and of general interest. These are Africa No. 1 that broadcasts to most West African countries, Horizon FM in Burkina Faso, Radio Multimedia and Radio TSF in Cape Verde, *Radio Jeune Afrique Musique* and *Radio Nostalgie* in Cote D'Ivoire and Sud FM in Senegal.[25] Most of these stations however are concentrated mainly in the cities and reflect the Western way of life and leisure culture. Radio broadcasting in Africa is overall the most extensive and effective communications system.

Television Essentially an Urban Phenomenon

Television as a broadcast medium has hardly impacted the continent and its peoples; the geographical coverage and audiences are very low in most countries. African countries as a whole have the fewest telecommunications infrastructures, and audiovisual equipments and programmes are distributed/disseminated mainly in the metropolitan areas. More than 80 per cent of the continent's population, particularly in the rural areas, do not have access to television. According to a Survey, in Cote D'Ivoire for example, only 20 per cent of the rural population had access to TV compared with 60 per cent city and town dwellers.[26] The state of underdevelopment of the television network is reflective of the poverty and limited availability of funds in most African countries. Besides, recession forced these countries to submit to the Structural Adjustment Programmes that obliged a cutting down of expenditures. And since television was never considered a priority for national development, it barely received any funds for its infrastructural development. Resultantly, transmitters were not upgraded and till very recently television viewing remained totally confined to the urban areas as an exclusive preserve of the city dweller who alone could afford to have a receiver.

Television in Africa had modest beginnings. In the 1960's when most African countries moved into Independence television was almost unknown. In 1965, BBC estimated the total number of television sets in Africa at 500,000—only two receivers for every 1000 peoples. By 1980, the total number of sets had grown to more than 6 millions and a few years later it was 14 millions; the number of sets per 1000 being 29.[27] The audiovisual developments over the same period in other Third World developing regions has been more heartening. Asia shows the fastest growth in any part of the world—from the modest 500,000 sets in 1965, the numbers increased to 1.9 millions in 1970, to 19 millions in 1980 and to 49 millions four years later in 1984. The increase per 1000 figures from 0.3 in 1965 to 9 per 1000 in 1980 and 20 in 1984. The Latin American scenario is even better; from 6.5 million TV receivers in 1962, the numbers increased to 50 millions in 1984. The number of sets per 1000 increased from 29 in 1965 to 134 in 1984.[28]

In recent years following globalisation, liberalisation, marketisation, the advent of Democracy and above all the internationalisation of communications through the nineties, the numbers and reach of television has grown. From being essentially a state controlled enterprise like the radio and the print media, television in the nineties has become freer and been influenced considerably by the international private operators who have made an entry into the continent. These latter, operating in tandem with the indigenous elites have diversified the programme content to include widespread Western-oriented entertainment and leisure programmes similar to the ones beamed in the Western capitals—London, Paris or New York. They recognised the TV, as Stevenson had said earlier for the African elites of the sixties and the seventies, as a symbol of modernity, "a new medium, powerful beyond anything that had come before it to raise expectations and demands that seemed capable of leaping the gap between the old and the new faster and more efficiently than all other media combined."[29] Besides, the use of sophisticated satellite equipments has helped to extend the network and attract large numbers of subscribers. Expansion and extension notwithstanding, television in Africa still remains at low levels of development. According to the most recent figures of 1996, sub-Saharan Africa has only 43 television sets per 1000 inhabitants. These figures when compared with those in other parts of the developing world, speak for the low levels of the spread of the audiovisual media in Africa. South Asia, for example, had 53 sets per 1000 people, large regions having between 100-200 receivers per 1000 inhabitants; West Asia and North Africa had 145; while Latin America and the Caribbeans had 217. Latin America having the second largest audiovisual market world-wide, remains ahead with a high proportion of 70 per cent of its population having television sets.[30] Only one country in Africa—South Africa had more than 123 receivers per 1000 inhabitants; 7 had less than 100; 4 less than 50; 10 less than 30; while 8 had less than 10. For a breakdown see Table 4.2.

Taken overall, barely 4 Africans in every hundred have a television set, *i.e.* 14.2 per cent of all inhabitants. The figure is far behind that of Asia where television is available to 55.3 per cent of the peoples. The worst sufferers in Africa are the rural populations; more than 80 per cent do not have access to television.[31] The Sahelian

Table 4.2
Country Breakdown of Television Sets per 1000 Inhabitants in Africa 1996

Sr. No.	*Country*	*No. of Sets per 1000 Inhabitants*	*Sr. No.*	*Country*	*No. of Sets per 1000 Inhabitants*
1.	Angola	51	17.	Madagascar	24
2.	Benin	73	18.	Mali	11
3.	Burkina Faso	6	19.	Mauritania	82
4.	Burundi	2	20.	Mozambique	3
5.	Cameroon	75	21.	Namibia	29
6.	Central African Rep.	5	22.	Niger	23
7.	Chad	2	23.	Nigeria	55
8.	Congo Democratic Rep.	41	24.	Rwanda	—
9.	Congo Republic	8	25.	Senegal	38
10.	Cote D' Ivoire	60	26.	Sierra Leone	17
11.	Ethiopia	4	27.	South Africa	123
12.	Gabon	76	28.	Tanzania	16
13.	Ghana	41	29.	Togo	14
14.	Guinea	8	30.	Uganda	26
15.	Kenya	19	31.	Zambia	80
16.	Lesotho	13	32.	Zimbabwe	29

Source: Figures culled from *World Development Report: Knowledge for Development 1998/99* (World Bank, Washington D.C. 1999).

belt of least developed countries—Burkina Faso, Chad, Rwanda, Burundi, Niger, Mali, Central African Republic and Ethiopia—and the former Portuguese colonies have the lowest levels of television development that reflects their state of socio-economic backwardness. Most of these countries still rely on a single national channel with limited airtime (broadcasting only in one language) that caters to a restricted urban audience—while the rural population has little access to even the basic infrastructures. Given this perspective, it is interesting to note that Burkina Faso was in 1963, along with Senegal and Congo, one of the very first African country to have television at all. In 1996, even though the number of television receivers increased to 80,000, as against 6,000 in 1978, the country's national television network covered only 15 per cent of the territory and was seen by no more than 20 per cent of the population having less than 100 receivers per 1000 inhabitants.[32] This is largely because of material, infrastructure and financial constraints that have seriously restricted programming and production. Again, whatever the increase and extensions of air time in these countries, it was largely because of the import of regional and international programmes that opened windows to the world but at the cost of network expansions.

Other countries on the continent, particularly, the former French colonies in West Africa and those in southern and eastern Africa, may be categorised as average growth rate countries. Their growth was essentially the result of increasing national air time and the entry of private regional and international operators often in collaboration with local partners. Thus for example, while most former French colonies have programmes beamed *via* satellite from France and other European countries, South Africa broadcasts in several languages, including the minority languages, through terrestrial networks in the neighbouring countries. South Africa is the only country on the continent that has a highly developed infrastructure of national television and another 30 private and public stations.[33] South Africa's progress and advancement is a development of the post-apartheid and democratisation phase of the nineties. It was in this period that the country acquired the most dynamic state of the art technology and developed digital broadcasting *via* satellite. Liberalisation also opened the doors to private operations and growing markets. By 1996, South Africa with its 40 million inhabitants had approximately 12 million, viewers, just under 257 receiving sets per 1000 peoples.[34]

IMPACT OF MEDIA GROWTH ON DEVELOPMENT

Impact on Society and Social Development

Media and communications growth has considerably impacted the continent. It extends to and influences all spheres of development—social, economic, cultural and political. But it is the broad transformation across board of society and social relations that is the most important, having both positive and negative implications. On the positive side, the advent of the radio and the television in the 1960's opened up for the first time the isolated centuries-old culture of the continent to that of the developed and wealthy industrialised Western societies. The programmes diffused on the network helped to educate peoples, impart literacy training, techniques for growth, management and development skills. Soon radio and television were accepted as the legitimate "multipliers" of knowledge and the medium for the upgradation of human resources as their programmes substituted for the lack of trained teachers in the immediate post-independence period and extended opportunities for learning well beyond the school to the community and the home. Overall, the mass media network facilitated education in a region of widespread illiteracy. In Malawi, for example, in 1960 fewer than 800 of its population had completed secondary school and only a small percentage had been to a University or college. In the entire country there were only half a dozen doctors, one lawyer, one engineer and no scientists. There was not a single person trained to be a secretary. On the other hand, in the UAR which had large numbers of trained graduates, literacy at the lower elementary and secondary levels (more useful and more needed by the villagers for their day to day activities and livelihood) remained at a low of 25 per cent and the community was short of technicians and skilled labour.[35] Exposure to the non-formal educational techniques and training helped reduce ignorance, liberated people, opening to them the wider horizons of knowledge. The media network thus acted, as visualized by Daniel Lerner, as a "prime mover in the modernization of every aspect of life...the basic personal skill that underlies the whole modernizing sequence" and opened to the heretofore isolated traditional societies a bridge to the wider world.[36]

In Africa, as in other developing countries, it is human resource growth that media has impacted most. Nonformal education, training, development of skills and techniques of growth imparted through the audiovisual network have facilitated a broad transformation of society and upgraded human resources building a trained pool of human capital. In turn the application of these skills has quickened the general pace of development of social overheads such as basic transport, irrigation and power facilities and the communications network so important for economic progress. And as emphasized by developmental theorists, it is this development of peoples that is so necessary for any change in society.[37] In this perspective, programmes diffused have attempted to maintain the need for developmental and social change orientation and services have been formulated to secure community participation at all socio-economic levels of social, religious, ethnic and other groups. These public service networks which evolved over the last several years are fairly widespread on the continent facilitating free flow of information and promoting dialogue and instruction through participation between diverse groups. And this is fairly useful in a scenario where more than half the population continues to be illiterate. As already noted before, community specific radio and television networks that have time allocated for educational and training programmes, cultural and recreational programmes, programmes promoting health campaigns, women's conferences or training for small farmers are present in almost all countries on the continent, even while the scale and impact vary. Thus for example while the countries of North and West Africa have highly developed community specific developmental programmes, those in Central Africa and the Sahelian region still continue to be in an underdeveloped state largely because of the less developed status of the communications networks in these regions. In more recent years however, technological advances, the internationalisation of communications and the end of the state monopoly of the broadcasting and television networks has facilitated the extension of community services on the continent.

In the long-term then the positive benefits of mass media growth on the continent lie in the development of human capital and the widening of its horizons from a clustered traditional socio-economic community existence to that of an environment of information and empathy with life patterns as exist in the modern well developed societies. It was as stated by Wilbur Schramm, quoting a wise African, like magic, as it would 'take a man upto a hill higher than any we can see on the horizon and let him look beyond.' Mass media, the wise African went on to add, was perceived by many in traditional society as having the quality of magic as it would 'let a man see and hear where he has never been and know people he has never met.'[38] By disseminating news and views of developments in other parts of the world—political, economic, social and cultural—the communications media not only helped to bridge the transition between traditional and modern society but also acted as an important agent of social change. It stimulated an intellectual climate making people think of future perspectives based on new technologies, practices and social relations.

But it is the negative socio-cultural impacts on the peoples exposed for the first time to new and alien concepts of knowledge and information that have been quite devastating and which far outweigh the positive features of communications development.

While the latter aroused hopes of a knowledge based better future through the sixties and the seventies, the flood of communications based on the power of technology of the later decades enabled the exercise of influence and control over opinion making. For example, the movies and TV programmes disseminated world-wide through the Western communications conglomerates, especially those of the United States (the US makes less than 10 per cent of the long films produced annually but it dominates the international trade in movies), spread the American "popular culture" world-wide and this has naturally impacted society and social relations. While the elites of the developing countries, through whom the imperialist control was intended, were naturally drawn to and influenced by the Western mores and consumer-oriented patterns of life, the rural poor remained alienated, deprived and frustrated as they did not have the wherewithal to acquire all the products of the good life portrayed. Joseph Nye in a study of the dynamics of power— how power actually operates— has succinctly analyzed the use of communications as a power resource. The spread of American "popular culture" world-wide, he describes as a source of "soft power" for the United States. There is, he says, "an element of triviality and fad in popular behaviour, but it is also true that a country that stands astride popular channels of communications has more opportunities to get its messages across and to effect the preferences of others." The millions across the world who are investing in satellite reception dishes, Nye adds, are in fact buying into a process that gives the Western world the ability to exercise power over them both through communication and information.[39] International communication is thus inherently strategic in nature. Being the sole transmitter of TV news and entertainment to Africa's two million households was certainly a source of power for the United States; this power it could not have exercised if African countries had been able to select their own programmes.

Even way back as 1965, African statesman Kwame Nkrumah of Ghana had expressed an awareness of the strategic character and potential of international communications. In his *Neo Colonialism: The Last Stage of Imperialism* he wrote:

> Even the cinema stories of fabulous Hollywood are loaded. One has only to listen to the cheers of African audiences as Hollywood's heroes slaughter Red Indians or Asiatics to

understand the effectiveness of this weapon. For in the developing continents, where the colonialist heritage has left a vast majority still illiterate, even the smallest child gets the message contained in the blood and thunder stories emanating from California. And along with murder and the Wild West goes an incessant barrage of anti-socialist propaganda in which the trade union man, the revolutionary, or the man of dark skin is generally cast as the villain, while the policeman, the gum shoe, the Federal agent—in a word, the CIA type copy—is ever the hero....[40]

Nkrumah went on to add about the power of the international structures of communications—

> While Hollywood takes care of fiction, the enormous monopoly press, together with the outflow of slick, clever, expensive magazines, attends to what it chooses to call 'news'. Within separate countries, one or two news agencies control the news handouts, so that a deadly uniformity is achieved, regardless of the number of separate newspapers and magazines; while internationally, the financial preponderance of the US is felt more and more through its correspondents and offices abroad, as well as through its influence over international capitalist journalism. Under this guise, a flood of anti-liberation propaganda emanates from the capitalist cities of the West, directed against China, Vietnam, Indonesia, Algeria, Ghana and all countries which hackout their own independent path to freedom.[41]

Thus through international communications, the North effectively and skilfully influenced and controlled the minds of people. But the socio-economic changes that occurred in the rural areas consequent to the processes of modernization and development had their own impact highlighting the dichotomy between them and the urban dwellers. The latter, the country's elite, ruled and dominated the state, its infrastructure and its policies and were also the beneficiaries of the international market systems. On the other hand, the vast mass of the country's people, who remained deprived and exploited because of the state's uneven development policies that favoured a few, came to be frustrated and alienated socially. Social discontent increased and quite often erupted in clashes and conflict situations. Even though these were sparked off by a variety of factors, socio-economic deprivation of one group by another was the main cause. Of such a scenario, a well-known watcher of the Nigerian political scene states—the African State squatted on the people like a bloated toad simultaneously 'overdeveloped' and 'underdeveloped,' captured by and used for private interests, unwilling and unable to serve any conception of the public good. It is linked to its social formation by exchange relations, 'a what's in it for me and my group,' political rationality.[42] And as the gap between the aspirations aroused and the reality widened, social, religious and ethnic strife also increased and conflict situations were widespread throughout the continent.[43] And in all these situations, the media helped to bring the issues into the arena of public discourse enabling peoples to become aware of the problems and to highlight them socially and politically.

Accompanying the negative social impacts is also an adverse impact on and imbalance of indigeneous cultures in Africa, as in most other developing countries. This is largely the outcome of international trade in cultural products—movies, TV programmes, music shows, books and periodicals, and above all international advertising—on which the developing countries have been forced to rely. In the context of the present paper, we would discuss here only the impact of the electronic software imported, programmes disseminated over the broadcast network and international advertising. And this impact has not only been considerable but has also received an impetus/momentum because of the underdeveloped status of these countries and their dependence perforce on the value-added standardised services offered by the Western communications conglomerates, all based in either Japan, the United States or Western Europe. The dependence on these global players has not only restricted the freedom of the developing countries but is also a threat to the religious and cultural perspectives and products of these smaller markets resulting in an overall impoverishment and disappearance of community cultures, weakening of indigenous cultural foundations and the imposition of cultural domination. It also amounted to an affront to and a surrender of national sovereignty to supranational communications organizations in the field. Thus for example, by the 1980's most international networks such as CNN, BBC and MTV circumvented national stations diffusing *via* satellite live entertainment programmes, news and advertising that no longer needed to be imported on films or video cassettes.

Even while appreciating that such TV programmes and TV reruns cost the host country a fraction of what it would take to make films locally (and this was naturally important for these cash strapped economies), they did introduce into the underdeveloped societies a 'cultural imperialism of their own.' 'Cultural imperialism' has been identified by Johan Galtung in his discourse on the Structural Theory of Imperialism[44] as one of the five imperialisms that characterize relationships between 'centre' nations, those with power and 'periphery' nations those without power. The other imperialisms he specifies are 'communications imperialism' (domination by the 'centre' nations of news and the means of international communications); 'economic' (control of the means of production and the processing industries); 'political' (reliance on the 'centre' nations for decisions and models of government) and 'military' (dependence on the centre for protection and weapons). 'Cultural imperialism,' a configuration of power relations—the 'centre' nations providing instruction to the 'periphery' states that are dependent on them for scientific and technological knowledge—says Galtung, is taking place in the world all the time. Even while the 'periphery' states are independent, the ruling elites of both the 'centre' and the 'periphery' maintain a harmony of interests through their interactions in international organisations and through international communications for the pursuit of all imperialisms. And because of this cultural and communications imperialism the Third World generally is kept in a passive state of being receivers of world views of others. Also since most of them lack the advanced communications capability they are perforce obliged to remain at the receiving end dependent on the institutionalized Western cultural communications networks and the diffusion of its multi-media products designed to cater to its own social needs. This has naturally had an adverse impact; it has not only exerted an economic control by presenting Western systems, images and products in a more favourable light but has also influenced habits, consumption patterns and popular culture in the developing Southern countries.

Thus for example, food and dress habits have undergone vast changes as a result of advertising by the global communications systems. Most developing countries' social elites exposed to the global flow of foreign images, ideas and cultural products have not only been influenced by but also altered their tastes accepting the cultural imperialism of the West regardless of its shortcomings. Singham and Hune in their study of the politics of NAM testify to the impact of advertising on peoples food habits in the region. They state:

> "The non-aligned world has experienced radical shifts...in its food habits, largely as a result of advertising by the global communications systems. New food tastes, such as bread made of white processed wheat flour, and powdered milk formulas for infants, are promoted as items of modernity and status. Such consumer items have not only altered the diet and nutritional levels in the Third World, but also have a detrimental effect on the domestic economy since these purchases generally have to be imported with hard currency."[45]

Western cultural hegemony is quite common in most developing countries; this largely because of a complex intermingling of political and social factors. The elites of the developing 'periphery' working in tandem with the elites of the 'core' countries politically and socially have facilitated the spread of Western cultural products. Consequently, such cultural hegemony is also the most difficult to resist and check.

The entry of a large number of foreign players on the African information and communications scenario in the nineties has completely altered the earlier traditional State political control structures. It has become freer. Radio France Internationale, BBC, Radio Vatican and Radio Swiss International have acquired licenses to broadcast programmes on Africa's domestic airwaves *via* satellite. Similarly, the audiovisual environment has also been overtaken by free enterprise and the advent of Democracy on the continent has provided the necessary impetus to the entry of small private operators. These foreign players are the major programme suppliers controlling more than 70 per cent of the continent's broadcast programmes, even while some countries such as Cape Verde and Djibouti import more than 90 per cent of their programmes. France is the major foreign player on the continent. Its networks such as Canal Horizons and TV 5 beam programmes from Paris *via* satellite to most parts of French speaking Africa.

While the network Canal Horizons had by 1995 gained more than 90,000 subscribers of whom as many as 18,000 were in Abidjan,[46] TV 5 diffused Canadian, French, Belgian and Swiss programmes to most French speaking countries in West Africa—Benin, Burkina Faso, Cote D'Ivoire, Gabon, Mali, Niger and Senegal. Other international networks that dominate the continental TV programmes are those of the United States that diffuse cultural and scientific programmes, Germany *via* the Transtel Network, and Deutsche Welle TV and the UK through the BBC World Service.

South Africa and Nigeria are the only national players that have emerged recently on the broadcast and the audiovisual scenario having large transnational services. While Nigeria broadcasts for about 120 hours per week in Arabic, French, Hausa and Swahili to the entire continent, South Africa has developed and widened the scope of its independent and community radio programmes. In the audiovisual sector South Africa's private and public networks have large infrastructures that cater to regional needs; by 1995 it had more than a million subscribers (90 per cent in South Africa) and diffused programmes to more than 35 countries on the continent. Nevertheless, as against the foreign operators their role is indeed limited and confined to their respective regions.

The monopoly for programme supplies lay with the global communications networks and it is they who exercised a cultural hegemony in the African countries. Most of the programmes they aired exposed the local peoples to seemingly innocent entertainment items, music and films, but in actuality they inculcated among the peoples the urge to imitate Western mores, tastes and the developed country consumer norms. They hardly reflected or portrayed indigenous culture and the morals of the people, rather they served the needs and priorities of the countries that generated these products. These ideas made the relationship between international power and international communications appear quite threatening enabling the powerful to disseminate their own propaganda and images creating their own scenarios in the minds of the foreign populations. The result was an uprooting of the traditional society and its replacement with bits and pieces of Western culture. As one writer of communications development states: "It was the incongruity of urban slum dwellers watching American television programmes in shacks where the only electricity flowed through a jerry built line to the TV set. It was the ubiquity of Coca Cola in countries where most of the population lacked access to clean water."[44] Besides, the poverty of African countries forced them to accept at low costs the standardized old programmes that had already had their run in the countries of their origin. Overall these programmes had their own repercussions in the developing societies. Of the impact of such a scenario of interactions between communications and society, and especially of the interactions between the two at different levels of their development, Schramm aptly states:

> Undoubtedly there is a powerful interaction: new developments in communication affect society, and new developments elsewhere in society affect communication. The important thing is that a certain level and stage of communication development have to accompany a certain stage and level of social development generally. Without a sophisticated and efficient development of communication, the base of population, cooperation, industrialization, education and skills needed in modern industrial society cannot possibly be established. It goes without saying that underdeveloped countries have underdeveloped communication systems too.[48]

Thus through the communications and media network Africa has come to be culturally dependent on the economies (including technologies) and the social mores of the advanced capitalist and industrialised societies. And African countries continue to be the poorest as regards telecommunications infrastructures and audiovisual resources. As recently as 1996, with a few exceptions, the African continent had only one telephone line for every 100 inhabitants, while barely 4 Africans in every 100 had a television set and these were available only in the urban centres while the rural areas remain deprived. Besides, since the programme content of the audiovisual networks hardly reflected or were sympathetic to the socio-cultural norms or the needs of the people, their dependence on the Western communications networks accentuated the wide diversities between the haves and the havenots and remained totally out of sync with the continental life patterns.

Political Impact and Political Use of Media and Communications

The media and communications network in Africa has extensively influenced the continent's political elites and its political systems, and given its potential, the media infrastructure has been widely used by them (the ruling elites) as a propaganda and power tool to influence policies and promote their interests. It was in fact quite early in the post-independence period that the political elites on the continent became aware of media's power and potential. Most ruling, authoritarian or single party leaderships—and Africa has had a fair share of them—did not take too long to realise this and exploit the sweep and power of the media. Radio and the radio broadcasting network has been most widely used since that arm of the media not only had an extensive reach but was also all encompassing of all strata of society both in the urban and rural areas.

Overall, when used for political purposes, particularly in the hands of the authoritarian rulers, its power has been quite awesome. Not only has media enabled the ruling elites to use it as an instrument for publicity and propaganda but at the same time it has been an effective means of control and self promotion. For example, at the time of a military *coup* or overthrow of a ruling government, control of the state radio station was as important as the seizure of the palace or seat of authority, and this happened ever so often. Nyerere used it to help advocate his socialist ideology and accelerate the implementation of social goals. Similarly, Mozambique and several other countries used the broadcast media to propagate systems of governance favourable to the ruling elites. Besides, the concept of "protocol" news—the news of ceremonial comings and goings of the public officials and coverage of ceremonial meets, conferences and other functions—were used by the top state functionnaries to promote themselves. It soon came to be an important weapon in the hands of the ruling elites. An example is the blatant use of the Mille Collines', "free" radio station in Rwanda for propaganda and hate mongering. Above all radio in Africa provided a window to the outside world and played a decisive role in the evolution of democratic pluralism.

It was only in the late eighties and the nineties that transnationalisation of the media and communications networks that swept the continent following globalisation, technology development that opened up the widespread use of satellites and other global networks for wider diffusion of audiovisual images, democratisation and the push of market forces that completely transformed the content and control systems of the existing media and communications infrastructure. At the same time, the emergence of new normative concerns of economic equity and upliftment of people also made the State diversify its media programmes to make them education and development-oriented. Control of the media and the communications network, till now managed entirely by the ruling government and the bureaucracy, came to be diversified between the government and the international information and communications conglomerates. While the former continued to handle news and developmental programmes, the latter new entrants on the scenario, monopolised and controlled the content and the diffusion of the bulk and the wide variety of international news, entertainment and other commercial programmes. In such a scenario several African states, particularly in West Africa—Senegal, Mali, Guinea, Benin and Burkina Faso—developed new control mechanisms for the media infrastructure. Similarly in South Africa, the post-Apartheid society adjusted to the winds of change ushered in by globalisation and by 1997 opened its communications network to private operators. But instead of becoming free and independent in its operations most African countries were perforce dependent on the international broadcast conglomerates that retained a nexus with the indigenous political and professional elites largely because of the very nature of their exogenous socio-economic and political links. And this had its own repercussions

The scenario was similar in the print media sphere; most African governments realising its power and potential lost no time in acquiring its management and control. They also did not hesitate to use the media to their own advantage. The state of the media then, in the decade following independence, reflected the nature of the State and the levels and patterns of its politico-economic development. In fact, as political freedom came to Africa, press freedom disappeared.[49] State control was extended to ownership of newspapers, radio and television development on the pretext of their inability to survive without subsidies, the need for employing indigenous staff and the need to create and control new styles of pluralism reflecting and supporting national developmental objectives. In reality however, newspapers soon became mouthpieces of the government and the independence and the creativity of journalists was curbed by formal and informal control systems.

African governments have over the years used various mechanisms to restrict and manage the media. In Zimbabwe, it purchased it outright. Resorted to a series of censorship procedures in the Cameroons where government officials used every means to suppress press independence.[50] In Ghana press control was extensive and even school magazines were expected to secure a license for publishing. Censorship laws were however never delineated and members of the Press were often incarcerated without justifiable reason.[51] In Malawi, President Hastings Banda tolerated no media criticism of his policies and quite often press personnel were indicted on the slightest pretext.[52] Governments in South Africa organized highly sophisticated campaigns to regulate the Press and used security and informal pressures in Kenya and Nigeria. In Kenya, where the Press is substantially privately and foreign owned (*e.g. Nation* and *Standard* of the Lonhro Group), the government has resorted to widespread intervention threatening the interests of the foreign investors and the local owners. Such interventions in media freedom reflect the government's political intentions of repression as a way of dealing with political opponents. In Nigeria also, the government exercised extensive interventionist tactics to influence, control and intimidate the Press, which is Africa's most vibrant network. Its news magazines, largely privately owned—8 dailies and 12 weeklies—constitute the most dynamic sector of the media. Since these publications were popular and widely circulated, the Government often adopted policies of intervention, checks and control. In 1986 for example, after the killing of Dele Giwa, Editor of the *Newswatch*, by a letter bomb suspected of having been planted by the state security agents, the magazine was suspended for publishing what the Government described as classified material—A Report of the Political Bureau set up by the government to draw up guidelines for the return to civilian rule.

Again in Tanzania, the Government under TANU (Tanzanian African National Union) resorted to policies of merger to ensure that sections of the privately controlled media would become a vital information arm of the government. Thus in 1972, the English language party newspaper *The Nationalist*, which had been heavily subsidised by the government, was merged with the nationalised *Standard* to form the *Daily Nation*. Originally both the *Nationalist* and *Uhuru* had been established "to give TANU and its government a mouthpiece both with Tanzania and the outside world."[53] Even President Kaunda of Zambia politically dominated the Press; he was known to appoint and fire journalists at will. Repression of journalists with a view to politically intimidate the media was also widespread in Uganda, Zaire and Equatorial Guinea.

In the Francophone countries the Press has been "an organ of propaganda" for the various governments and the political parties. Even in Senegal, which has a multi-party political system, *Le Soleil,* the country's most important daily, served the interests of the ruling Socialist Union Party *(Union Socialist Progressive)* and its governments in office.

Overall, most African leaders, whatever their political ideologies and affiliations, enforced measures of control and repression that would enable them to dominate the Press. The latter over the years has become an integral mouthpiece of governments. It has been "reduced to [being] a mere marionette which can only respond to the whims and caprices of the governments of the day, leaving the public it is supposed to serve in the lurch."[54]

APPRAISAL: EMERGING SCENARIOS

Media and communications development in Africa has thus come a long way from the first radio-broadcast on the continent which opened the floodgates of information and news to the great joy and excitement of the peoples. The communications network has since expanded and diversified to several areas of the continent. Besides, the technological advances and the development of the digital systems of transmission of programmes and images *via* satellite of the nineties' decade has revolutionised the entire communications structure, the structure that enables audiences to experience live images and pictures of current developments world-wide. Communications growth today is indeed complex; a multitude of interconnections, technological, political, cultural and economic have emerged and integrated into unified networks that profoundly affect socio-cultural and political developments on the continent. But while this profusion of new connections, technologies and information systems have opened wider horizons of knowledge to previously unlettered masses isolated to a community existence, it has had its own repercussions on them that highlight the inequities both at the national and international levels between the haves and the havenots.

Several distinctive features emerge from the foregoing analysis. The first is that media and communications development have had a far ranging and diverse impact on African countries both in respect of the availability of the number of receivers and the systems of networking. And this impact is directly related to the politico-economic developmental status of these countries—the imbalances of unequal economic development, the diversity of its political systems and the specific nature of its society. The development of the information society indeed reflects the distinct divisions between the industrialised developed world and the developing countries, including Africa, and also brings to the fore the issue of the inequalities between the rich and the poor within these. Like in other areas of economic development and political benefits, the differences in the information society are particularly wide in Africa and exist in the systems of telecommunications networking, the radio, television and the Press. Even as recently as 1994, Africa's development in this sphere was quite dismal as compared to other parts of the world. With 12 per cent of the world's population, it had only 1 per cent of the telephone lines available in the world. There were more telephone lines in the city of Tokyo than in the whole of Africa when the population of the continent is thirty times greater than that of the Japanese capital. Also, the differences in telecommunications development vary from one region to another—over the last decade the number of telephone lines per 100 inhabitants doubled in the Maghreb, while their numbers increased by 200 per cent in South Africa. But in the least developed region of sub-Saharan Africa, telecommunications development was almost stagnant reflecting the disparity between the affluent and the underpriveleged regions of the continent. At the same time the heavy concentration of telecommunication services in the capital cities and the provincial capitals is indicative of the benefits of the information system accruing only to the rich and the well-to-do. Thus for example in 1992 in the Ivory Coast, 71 per cent of the installed base of telephones were located in Abidjan; the subscriber line average for the whole country was 0.7 per cent compared with 4 per cent in Abidjan. In Benin, of the 25,500 lines available, 60 per cent were installed in Cotonou, which has only 10 per cent of the country's population. Again in Ghana, the country's 41,000 direct lines were concentrated in Accra, *i.e.* 2 per 100 inhabitants, whereas the overall rate in the country is 0.5 per cent and 0.1 per cent in the rural areas.

Similarly, even though the numbers of radio and the radio broadcasting networks have grown phenomenally over the last few decades, their growth when compared with the other parts of the developing world—Asia and Latin America—is low. To sub-Saharan Africa's 100 to 200 radio receivers per 1000 inhabitants and less than 12 hours daily broadcast time, most countries of Latin America had more than 200 receivers per 1000 inhabitants. In Africa itself there is wide disparity from one region to another; while several West African countries have more than 200 receivers per 1000, the least developed Sahelian belt countries have only between 100-200 receivers. South Africa and the Maghreb alone had more than 200 receivers per 1000 inhabitants. Meanwhile, the other media networks of the television and the Press have remained localised in the urban areas, and notwithstanding the development of the nineties, Africa even today has only 43 television sets per 1000 inhabitants—the lowest as compared to Latin America and Asia. The print media form has also remained in a state of underdevelopment. As recently as 1994, four Sahelian belt countries—Burkina Faso, Chad, Rwanda and Mauritania had no daily newspaper. Circulation has also remained limited to the educated elite and those who had the wherewithal to purchase a newspaper daily, and their numbers are small.

Secondly, the imbalances in media development and diffusion of its products as also the nature of African society, having widely differing levels of economic development, has enabled a techno-economic and socio-cultural hegemony of the West on the continent. This is largely because most developing countries do not have the advanced communications technological know how and are constrained by financial, technical and political factors that force them to rely on the industrialised West for developing their broadcast networks. In Africa, globalisation, liberalisation and marketisation have underscored these imbalances and distortions; resultantly communications have become standardized in content and are unidirectional in flow from the industrialised producer countries to the developing consumer states. Besides lack of resources and other developmental priorities have further prevented most African states from producing their own software for diffusion. Africa overall presents the worst case scenario amongst all the developing countries of such inequitous media development, even while over the last two decades the advent of Democracy in several states and the internationalisation of communications has made the media and communications sector freer, more varied and innovative.

Thirdly, techno-economic hegemony which affected every sector of the media and communications networks notwithstanding, it is the socio-cultural hegemonic control and the sociological upheavals it has wrought on society which are the most dramatic and which threaten the processes of development in Africa as in most other developing countries. And in this it is the crucial role of the television, which has come to be the primary cultural activity in most countries, that has to be underscored. The range and variety of programmes produced and diffused by the Western countries, mostly the United States, and their availability non-stop 24 hours a day through digital techniques *via* satellite have had their impact on developing country viewers exposed for the first time to such fare as pay TV, video games, sports, tele-shopping, films, serials, etc. However, most of these programmes have a uniformity and a standardized content that threatens to swamp developing societies marginalising their fragile community cultures. As says Schramm, people learn to like what they hear and see.[55] The particular power of the mass media lies in its ability to bring issues into the sphere of public discourse and to speed up the familiarization processes that have an effect on the formation of tastes. Quite often they also make these societies withdraw to their own ethno-religious beliefs and identities that oftentimes erupt in ethnic conflicts.

The perspective then is of an inequitious media growth process between the affluent industrialised North and the majority of the poor developing countries in the South. The disparity between them is growing even wider and the benefits of information and knowledge continue to accrue only to the rich advanced countries where databases, software and programmes are produced and concentrated. And it is these countries that dominate the audiovisual market, a market in which even the appearance and disappearance of programmes is controlled by the forces of demand and supply. The whole scenario is complex—control by a few countries of the content of the new information and communications technologies, access to them, the industrialisation of programmes and its diffusion to large numbers of people in the developing countries. And all these developments are linked to the current issues of globalization, development and Democracy.

On the African continent itself, the scenario of development is even more complex, and apart from other factors, generally relates to the exogenous sociological cultural influences on the elite groups in these countries and their dependence arising out of the colonial economic structural relations and ideological cultural ties. Besides, growth perspectives are comparatively lower than those in other developing countries. And while its thrust is widespread its impacts have been very often negative.

Given this overview of political control, cultural domination of transborder communications and data flows of economic, political and other information and its inequitious dissemination processes, several questions arise for the future. What can African countries, given their diversity and underdeveloped state of information and technology do for widespread dissemination of new mass communication trends that would enable development of all sectors of society? How can the wide diversity of knowledge and information between the rich and the deprived sectors of society be bridged?

As already stated before, African countries have taken several initiatives to widen and diversify its media and communications networks following political liberalisation and democratisation in the nineties. Some countries have launched independent private and commercial channels to meet the growing pressure of audiences for quality programmes. But the worsening economic situation on the continent has forced most African countries to prioratise their expenditures—resultantly they have been obliged to depend technically and financially on partnerships with other countries. In such a situation African countries must evolve indigenous national and sovereign policies to create an information society that would promote conditions harmonious to social, economic and cultural development that ensure access for the maximum numbers possible. Such access to knowledge and information would enable a positive contribution to the sustainable development of all sections of society. It would also be equally important for African countries to develop a cultural pluralism of ideas and opinions which would check standardization and uniformity of content in programmes. Diversity alone would enable a survival of the continent's varied culture and traditions without being linked and controlled only by market forces. But having said this, governments in Africa should not be unilaterally tempted to totally restrict and control access to the international communications highways which have their own role that allow for widespread information and knowledge. With these aims and directions, African countries would go a long way in evolving a sustainable communications system that has a wide sweep.

References and Notes

1 Several writers and researchers—Alvin Toffler, Peter Drucker, Regis Debray, Marshall Mcluhan and Joel de Rosnay—subscribe to the view that the West has evolved through three civilizational phases: the agrarian and feudal when economic activity was marked by an ample material base, but with little knowledge; the Industrial Revolution with its energy driven mass production techniques and now the Age of Information. This last phase, these writers assert is the age of new technologies when science and knowledge have become the critical vectors of the so called "value added" economies.
(For details see M. Cartier: *Les Inforoutes, mythes et realite* [Information Highways: Myths and Realities], Montreal, 1995.

2 Robert L. Stevenson: *Communication, Development and the Third World: The Global Politics of Information* (Longman, New York, London, 1988), p. 131.

3 Frank Okwu Ugboajah (Ed): *Mass Communication, Culture and Society in West Africa* (Hans Zell Publications, London, 1985).

4 UNESCO in its Report—*Mass Media in the Developing Countries 1961* states: As many as 100 states and territories in Africa, Asia and Latin America fall below this very low "minimum" level in all four of the mass media. The actual situation is even worse because the above criteria do not take into account the distribution of facilities within countries. In many underdeveloped countries over 60 per cent of the population live in rural districts, whereas the facilities for information are concentrated in a relatively few urban areas. Consequently, the above very general analysis does not fully reflect the dearth of facilities in the rural areas of most underdeveloped countries, and even of most semi-developed countries which otherwise stand above the "UNESCO minimum" level. An additional 19 countries, representing 2 per cent of the world population, fall below the "UNESCO minimum" in respect of three of the media. In short, nearly 70 per cent of the world's peoples lack the barest means of being informed of developments at home, let alone in other countries.

The above evaluation of development of the mass media in some 120 countries corresponds very closely with the United Nations' designation of countries which are generally underdeveloped. With due regard for the limitation of the method of classification used, the United Nations considers that a country is underdeveloped if the average per capita income is less than $ 300 annually. One hundred and one countries are found to be below this income level and an additional 16 countries fall within the $ 300 to $ 400 range. The countries in these two groups are, with few exceptions, those which fall below the "UNESCO minimum" for information facilities or which stand only slightly above that level.

Quoted in Wilbur Schramm: *Mass Media and National Development—The Role of Information in the Developing Countries* (Stanford University Press, Stanford, California, 1964), pp. 94-95.

5 Also when this figure is compared with the United States' 64 telephones per 1000 peoples, the gap between the two parts of the world is even more marked.
World Development Report—Knowledge for Development 1998-99 (World Bank, New York, 1999).

6 *Ibid.* Also see **Annexure I**, Table on *Information Flows.*

7 Ithiel de Sola Pool, who for many years studied information and communications related issues, in his study of the importance of telecommunications to rural development in Egypt, calculated a direct cost benefit ratio of 40 to 1, that rose to 85 to 1 when indirect special benefits were added. A telephone, Pool stated, not only facilitated the working of the local bureaucracy, but also made commerce more efficient and reduced the disruption and impact arising from emergency situations.
Ithiel De Sola Pool: *The Social Impact of the Telephone* (MIT Press, Cambridge MA, 1977).

8 Mustapha Masmoudi: "The New World Information Order" in *Journal of Communication* 29 (2), 1979, pp. 172-85, Quoted in *Communication Development and the Third World* By R.L. Stevenson (Longman, New York, 1988), p. 126.

9 Wilbur Schramm: *Mass Media and National Development—The Role of Information in the Developing Countries* (Stanford University Press, Stanford, California, 1964), p. 93.

10 *World Communications Report 1964* (UNESCO, Paris).

11 David Lamb, *Los Angeles Times* correspondent in *The Africans* (Random House, New York, 1982).

12 Frank Barton: *The Press of Africa—Persecution and Perseverence* (Macmillan Press, London, 1979).

13 It may however be noted that while some of these countries have a large number of dailies, their per capita circulation is low being offset by the fact that most of the dailies are circulated only in the

cities and towns while the rural areas remain neglected. India for example, has 800 dailies but the circulation figures are 20 dailies to a 1000 inhabitants.

14 1964 figures culled from *World Development Report 1998-99—Knowledge for Development* (World Bank, New York, 1999).
15 *UNESCO Statistical Yearbook 1996* (UNESCO, Paris, 1997).
16 Emile G. McAnany: *Communication in the Rural Third World: The Role of Information in Development* (New York, Praeger, 1980).
17 Daniel Lerner: *The Passing of Traditional Society : Modernizing the Middle East* (Free Press, Glencoe IL., 1958) Paperback edition published in 1964.
18 Wilbur Schramm: "Mass Media and National Development—1978", *UNESCO, Document No 42* submitted to the Macbride Commission, 1978.
19 Wilbur Schramm: n. 4, p. 271.
20 Graham Mytton: *Mass Communication in Africa* (Edward Arnold, London, 1983).
21 Source: *UNESCO Statistical Year Book 1996* (UNESCO, Paris, 1997).
22 *Le Pluralisme Radiophonique en Afrique de l'ouest* [Radio Pluralism in West Africa] Vol. 2 (L'Harmattan, Paris, 1993).
23 *Report of the Sixth World Conference of Community Radio Broadcasts Dakar, Senegal, 23-29 January, 1995:* "Women's Station Hits the Airwaves" *Inter Radio* (Montreal), Vol. 7, no. 2, 1995, p. 4, Quoted in *World Communications Report, 1997.*
24 "Rural Radio in Africa," *Development of Rural Radio in Africa,* International Workshop, Ouagadougou, Burkina Faso, 10-14 June 1996.
25 *World Communications Report* (UNESCO, Paris, 1997).
26 A.J. Tudseq: *L'Afrique Noire et ses televisions* (Paris, 1992), Quoted in *World Communications Report, 1997.*
27 Robert L. Stevenson: n. 2, p. 109.
28 *Ibid.*, pp. 112 and 114.
29 *Ibid.*, p. 70.
30 *World Development Report: Knowledge for Development 1998/99* (World Bank, Washington D.C., 1999).
31 *World Communications Report, 1997.*
32 1996 figures taken from *World Communications Report, 1997.*
33 See L.M. Bourgault: *Mass Media in Subsaharan Africa* (Indiana University Press, 1995), pp. 105, 127.
34 *World Communications Report, 1997.*
35 Frederick Harbison, "Education for Development" in *Scientific American* 209, no. 3, 1963, pp. 144-47. Quoted in Wilbur Schramm: n. 4.
36 Daniel Lerner: "Towards a Communication Theory of Modernization" in Lucian Pye: *Communications and Political Development* (Princeton University Press, Princeton, 1963), p. 341.

37 See M.F. Millikan, and D.L. Blackmer, *The Emerging Nations* (Little Brown, Boston, 1961) p. 47 ff, for an exposition of the development process.
38 Wilbur Schramm: n. 4.
39 Joseph S. Nye Jr., "Soft Power" in *Foreign Policy*, No. 80, Fall 1990, pp. 153-71.
40 Quoted in Mark D. Alleyne: *International Power and International Communication* (Macmillan in association with St. Antony's College, Oxford, 1995), p. 10.
41 *Ibid.*, p. 11.
42 R. Joseph, "Class, State and Prebendal Politics in Nigeria," *The Journal of Commonwealth and Comparative Politics*, Vol. 21, no. 3, pp. 21-38.
43 In Gambia, Central African Republic, Nigeria and Kenya, the deprived groups challenged the authority of tradition and prevailing patterns; in Chad after the fall of Tombalbaye, in Liberia 1990/91, in Uganda under Idi Amin, in Zaire through the entire period of Mobutu's rule and in Mozambique since 1980, conflicts occurred because of economic hegemony and coercive tactics of the State; in Angola, Mozambique, Ethiopia, Madagascar, Congo, Zimbabwe, etc., socially discontented groups challenged authority and yet in others—Chad, Sudan, Nigeria, Zaire, Uganda, Equatorial Guinea, Rwanda, Burundi, Mauritania and Liberia ethnic and religious strife was considerably aggravated by socio-economic differences and deprivations extending from one ethnic group to another.
44 Johan Galtung: "A Structural Theory of Imperialism," *Journal of Peace Research*, Vol. 8, no. 2, 1971, pp. 91-94.
45 A.W. Singham and Shirley Hune: *Non-Alignment in an Age of Alignments* (Lawrence Hill and Co.: Westport, Conn: 1986, pp. 350-51.
46 Canal Horizons se developpe en Afrique [Canal Horizons is Progressing in Africa], *Le Monde*, Paris, 15 September 1995. Quoted *in World Communications Report*, 1997.
47 Robert L. Stevenson: n. 2, p. 69.
48 Wilbur Schramm: n. 4, p. 41.
49 F. Barton: *The Press of Africa* (London, Macmillan, 1979).
50 Baffour Ankomah: "Cameroon's Forbidden Topics" in *Index on Censorship*, February 1988.
51 *West Africa* (London), 15-21 October 1990, p. 2648.
52 *Ibid.*
53 Graham Mytton 1983: n. 20.
54 Niyii Alabi: "Publish and Survive" in *New African*, May 1988.
55 Wilbur Schramm, n. 4, p. 137.

ANNEXURE I

Information Flows

Country	*Main Telephone Lines*		*Televisions*	
	Per 1000 people Index 1996 (1990=100) i.e. data refer to change in total value 1996		*Per 1000 people Index 1996 (1990=100) i.e. data refer to change in total value 1996*	
High Human Development				
1 US	640	125	806	110
			data refers to 1995	data refers to 1995
2 Japan	489	113	700	117
3 France	564	117	598	114
			data refers to 1995	data refers to 1995
4 Germany	538	138	493	106
5 Switzerland	640	115	493	128
Medium Human Development				
1 Malaysia	183	238	228	178
2 Phillippines	25	293	125	300
3 Brazil	96	161	289	148

(Contd.)

	Country	*Main Telephone Lines*		*Televisions*	
		Per 1000 people	*Index 1996 (1990=100) i.e. data refer to change in total value 1996*	*Per 1000 people*	*Index 1996 (1990=100) i.e. data refer to change in total value 1996*
4	China	45	802	252	172
5	South Africa	100	128	123	141
6	Algeria	44	161	68	115
7	Swaziland	22	151	96	600
				data refers to 1995	data refers to 1995
8	Namibia	54	161	29	150
9	Gabon	32	169	76	233
				data refers to 1995	data refers to 1995
10	Zimbabwe	15	141	29	107
				data refers to 1995	data refers to 1995
11	India	15	287	64	222
12	Cameroon	5	175	—	—
13	Congo	8	135	7	154
14	Kenya	8	149	19	141
				data refers to 1995	data refers to 1995

Low Human Development					
1	Congo Democratic Republic	1	106	41	4500
				data refers to 1995	data refers to 1995
2	Sudan	4	160	80	124
				data refers to 1995	data refers to 1995
3	Togo	6	229	14	273
4	Nigeria	4	140	55	174
		data refers to 1995	data refers to 1995	data refers to 1995	data refers to 1995
5	Madagascar	3	125	—	—
6	Mauritania	4	174	82	664
7	Zambia	9	120	80	264
8	Senegal	11	214	38	121
				data refers to 1995	data refers to 1995
9	Cote d'Ivoire	9	178	58	117
10	Benin	6	221	73	533
				data refers to 1995	data refers to 1995
11	Tanzania	3	127	—	—
12	Uganda	2	172	26	292
13	Malawi	4	133	—	—
14	Angola	5	75	51	965
				data refers to 1995	data refers to 1995

(Contd.)

Country	Main Telephone Lines		Televisions	
	Per 1000 people	Index 1996 (1990=100) i.e. data refer to change in total value 1996	Per 1000 people	Index 1996 (1990=100) i.e. data refer to change in total value 1996
15 Guinea	2	143	8 data refers to 1995	133 data refers to 1995
16 Chad	1	149	2	150
17 Gambia	19	346	—	—
18 Rwanda	—	—	—	—
19 Central African Republic	3	194	5	131
20 Mali	2	191	11	150
21 Eritrea	5	—	7	—
22 Guinea Bissau	7	133	—	—
23 Mozambique	3	126	3 data refers to 1995	150 data refers to 1995
24 Burundi	2	191	2	240
25 Burkina Faso	3	210	6	138
26 Ethiopia	3	119	4 data refers to 1995	217 data refers to 1995
27 Niger	2	166	—	—
28 Sierra Leone	4	129	17	177

Source: ITU (International Telecommunication Union) 1997 *World Telecommunication Indicators*, (Database Geneva).

5

Arab Attempts at Journalism

*S.N. Asad Rizvi**

In 1690 a Moroccan Ambassador, Mohd. bin 'Abdal-Wahab al Wazir al-Ghassani, went on a state mission to Spain to discuss with King Carlos II the release of Moroccan prisoners and other matters of common concern. Recording his impressions from his first visit, Ghassani noted a curious phenomenon. In Madrid, he reported, there exists a house with a 'writing mill' (*qalib al-kitaba*). Its owner gathers news items from remote lands, prints them on sheets (*qaratis*) in thousands of copies, then sells them for a modest fee to those interested. These papers, Ghassani observed, "are full of exaggerations and lies." They are called *kasita* (gazette, Spanish *gaceta*), a name that sounds as strange as the idea itself.[1]

Three centuries later, Ghassani's account of European newspapers is no more than a curiosity. Thousands of periodicals have since appeared in West Asia itself, most of them in Ghassani's own language, Arabic. Hundreds of Arabic newspapers are currently being published inside and outside of the region. In format, reporting methods, distribution mechanisms, and graphic arrangements, they do not differ markedly from their European counterparts; some indeed compare favourably with most Western periodicals in more ways than one. The medium now has a universally accepted name, or rather two interchangeable names of pure Arabic origin: *jarida* (*pl. jaraid*) or *sahifa* (*pl. suhuf*). And after some 160 years of growth, its history is fairly fully recorded

* Dr. Rizvi was formerly Lecturer at the Academy of Third World Studies, Jamia Millia Islamia, New Delhi.

in scores of published studies. It seems, then, that the Arabs have devised their own version of what was once a foreign oddity, and have made it a permanent feature of their social, political, and cultural reality. To what extent, one may ask, do these similarities in format and techniques reflect resemblances in other, more significant aspects such as the role of the Press in the political community, the degree of its freedom, its social functions and cultural roles, its public image, and the standing of those associated with it? In other words, do the terms *jarida* and *sahifa* differ markedly from newspaper or journal in their semantic range and accepted connotations? And to the extent that they do, what in the Arab socio-political and cultural legacy has caused the Arabic Press to evolve in a manner distinct from its European prototype?

Thus phrased, the question is broad and complex enough to call for an extensive study. The purpose of what follows must be more modest: to identify some basic characteristics of the Arabic Press during the phases of its evolution, and to point out some of the major factors which have shaped its unique nature. The discussion will focus on the political Press only. Non-political periodicals have, of course, played a major part in modern Arab history and have made an invaluable contribution to Arab culture, education and science. It is precisely for this reason that a proper appreciation of their role requires and merits, a separate study.

Historical surveys of the Arabic Press, most of them by Arab authors, tend to follow a standard pattern. They start from a point in the late eighteenth century, with the French invasion of Egypt and the printing shops General Bonaparte set up there; they proceed to describe the early journalistic projects of the governments in Cairo and Istanbul, then move on to recount developments during the phase of non-official journalism, often taking the two World Wars as two major turning points. If these surveys differ from one another, it is primarily in the amount and accuracy of the details which they provide. Most of them are little more than chronological catalogues of the appearance and disappearance of the region's many newspapers. As such they make for rather dull reading.

Some authors, however, endeavour to lend more meaning to the story of Arab journalism by tracing back its roots to earlier Islamic periods. For example, the Lebanese Adib Muruwwa, an oft-quoted authority in this field, seeks "the seeds of (Arab) journalism" (*budhur fann al-sihafa*) in the first century of Islam.

Outlining the evolution of the Press *al-sihafa*—during the Ummayyad, Abbasid, and Mamluk periods, he counts men such as Ibn al-Muqaffa, Jahiz and Maqrizi as *kuttab sahafiyyin*, 'journalists,' and Ibn Hawqal as *katib riburtaj* 'a reporter.'[2] Moving on to consider the modern phase, Muruwwa depicts the Egyptian historian 'Abdal-Rahman al Jaborti as the "first Arab to have engaged in journalism (*marasa al-sihafa*) in a practical way;" his book *'Aja'ib al-athar* was "*a sihafa* in every sense of the word, since it registered events day by day... in a manner no different from that of present day journalistic reporting." Others, too, have offered such interpretations.[3]

Al-sihafa al-abbasi 'the Abbasid Press,' is evidently an anachronistic (anything out of its proper time in history) compound—unless of course the sense of *sihafa* is stretched far beyond its accepted meaning, historical or contemporary. As Muruwwa himself rightly notes,[4] the word *sihafa* for 'Press' is a nineteenth century neologism (a new word or a new meaning for an established word). It was derived from *sihafa*, 'newspaper,' itself a new term which had acquired this modern sense earlier in the century. Previously *sahifa* had meant a 'leaf,' 'page,' 'a letter' and most commonly, 'a book.' Nor was there another Arabic word for 'newspaper' before the nineteenth century, since the notion itself was hardly known. Had there been one, Ghassani would not have had to employ a foreign expression, *sihafa*, reflecting the novelty of the idea in West Asia, just as reporting to an alien world where none existed in Arabic had attested to its foreignness two centuries earlier.

The study of nineteenth century Press/government relations in West Asia reads very much like that of Europe in the seventeenth and eighteenth centuries. Royal efforts to circumscribe the spread of printed opinion through coercion, temptation, censorship, suspension, prosecution, or subsidies and other kinds of assistance, had marked the evolution of journalism in Western Europe as it did in West Asia. Like their European colleagues, Arab journalists sought greater freedom but were markedly more docile. Only a few were bold, and having been convinced that Western political values were applicable to their society, demanded fuller liberty. Among them were men like Adib Ishaq, Abd Allah Nadim, Yaqub Sannu and a handful of others;[5] they were exceptional. The nineteenth century bequeathed the phenomenon of both docility and daring to the twentieth.

During its infancy the Arabic Press had proceeded tardily on the long road to political independence. While playing a major cultural and educational role, it was a less effective instrument for mobilizing public opinion and for increasing public involvement in political affairs. Impatient journalists who sought a quick transformation of these realities found themselves forced out. They moved from Hamidian Syria and Lebanon to Egypt, where the atmosphere was more congenial and from there to London and Paris. But the great majority of journalists preferred to stay, accepting caution and compliance as necessary ground rules for their new journalistic endeavours.

In the late nineteenth century, *i.e.* during the early adolescence of the Arab Press, the political environment had a far-reaching effect on Arab journalism. Dominating the political scene, 'the struggle' claimed a great deal of the writers' energy at the inevitable expense of objective reporting. Often enough, when a person chose to become a journalist he in fact chose to join a battle. Partisanship became an accepted standard, and journalism became synonymous with it. Reporters trained themselves in taking the offensive rather than in seeking the truth, and came to regard fighting for a cause as their primary objective, conveying information as merely a secondary task. Excited by the new opportunities, yet not always aware of the full might and risks of free expression, they frequently misused their medium, employing it indiscriminately and with excessive aggressiveness against government and colleagues alike.[6] The Arab Press of this period, with some well-known exceptions, was typically 'a Press of commentary' *sihafat maqala* rather than 'a Press of news' *sihafat khabar*;[7] to wit the kind of Press in which the line between reporting and opinion is of little significance and often blurred. And since there would be many causes worth fighting for even after national independence had been achieved the experience was carried forward as likely to be useful in later years as well.

During the inter-war period, the Arab Press made impressive strides. But soon after the attainment of national independence following the Second World War, military *coups* in various parts of the Arab world clouded the silver lining. These regimes silenced all criticism by launching new official organs and when this did not prove to be satisfactory, the Press was nationalized. Journalists now a part of the bureaucracy were confined to a mere recording of the events.

In countries where no revolutions took place, like Jordan, Saudi Arabia and the Gulf States—newspapers were expected to show loyalty to the government. Unlike in the military revolutionary regimes, newspapers were not absorbed into the bureaucracy. They were allowed to remain in private hands (though sometimes owned jointly with state agencies). But much like the Press in the revolutionary regimes, they were expected to take their political cue from the authorities, give overall support to government policies and take no independent political initiatives. Journalists in these states were somewhat freer than their colleagues in the revolutionary states.

On this *mise en scene* two places stand out distinctively. One was post-Second World War Lebanon: the country's pluralistic composition and the absence of an authoritarian government allowed the growth of an independent and politically varied Press. Until the 1975-76 Civil War, the Lebanese Press served as an outlet of free speech in an otherwise tightly controlled system. Newspapers which survived the turbulence of the civil war and ensuing developments continued to enjoy considerable degree of liberty, guaranteed by the lack of a strong, or indeed any, central government. The other place where printing was free was abroad, where forced or voluntary exile had opened the road to free expression for Arab journalists.

In recent years there have been changes. In Kuwait, a high quality diverse Press has emerged of late to replace its Lebanese counterpart as an arena for inter-Arab dialogue. Here the Press seems to be quite distinguishable in certain important respects from that in other Arab countries, and hence to lend an additional tint to the contemporary meaning of *sihafa*. In Egypt, licensed political parties have been allowed to publish their own newspapers and propagate even their own antagonistic views.

In several ways the Arab Press may well be a reflection of its complex history, the history of an important institution, based on foreign example, struggling to be assimilated into a society reluctant to relinquish its traditional conventions.

References

1 Bernard Lewis, *The Muslim Discovery of Europe* (New York, 1982), p. 303.

Muhammad bin 'Abdal-Wahhab al-Ghassani, *Rihlat al-wazir Fi 'Ifikar al-asiv*, (Ed.) (Alfredo Bustani, Tangier, 1940), p. 67.

2 Adib Muruwwa, *Outline of Press in Arabia* (Beirut, 1961), p. 75.
3 *Ibid.*, p. 158.
4 *Ibid.*, n. 2, p. 15.
5 Tom J. McFadden, *Daily Journalism in Arab States* (Columbus, 1953), pp. 28-31.
6 Rafiq al-Maqdisi, *The Art of Journalism* (Damascus, 1946), pp. 90-91.
7 Saluma Musa, *A Chronicle of Arab Press* (Columbia, 1962), pp. 71-76.

Section II

Freedom of Information and Repercussions of Political Control

6

Media in the Third World: Freedom and Social Responsibility*

Ajit Bhattacharjea **

The importance and timeliness of a discussion on *Media and Communications in the Third World* cannot but be underscored. Throughout the world, media is going through a period of intense self-examination. Professional journalists are questioning their role in the society. They are finding it difficult to cope with pressures emanating from the global market forces, reinforced by rapid advances in media technology. They are faced with forces that attempt to treat news as a commodity to be evaluated more by its packaging than its content. This naturally goes against their professional ethics. Noted French media critic, Dominique Wolton, Director of the Laboratory of Communication and Politics, Paris, has put it very succinctly: "News is different from merchandise in a fundamental way: it is either true or false." The role of editors hinges on this belief. But packaging has been simplified by computer programmers and profit is of the highest value in the cult of the market. As a result managers and designers have begun to supervise news operations. Even the Americans have expressed

* Keynote Address at Seminar-Media and Communications in the Third World, organised by the Academy of Third World Studies, Jamia Millia Islamia.

**Ajit Bhattacharjea is Director, Press Institute of India, New Delhi.

concern at these developments. Prof. Daniel Hallin of the University of California writes:

> Economics has eroded the barriers between journalism and the profit-making business of selling audiences to advertisers. And this is likely to bring into question both the notion of journalism as a public trust and the existence of the common public culture that news once provided.

Random interviews conducted by the International Press Institute about a year ago reveal the depths of public disillusion with the media. Sample opinions of readers were: In Paris—"I don't pay attention to the media because I don't believe any of them." In Rome—"When I buy a newspaper, any newspaper, I'm perfectly aware that the information I get is biased. Papers are controlled by publishers, and publishers have opinions." In Buenos Aires—"I do not have confidence in any newspaper. They are all subjective." In Bangkok—"There's a lot of criticism of unreliability of newspapers." These were typical reader responses in most countries. In South Korea, Press credibility had deteriorated so much that legislation was being drafted to limit monopoly ownership by 'chaebols,' the giant financial conglomerates that dominate the economy. Even in Britain, competing Press barons have damaged the reputation of what were once known to be quality papers. Meanwhile, the tabloids which pry individual privacy and subscribe to presenting salacious accounts of crime, sex, violence and some of the worst features of social life, prosper and increase their circulation.

Yet mass media continues to be an essential pillar of the democratic structure. There is no alternative channel to keep the electorate informed of what is happening in the country and about the adequacy of government structures, at all levels, in resolving national problems. It must perform the no less vital job of keeping those in authority informed about trends in public opinion. Indeed, if cynicism about media grows, democracy may not survive. Newly-independent nations, with delicate democratic structures, are particularly vulnerable. Their self-confidence is also shaken by media's traditional preference for the negative, sensational happenings. Normalcy and progress seldom make news. There are however, no simplistic solutions to this problem. Circulation graphs attest to a clear reader preference for a regular dose of negative news. Eliminating them would mean loss of circulation and advertisement revenue. The very same reasons are cited for the excess of Bollywood-style entertainment on TV. And it is essential that media be financially viable if it is to function independently. Whatever its compulsions however, the cost to society will be much higher if media's functions in a democratic society are sacrificed at the altar of profit.

This is the dilemma we face. media must obviously be free from governmental authority and influence if it is to perform its role of watchdog and evaluate governmental performances objectively. At the same time if freedom is taken to mean freedom to pursue commercial profits at the cost of favouring moneyed interests, while ignoring the plight of the poor and underprivileged, media abuses its power. The conflict between profit and social responsibility is particularly sharp in a Third World country, for the poor form the bulk of the population. The conflict has been heightened by the rapid advances in media technology in the last decade and the spread of the culture of the market. We have yet to evolve an effective way to encourage media to perform its democratic role without curtailing its autonomy.

India is experiencing the impact of advancing media technology more intensively, perhaps, than most other countries. Like much of the Third World, it is under pressure to open upto the forces of economic globalisation. Even while I do not intend to discuss the pluses and minuses of the economic argument, I would like to state that the forces of technological and economic globalisation divert media attention from the conditions of the poor and underprivileged. The latter do not count in a market-dominated society; in the harsh world of media economics, they do not generate advertising revenue.

Advances in media technology have been a mixed blessing for India. The country has witnessed unprecedented growth in both the print and the electronic media. Television is doing even better than print and is likely to do so even more despite the widespread poverty and limited access to electric supply. This is because illiteracy is no barrier to TV, it reaches out to millions who have no other source of information and entertainment. As a result they tend to be uncritical taking the screen as reality. This gives great incentive to advertisers who are financing an increasing number of TV channels. Satellite transponders are also available on hire. Cable facilities enable viewers in Delhi and other cities to access at least fifty channels. Due to limited uplinking facilities most foreign satellite channels emanate from stations sited in Hong Kong. Even while these stations beam programmes beyond India, they generally cater almost exclusively to India. As a result a large number of these programmes are dubbed into English and Hindi. Besides, the Indian middle class—an estimated 300 million provides an attractive and large market for consumer products. This is more than what an European country can offer. Consequently, there is no dearth of multinational companies eager to buy advertisement time. Since the large section of the middle class can afford to pay, the advertisers spare no effort. Resultantly, most TV programmes are designed to entertain rather than educate. News programmes, usually depict personalities rather than issues; and grass-roots problems of poverty and deprivation seldom receive much attention.

The end result of these programmes and those thriving on sex and violence is beginning to tell. The impact of TV commercials is even more damaging, especially for children. They also promote social envy and family discontent. A 1996 study titled *The Impact of Television Advertising on Children* (Sage), found among other things, "the affluent child may feel convinced that only his or her class of Indians really counts. On the other hand, the child from a poor family may be forced to acknowledge that the lifestyles of the affluent are the only legitimate ones." Many commercials thus target this very impressionable group.

While on this subject, UNESCO must be congratulated for undertaking a global study recently on the impact of media violence on children. The report is highly disturbing showing that TV dominates the life of children throughout the world; it promotes and justifies violence, aggression and other forms of anti-social behaviour. Horrifying evidence of this was seen in America recently when two school children shot dead five of their classmates and injured others in a TV-style shooting spree.

In India, when TV was started in 1975 it aroused very different expectations of its benefits. The Government of India sponsored a path-breaking demonstration of the use of satellite television to extend primary education and socio-economic development to remote villages. The occasion was the loan of an American satellite for one year. With software devised in India, the Satellite Instructional Television Experiment, or *SITE*, beamed programmes on agriculture, health and primary education to 2,400 villages. Researchers evaluating the experiment found that many recommended practices in agriculture, health, hygiene and family welfare had been adopted. The experiment ended when the satellite was withdrawn and was not revived even after India launched its own communications satellite in 1982. By then, Doordarshan was accepting commercials to meet its expenses. A programme meant for poor remote villages was unlikely to earn revenue; the most important unquantifiable non-commercial benefits were totally overlooked.

But, unlike in the developed countries, advances in television have not inhibited the growth of the print media. New technologies, such as desk top printing, modems and better communications have facilitated the growth and circulation of newspapers country-wide. A large number of regional newspapers which service remote areas have also emerged. All this has been facilitated to a considerable extent by computer programmes that provide scripts in many languages. This has not only simplified production but has also helped to design modular layouts and colour prints that make newspapers more attractive. Even while such layouts encourage only brief action-oriented news reports and entertaining colour features at the cost of detailed investigations they have not inhibited the growth of print media. In fact, according to the latest figures (1996), provided by the Registrar of Newspapers for India, news journals appeared in 19 languages and 81 dialects. The total number was 37,254; an increase of 1,653 over the previous year. The overall circulation amounted to as much as 79,283,000. The number of daily newspapers was 4,236, an increase of 197. In terms of figures, the Press undoubtedly is flourishing. Besides, respect for the printed word being deeply ingrained, has helped give considerable momentum to the development and growth of newspapers and they have remained beyond the pale and implications of the market forces.

In the final analysis, while technological advances have encouraged growth and development of the print media, it has considerably discouraged detailed investigations. There is no space for lengthy reports however important the occasion. The patchy coverage of the Lok Sabha debate on the Vote of Confidence on Prime Minister Vajpayee's Government is the latest example. Bigger newspapers are increasingly dominated by advertisements and their area of coverage is narrowly focused on the metropolitan region. These contain the affluent ten per cent of the population that is the primary target for advertisers. Since the vast majority of the people of India live in villages and small towns their socio-economic conditions goes virtually unnoticed.

Media failings have been used by some governments to justify censorship and other forms of regulation. In every case, the remedy has proved worse than the disease. It has inevitably been used to black out criticism and project an unrealistically positive view of authority. As a result, the credibility of the media is entirely lost and whatever the authorities say is suspect. The outcome is worse than before, as Prime Minister Indira Gandhi discovered after censorship was imposed under the Emergency of 1975-76.

The dilemma of choosing between a free but often irresponsible and a controlled but subservient media remains the most crucial problem facing countries that have chosen the democratic path. The only way out is to promote a culture of self-regulation combined with greater awareness of the media's role in society. Certain developments have helped. The advantage of immediacy that TV enjoys in covering spot events has induced some papers to focus more on covering histories and backgrounds. *The Los Angeles Times* gives space and prominence to reports on social processes rather than events. *The Globe* and *Mail of Toronto* have instructed its correspondents to report on processes, leaving events to news agencies. This is the route major papers must take if they are to survive. But newspaper establishments and some journalists are reluctant as process reporting takes time, study, fieldwork and money. Happenings involving sex, violence, scandal, corruption and the rest are easier to locate, easier to write, easier to headline and easier to sell. And the remaining space between advertisements can be filled cheaply with featurised entertainment material.

Nevertheless, the media will have to counter public disillusion if it is to survive. *The Los Angeles Times* has shown the way the more serious national papers will have to go. In most Third World countries, the regional Press which is still developing, provides room for hope. It is less subject to market forces and is in closer touch with local opinion. Local journalists are less cynical about their vocation than their metropolitan and foreign counterparts. Given encouragement and recognition, they may change the face of grass-roots papers. Television too, is responding to charges of entertainment excesses. It has started to offer more news and current affairs programmes. The *Discovery* channel demonstrates that popular education need neither be dull nor unviable, if imaginatively handled. The future thus may not be as black as it appears today.

7

UNESCO's Commitment to Free Flow of Information*

*Prof. Moegiadi***

Prof. Moegiadi thanked the Academy of Third World Studies for inviting him for the Inaugural Function. As a UNESCO representative in the region, he said, he was happy that the Seminar would focus and interact on various issues related to media and communications, especially issues of social and global impact of media development, religion and media, and political control over media in the Third World.

The role of the media in the changing world is now more important, more relevant than ever; it involves a mobilization, a call which has to emanate from the people, who can and must participate.

UNESCO reaffirms its commitment to the *"free flow of information"* in order to encourage the free flow of ideas by word and image and a wider and better balance, dissemination of all forms of information contributing to the advancement of societies without any obstacle to freedom of expression, both through the traditional media and the new electronic media systems.

We in UNESCO have also endeavoured, in recent years, to promote the educational and cultural dimensions in the media,

---

* Inaugural Address at Seminar—Media and Communications in the Third World.

**Prof. Moegiadi is Director, UNESCO, New Delhi.

highlighting in particular the mission of public service broadcasting in this respect, whether financed by the state or by the private sector. The establishment in 1993 of the World Radio and Television Council was an important landmark in the direction. This move has also made it possible to disseminate information on the action taken by professional organisations to reduce violence in the media and win recognition—through the adoption of the Toronto and Beijing platforms for action—of the need to facilitate access by women to expression and decision-making in the media.

Women have been underrepresented in technical posts and on managerial boards. Resultantly, their influence in decision making in their organizations is limited. The question of their influence over content is a more complex issue owing to the wide variety of situations to be found within the media (women's magazines, television programmes, newspaper articles and others).

UNESCO's Constitution states that it is necessary to foster 'the free exchange of ideas and knowledge to develop and increase the means of communication between peoples and to employ these means for the purpose of mutual understanding and a truer and more perfect knowledge of each other's lives.'

For the current biennium 1998-99, freedom of expression and freedom of the Press is still one of UNESCO's major programmes. In the World Press Freedom Day to be celebrated on 3 May, 1998 UNESCO's Guillermo Cano World Press Freedom Prize will be awarded. It is expected that all member states would make a special effort to celebrate the occasion which marks the fiftieth anniversary of the Universal Declaration of Human Rights. UNESCO's sub-programme on "*Media and freedom of expression*" during 1998-99 will focus on the following lines of action:

(*i*) Freedom of expression and freedom of the Press;
(*ii*) Promoting independent and pluralistic media;
(*iii*) The educational and cultural mission of public service broadcasting; violence on the screen; and
(*iv*) To enhance the role of Women in the media.

To have "*access to information and new technologies*" a *project on Ethical and Sociocultural Challenges of the New Information Society* is planned and will be implemented jointly by sectors of Communication, Information and Informatics, Culture and Education. This inter-sectoral project is aimed at strengthening

UNESCO's role as a forum of reflection and clearing house on the impact of new information and communication technologies.

UNESCO is also committed to *capacity-building in communication, information and informatics* to help member states, particularly the developing countries and disadvantaged communities world-wide to strengthen their capacities in communication, information and informatics. The main lines of action for this biennium are:

(*i*) assistance to projects for the development of communication;
(*ii*) training of communication professionals;
(*iii*) development of Community media.

In this connection we will continue our efforts, assisting the countries in South Asia to develop an approach using expertise available in India.

UNESCO will also continue to support the development of library and information services at the national and regional levels. Particular emphasis will be placed on helping information institutions master the new technologies in co-operation with the Inter-governmental Informatics Programme, and on promoting the role of public libraries as community information centres. The main lines of action are:

(*i*) Development of library and information services;
(*ii*) Restoration of world libraries;
(*iii*) Upgrading of archival services.

The UNESCO Network of Associated Libraries (UNAL) will be further expanded and strengthened. Cooperation, particularly, in the use of new information and communication technologies, between UNAL and UNESCO Clubs, Centres and Associations will be encouraged. Regional initiatives such as the network of virtual libraries in the Mediterranean area will also be supported. In the field of archives, efforts will focus mainly on extending archival infrastructures and improving training of archivists in developing countries and countries in transition to Democracy—in particular training in the use of new information technology.

In 1998-99 UNESCO would also work for the *development of informatics and telematic applications*, building upon the results already obtained in the implementation of selected interdisciplinary pilot projects (development of appropriate telematics applications: use of interactive television technology for educational applications in developing countries; virtual laboratory projects, etc.) A new emphasis will be put on providing an active and effective technological support for development projects in all UNESCO's fields of competence. The main lines of action intended are:

(*i*) Expanding access to global information flows;
(*ii*) Electronic networks for increased cooperation in science, education and culture;
(*iii*) Virtual learning communities and virtual laboratory applications;
(*iv*) Training of computer specialists, trainers and users.

Thus, within the basic frameworks of freedom of expression and freedom of free flow of information, UNESCO is engaged the world over in promoting the educational, cultural and developmental dimensions. The forthcoming World Conference of Communications and Culture in year 2000 is intended to discuss issues having an adverse impact following the globalization of communications. Even while UNESCO promotes free flow of information, it is concerned with the threat that such free flow pose to the cultural identity of states. Diversity must be preserved and media and telecommunications should remain a tool in our hands.

8

State of Media in Pakistan: The Last Decade

*Sushant Sareen**

Post-Script

The military coup in Pakistan happened right in the midst of the penning down of this paper. Suddenly it appeared as though the paper had been overtaken by events. Since the focus of this paper was on the state of Media in Pakistan during the last decade, a period during which Pakistan was under a multi-party democratic dispensation, the reversion to an authoritarian military dictatorship seemed to make redundant the entire premise of the paper. Democracy with all its anarchy and chaos, protest and turbulence, factiousness and fractiousness, allowed the Press at least a modicum of freedom. For a moment it seemed that all this was going to change after the coup.

However, a deeper analysis of the situation in Pakistan and indeed of the theme of the paper made one realize that despite the reversion to an authoritarian military dictatorship, there is no paradigm shift as far as the issue of independence and freedom of the Press in Pakistan is concerned. Nor for that matter does the new dispensation mark a paradigm shift in the struggle of the independent media to maintain its hard-found and hard-fought freedom. Notwithstanding the trappings of a multi-party liberal

* Sushant Sareen is Executive Editor of **POT** *Public Opinion Trends, Analyses and News Service*, New Delhi.

democracy, the Press in Pakistan has always had to contend with myriad pressures, generally subtle but often brazen, from whichever government in power during the decade or so of liberal multi-party democracy from 1988 to 1999.

Of course, a sense of trepidation did seize the normally unrestrained and voluble Pakistani print media just after the coup. As a reporter in the monthly news magazine **Herald** *writes, "The memories of Majors sitting in newspaper offices to vet everything before it could be sent to the Press may have faded a bit over the last fifteen years or so, but they haven't gone away entirely. Was the rather longish honeymoon that the Press had with freedom, then, finally over?... the Press went into a mode of extreme caution. The extent of self-censorship employed by the Press in the days following the October 12 coup has not been seen in Pakistan in the last fifteen years...."[1]*

The first few days under the new military dispensation have however belied some of the fears of the Press community, at least for the time being. The new Chief Executive of Pakistan, Gen. Pervez Musharraf, in his first policy address to the nation declared: "Media forms an integral part of statehood in this era of information, I have great regard and respect for the media. I trust it to play a positive and constructive role. I am a firm believer in the freedom of the Press and am even considering liberalizing the policy on the establishment of private television and radio channels".[2]

While this might have reassured mediamen, its still an open question as to how long this military-media honeymoon will last. As of now the Press is going to town publishing stories of the kind of venality and corruption the Nawaz Sharif Government indulged in. For a military regime seeking to establish its legitimacy, such stories about the previous government serve its purpose adequately as they provide the military junta with a modicum of justification for overthrowing an elected government. But soon the Press will start to highlight the corruption and venality of the military regime. And this is when the professed commitment of Gen. Pervez Musharraf to freedom of the Press will be tested. In his subsequent comments the new Pakistani dictator has hinted that the Press needs to be more circumspect while reporting stories.

During a meeting with a delegation of the All Pakistan Newspapers Society, General Musharraf said he firmly believed in the freedom of Press, but certain misinformation, dis-information or irresponsible stories did appear in the Press which should be avoided. There should be a system in which such things should be settled. He viewed that he had not seen anything against national interests in the Press of a neighbouring country, but unfortunately statements of foreign leaders are highlighted in the Pakistani Press. The foreign newspapers do not give such coverage to Pakistani leaders. There should be no compromise on national interests and even if one had correct information which may harm national interest, it should not be published, he said. The Chief Executive further stated that the government wanted to set up a monitoring system in this regard and the issue had already been discussed at the Corps Commanders Conference. He said: "In the light of our discussion, I would think and analyse the issue of making a Media Committee which would draw up a media policy. Representatives from newspapers would be included in this committee." He further advised, "forget about the past and write whatever you like but always write true after confirmation. Try to accommodate every point of view."[3]

Obviously then, after these comments, it is clear that the military junta even as it professes its commitment to freedom of the Press, expects the Media to exercise a degree of self-censorship by anticipating what the junta wants should appear in the Press. Most likely, the Press will now function in Pakistan under a system of controlled freedom, and the control will not only be self-imposed but also institutionalized. The institution that Pakistan's new Chief Executive seems to have in mind is some kind of a Press Council—an idea which by no means is new as many democratically elected governments in Pakistan have often considered ushering in this kind of institutionalized control over the independent media. Under the garb of enforcing a code of ethics on the media, this Press Council will be used to keep a check on what appears in the media. How the Press stands up to this kind of a censorship policy remains to be seen. Also, the reaction of the junta to any deviation from the norms that it expects the media to follow, is still to become clear. Of course, if history is any guide, once the going gets tough for the junta, the media will inevitably have to contend with majors vetting everything before it could be sent to the Press.

INTRODUCTION

The now defunct English daily, *The Muslim*, used to carry on its masthead the legend *"The Press and the Nation-Rise and Fall*

Together." As a testimony to the level of commitment and degree of seriousness with which many Pakistani journalists take their job, especially those attached to the independent media, the legend on *The Muslim's* masthead is most appropriate. But the legend is also an eloquent statement, almost prophetic, of the immutable linkage between the state of the media and the state of the country, particularly in the context of present day Pakistan. Given the impending collapse of the almost bankrupt Pakistani economy, the financial collapse of *The Muslim* might well be a sign of things to come for Pakistan itself.

The vicissitudes of the media in Pakistan and how these have been reflected in the state in which the country finds itself have been aptly summed up by a Pakistani columnist who recently titled his article "Is Pakistan going the *Pakistan Times* way?".[4] The story of the decline and fall of the *Pakistan Times*, a newspaper which at one point was described by the *Time Magazine* as the "best edited English language newspaper outside the English-speaking world" is, in a sense, the story of the pulls and pressures that the media in Pakistan faces and the crises with which it has had to and continues to contend. According to the above mentioned columnist, Lahori, an appropriate epitaph for the *Pakistan Times* should read: "The *Pakistan Times*: founded by the Quaid-i-Azam, confounded by Field Marshal Ayub Khan and dumbfounded by Gen. Ziaul Haq."[5] These words describe succinctly the phases through which Pakistani media passed in the first four decades after Independence.

The media in Pakistan has never really had an easy time what with having to function under a clutch of authoritarian regimes, civil and military that have ruled Pakistan. The first decade of Independence saw the spirit of freedom permeate to the media. In a way this was the golden period of the Pakistani Media, which was flush with a sense of idealism that only new found freedom can instil. However, with governments falling like nine-pins every few months, and politicians unable to frame a constitution for the country, the media soon turned cynical. The first decade ended with Gen. Ayub Khan imposing martial law in 1958. The next three decades saw the media severely shackled.

The Bhutto *interregnum* (1972-77) was hardly an improvement over the martial law regimes that preceded it. In a way, the Bhutto era left the media confused about the degree of freedom it actually enjoyed. Despite all the formal trappings of Democracy, Bhutto was quite intolerant to criticism. Journalists who dared to criticize or question Bhutto did so at their own peril. Nevertheless, a number of journalists took their chances and many got away unscathed. The Gen. Ziaul Haque years (1977-88), were however a dark period for the Pakistani media. Control over the media was stifling, with strict and unsparing censorship as the norm and criticism of the regime a taboo. To their credit, even during the dark and diabolical Zia era, some intrepid Pakistani journalists evolved a way of saying their bit between the lines.

With restoration of multi-party Democracy in 1988, the period on which this paper will concentrate, many in Pakistan believed that an era of freedom had dawned for the media. Events and attitudes over the last decade have, however, belied these hopes. The pulls and pressures on the media have hardly ceased. What has changed, however, is that unlike earlier periods, the independent media now tries to resist Government attempts to restrict its freedom. The media in Pakistan now jealously guards its freedom and while valiant attempts by the media to resist official arbitrariness might not have always succeeded, they have nevertheless managed to raise the credibility of the independent media among the public.

What has also changed, and quite dramatically at that, is the breaking down of the information barriers set up by the State with the advent of the information revolution. The global information revolution, which has coincided with the period under discussion, has made a significant impact on the development of both the electronic and print media in Pakistan. Satellite television and internet have broken the State's monopoly over the electronic media. At the same time archaic laws, for example those forbidding exchange of newspapers with India, have become anachronistic with newspapers easily accessible on the internet. And while winds of change are sweeping the field of media and communications, the State seems to have adopted an ostrich like attitude of putting its head in the sand in the hope that the storm will pass it by. As a result the response of the State in the face of the information revolution has been, to say the least, typically bureaucratic.

While the changes being forced upon the Pakistani Media by the information and communications revolution are obvious, there remain a range of areas where this revolution has made little difference. In this paper we evaluate the impact of the information revolution on the information industry in Pakistan, as well as other issues of critical importance that determine the role, influence and impact of the media in Pakistan.

ELECTRONIC MEDIA AND THE STATE

The impact and influence of media in any society is determined by a variety of factors. Probably the single most important factor is the relationship between the State and the media. The State, through its policies and attitudes, determines the reach of media and its influence on the masses. In Pakistan while the electronic media is a state monopoly, the print media is dominated by private and non-state players. Given the low levels of literacy, the impact and influence of the print media is by definition limited. While the power and influence of the electronic media by its very reach is considered to be much greater than that of the print media, in countries like Pakistan with low levels of literacy the impact of the electronic media is that much more. The fact that the influence of the electronic media is inversely proportional to the level of literacy makes the electronic media a very potent weapon in the hands of the State. While people might not be able to read and understand the written word they can very well understand and absorb what they hear on the radio or what they see on television. Within the electronic media the power of television is far greater than that of radio. Images are more compelling and make a greater impact than a voice on the radio.

Use of the electronic media for propaganda purposes is not limited to Third World countries alone. Even in the developed world media organizations serve as a hand-maiden to their governments. And despite the veneer of objectivity and dispassionate information dissemination adopted by news organizations like the BBC and CNN, their bias in favour of their own governments is quite obvious. There are two possible reasons for this sort of a bias in news coverage. The first is that such a bias is inherent among media managers and journalists because they genuinely believe in the righteousness of their own government's position. Moreover, the fact that they are the products of a particular socio-political milieu, brings into play an element of insidious indoctrination that leads to biases in news reporting and analysis. The biases of the international media are, therefore, partly by design and partly by default. The second reason is that most of these media organizations depend critically on their governments for news gathering operations. Therefore, any damaging news story could well lead to the government adopting an unco-operative attitude and blocking access normally granted to these organizations in their news gathering operations. A case in point is the hasty retraction by CNN of the story on the use of chemical weapons by the US armed forces in Vietnam. The element of coercion was apparent in the retraction. News organizations like CNN thrive on war reporting and cannot do without the support of the US armed forces in conflict situations, especially since such cooperation would be extended to rival news organizations.

But there are crucial differences between international media organizations and Pakistan's state controlled electronic media. One, where there is an element of design and default in the biases of the international media, in Pakistan's case the biases are almost entirely by design. There would of course also be an element of indoctrination that would be reflected in programming, but the degree to which bias creeps in by default is possible to estimate only if there is at least a semblance of independence for the media. Two, unlike the international media where subtlety is the key to propaganda, the Pakistani state controlled media is so blatantly biased that its propaganda enjoys no credibility whatsoever. Three, while the international media tends to be biased in its coverage of international affairs, it is generally neutral and objective in its coverage of domestic political affairs. In Pakistan's case, the media toes the government line in both international as well as domestic affairs. Finally, there is a difference in the focus of news. The international media caters to a global audience and so its primary focus is on international news. The Pakistani electronic media on the other hand has hardly any viewership outside of Pakistan. Therefore the primary focus of the electronic media in Pakistan is domestic politics. Since it is controlled by the government the electronic media acts as a government mouthpiece and serves as an instrument for building the image of the government in power. There is an international dimension to Pakistan's electronic media. But even here the focus is only Kashmir, with lots of India-bashing thrown in for good measure.

In a sense the State controlled media in Pakistan functions no different from such media in any other country. But unlike the subtle propaganda in the media in the developed world or even the independent electronic media in India, the blatant propaganda carried out by the Pakistani State controlled electronic media robs it of all its credibility. According to Aslam Azhar, considered to be the father of television in Pakistan, "the difference between these networks and PTV and PBC needs to be understood. These networks serve the long-term interests of the State, and are therefore even enabled to be critical of their own governments in the short-term. Hence their apparent credibility. Our Pakistani media serves only the short-term interests of the government of the day, without regard to a perceived, well-defined and ongoing national agenda. Hence our own total lack of credibility."[6]

For any news and information media the loss of credibility and credulity implies the loss of its propaganda value. This is what has happened to Pakistan's State controlled electronic media. Before the advent of satellite television, the Pakistani people would turn to BBC Radio Service for getting authentic news and information. Radio Pakistan was not trusted by the very people towards whom it was directed. But while Radio Pakistan never enjoyed a monopoly, Pakistan Television (PTV) had a monopoly over television. In the border areas the Pakistani public could see Doordarshan but just as they never trusted PTV news, they trusted DD news even less.

This lack of choice in television news ended with the arrival of satellite television. The easy access to news channels like BBC and CNN made PTV news redundant, especially for breaking-news stories from the region. The PTV news programme the *Khabarnama* has become the butt of jokes and ridicule, and hardly anyone watches news on PTV, much less trust it. So much so that the decision of the Government of India to ban PTV during the Kargil conflict confounded many Pakistani commentators and provoked the former ISI chief Lt. Gen. Asad Durrani to comment that by banning PTV in India the Indian Government has done great disservice to the people on both sides of the divide as they have "conferred a certain credibility on our Goebbels."[7] While the *Khabarnama* suffers the pitfalls of State control over the electronic media, news analysis programming on PTV fares no better. The problem with most news analysis programmes is twofold. Firstly, such programming has been farmed out to the cronies of the government to oblige them. Secondly, since the hosts are cronies of the government they tend to present only the official, rather the government's, point of view. Often such programming is used to target political opponents.

While the media managers of the government believe that they serve the government loyally, the reality is that by presenting such clumsily biased propaganda, they have failed singularly in the task of image building. This is because neither the Pakistani politicians nor their media managers have understood the dynamics of television news. It is in the nature of television that the viewer, even if he is entirely sold to the government point of view, would like to hear the views of the opposing side. What he likes best is a good debate in which his side manages to effectively silence the opposing side. But a one-sided discussion can hardly hold the attention of the viewer, especially since alternatives are now available. According to Aslam Azhar, "PTV and PBC (Pakistan Broadcasting Corporation) have never ever succeeded in promoting the credentials of the governments under which they have operated; nor have they served the Pakistani society in its most crucial areas of concern. PTV and PBC have on the contrary contributed their share to bringing each succeeding government into disrepute and to distorting civic values and civil society.... The irony of Pakistani broadcasting has been that precisely these news and Current Affairs programmes have come to be the graveyard of both PTV and PBC, and by extension, of the governments that have decreed their policies."[8]

Nowhere did this dynamic and dialectic of television become more manifest than during the Kargil conflict. Kargil was really the first subcontinental television war and the power of television, credible television that is, came out unambiguously during this war. Pakistani commentators acknowledge that they were roundly and soundly defeated in the media war that the Kargil conflict unleashed. But an analysis of the reasons—the domination of Indian satellite television channels—for Pakistan's failure in the media war as well as the remedy suggested—creation of a media cell and a 24 hour news channel—for preventing this kind of failure in future are both faulty.

The reason why Pakistan's propaganda offensive during Kargil failed to convince anyone, even their own people, was that the entire propaganda campaign was geared to peddling a lie that no one was willing to buy. According to Lf. Gen. (Retd.) Kamal Matinuddin, Pakistan's media failed because it was "trying to hide something that could not have been hidden behind the lies."[9] Another reason was that Indian satellite television channels had already been functioning for a few years prior to Kargil, during which time they had established their credentials as independent and credible news organizations. As a result, rather than PTV most Pakistanis watched ZEE news for regular updates on the Kargil conflict. According to an Editor of a Pakistani national daily, ZEE TV, a private channel, enjoyed a certain credibility which government channels lack. The Editor stated that people trusted a private channel even while they were against being partisan. On the other hand, even if a PTV newscaster sweared by his faith that he was telling nothing but the truth few people will believe him.[10] Thus, a state controlled television news channel will have its credibility tainted by its very association with the government.

Apart from the inherent disability of State control over the electronic media, there are other factors that have limited the reach, spread, influence and growth of the electronic media in Pakistan. Most of these factors are the result of State policy regarding growth of electronic media as well the State's economic development and the role played by it in the economy. There are other factors also that inhibit the growth and penetration of satellite television in Pakistan. One of these factors is the digitization of satellite television channels. Ever since the process of digitization started, there has been a sharp drop in the viewership of satellite channels like *Star News*. Unlike in India, where private cable operators have divided the cost of decoding digital satellite channels among their subscribers, in Pakistan private cable operators are hardly present. Even where private cable services are available, the facility of decoding signals at the cable operator level for allowing access to subscribers at a nominal fee is generally absent. Since the cost of decoders is prohibitive, most people cannot afford to watch news channels like *Star News*. On the other hand, the great advantage of *ZEE TV* is that it's a free-to-air channel. Moreover, because *ZEE* is more earthy in its approach it has wider acceptability.

More important than the developments in satellite television, however, remains the policy of the Government on satellite television. The Pakistani Government has not allowed private broadcasters to air news programmes. For example the Network Television Marketing (NTM), a private television channel and the nearest to *ZEE TV* in Pakistan is not permitted to have its own news bulletins and is obliged to relay the PTVs *Khabarnama*. Commenting on this a Pakistani columnist Hafizur Rahman writes: It seems that the Government does not trust the private sector with the business of informing the public. This policy is not peculiar to the ruling regime. In fact this has been the only common factor between successive PML (Pakistan Muslim League) and PPP (Pakistan Peoples Party) Governments.[11] Although several Pakistani nationals have expressed an interest in starting private satellite channels, the Government of Pakistan has been reluctant in giving the go-ahead. The reason for this is simple: it is not so much the international news coverage that bothers the Government of Pakistan as the coverage of domestic news which may not be very complementary to the Government in power.

Even if the Government were to give the go-ahead, private satellite channel operators will have to contend with the immutable realities of not only Pakistan's power politics which would almost certainly lead to strong arm tactics to bring such a channel in line, but these channels will also have to confront the laws of economics. If the Indian experience is anything to go by, the market for satellite channels is still not so large as to be able to accommodate many players. As is the case in India which has a larger market of potential viewers and an economic and industrial structure that can support these channels. In Pakistan, neither the market nor the economic and industrial structure is large enough to support private television channels. Satellite television is extremely expensive, and more so in case of a news channel. Unlike commercial and entertainment programming, news gathering is more expensive, especially for a 24 hour news channel. Any such channel requires massive investment for creating the infrastructure not only for airing news but more importantly for news gathering. Moreover, it requires advertising support for sustaining its operations, which is a function of the general economy. The larger the industrial and economic sector of a country the greater the scope for garnering advertising support. In Pakistan the problem is that while the state has the adequate resources for funding such a venture, it has no credibility. On the other hand, the private sector probably will have the credibility, but will find it difficult to garner the necessary resources.

In addition to issues of state control and economic resources, there are important cultural and attitudinal issues related to media, especially the electronic media. The electronic media operates in a highly competitive world; it needs to keep up with the competition in the programmes it offers to its viewers if it wishes to stay relevant. One major problem that the media in Pakistan faces is the pressure brought upon it by the Islamic religious lobby. In 1993 the Islamic Ideology Council made some recommendations on media policy. These included no television after 10 p.m., restricted sports programming as it takes students away from studies, restrictions on advertisements that "excite sexual feelings," transmissions to stop for 30 minutes after the call of *Azaan* and to take steps to punish falsehoods in news![12] An editorial in *the Muslim* strongly castigated the tendency in PTV to succumb to such pressure saying "the most unengaging face of PTV is its moralizing, pontificating, in a hypocritical endeavour to pave the viewers' way to paradise. Intelligent viewers totally fail to see why PTV programme organizers don't realize that they have just no business to inflict priests and preachers with no known credentials *ad libilum, ad nauseum*, day in and day out on their viewers."[13]

Unlike India, where even if the Government perceives a bias in any news channel, it would be loath to use strong-arm tactics against it, in Pakistan the Government is loath to tolerate any such bias from a territorial channel. All sorts of pressures would be brought to bear on the offending channel which would end up destroying the credibility and objectivity of the news organization. If the Pakistani State and Government attitude towards the print media is any indication, the future of private electronic media in Pakistan does not appear very bright.

PRINT MEDIA AND THE STATE

Although the dominance of the electronic media in dissemination of news and information in a country with low literacy is natural, the print media has managed to hold its own in Pakistan, particularly in the urban areas. There are two reasons for this. First, since most people do not trust the State broadcaster, PTV, for giving authentic news their dependence on the independent print media is greater. Second, unless there is some major news story, most of the satellite channels cover events in Pakistan only in a very perfunctory manner, if at all. Generally the coverage is limited to headline news. Thus, for normal, day-to-day news the people have to depend on the print media.

According to a survey carried out by the Pakistan Advertisers Society, nearly 51 per cent of the people in urban areas read a newspaper and among them a predominant majority, 95 per cent, read Urdu newspapers while only 8 per cent read English dailies.[14] With newspapers serving as the primary source of their news and information, influence on the people and impact on events is enormous. Enough to make the State want to exercise control over what is published, by whom it is published and most importantly, for whom it is published. The State's task is, however, complicated somewhat by the fact that most newspapers, magazines and journals are published in English, Urdu and local vernaculars like Sindhi and Pashtu, differences in circulation, influence, and most of all, erudition, vary widely across languages.

Although the Urdu newspapers have far greater circulation than the English newspapers, the latter are relatively more influential. The fact that English is the language of the elite is what makes the English language Press so influential. But since there are not many English-speaking people in Pakistan, and there are at least three or four major English dailies, there are inherent limitations to the growth of the English language Press. Urdu on the other hand is the language of the masses. If the English language Press influences politics in the corridors of power, the Urdu language Press influences politics on the streets. And it is street power that has resulted in most of the political changes in Pakistan. Thus, while the English Press thrives on stability, the Urdu Press thrives on instability.

In the subcontinent, Urdu literature connotes elegance and sophistication. But when used in publishing newspapers the idiom changes drastically and the language metamorphoses into an anti-literature medium. Probably this has something to do with the audience that the medium seeks to address. The subcontinental mass culture is generally subjective and the element of objectivity is marked by its absence. Rather than objectivity, the vernacular Press (Urdu) thrives on high emotion, passionate rhetoric, ideological metaphors, nationalistic jingoism and religious symbolism.

Objectivity is really a gift, a legacy of the Western civilization. Thus, only that section of the people who have been educated in English or are familiar with Western literature, philosophy and thought have a degree of objectivity in their writings, even if these are in the vernacular medium. Nowhere is this more manifest than in the comparative analysis of Urdu and English language newspapers. According to Khaled Ahmad, a senior Pakistani journalist and intellectual, there exists "a permanent schism...between the Urdu and English Press, between the ideological and the objective. ....The ideological divide is there because of the language..."[15] Surprisingly enough, the vernacular newspapers in local languages like Sindhi and Pushto are more liberal, have a wider horizon as well as a world-view and to that extent greatly differ from the Urdu newspapers in their coverage and analysis of news. The reasons why provincial vernacular appears more objective and liberal than the national vernacular in newspapers is an issue that requires greater inquiry and analysis and is beyond the scope of this paper.

Unlike the electronic media, the State hardly has any formal presence in the print media, where private players dominate the scene. In fact, in the early 1990's the State gradually moved out of the newspaper business and left it to private individuals. Broadly, the ownership pattern of newspapers in Pakistan fits into three categories. Most of the newspapers are editor-owned. Then there are a few newspapers that are owned by business houses, the most notable example being the *Dawn* group of newspapers. Apart from owner-editors and business houses, political parties also publish their own newspapers. While the circulation figures of these party organs are nowhere close to those of privately owned publications, they continue to retain a fairly large and loyal readership base. A new initiative, and a very successful one at that, was taken in 1989 when a journalist's cooperative started the monthly *Newsline* magazine.

The domination of editor-owned newspapers unlike in India, where many large newspapers are owned by business houses has its advantages as well as pitfalls. In fact, many of the advantages also double-up as disadvantages and *vice versa*. With the newspaper being the sole pre-occupation of the owner, other business considerations don't often influence the editorial policy of the publication. There are no oil mills, sugar mills, cloth mills or paper mills, whose interest is sought to be promoted or protected through the newspaper. On the flip-side, the advantages that other business interests bestow on a newspaper, essentially of cross-subsidization are missing. This makes the newspaper solely dependent on advertising revenue. The economic structure of Pakistan is such that private sector advertisements constitute a small proportion of overall advertising revenue earned by a paper. The bulk of revenue comes from the Government. This makes newspapers susceptible to government pressure and there have been innumerable instances of newspapers succumbing to such pressure and towing the government line.

Most newspapers in Pakistan, as in many other developing countries, depend critically on the Government for their advertising revenue, the State thus has a very potent lever of control that it often uses over the print media. Without the revenue earned from government advertising, it is not viable to sustain a newspaper. If sufficient corporate and product advertising by private companies was available, the dependence of newspapers on government and public sector advertising would be that much less. But since this is not the case, newspapers survive on government advertising. The State can strangulate a newspaper by cutting off advertising support. According to the US State Department Report on Human Rights in Pakistan, "the Government has considerable leverage over the Press through its substantial budget for advertising and public interest campaigns, its control over newsprint, and its ability to enforce legislation."[16]

The State also exercises control over the print media by allocating newsprint quota to newspapers. By simply turning off the supply of newsprint the State can bring any newspaper to heel. Since most of the newsprint is imported, the State has monopolized its allocation. There is also an element of subsidy built into the newsprint that the Government supplies. This allows the Government to oblige friendly papers by allotting to them newsprint in excess of their requirements or entitlement so that these papers can then sell the same in the open market and pocket a nice profit. At the same time denial or obstruction of supply of newsprint to an unfriendly paper is often used as a tactic to bring the newspaper management in line.

Privately owned newspapers had existed in Pakistan since independence; the restoration of multi-party Democracy saw the proliferation of independent newspapers and the simultaneous fading away of those that were Government-owned. The fact that independent newspapers have survived and thrived in Pakistan despite long years of martial law is in itself something of a paradox. Normally, its difficult to associate the existence of independent newspapers in a country with authoritarian regimes. But in Pakistan, a combination of circumstances ensured the survival of private newspapers even under military regimes.

Owners of newspapers like the mass circulation English daily *Dawn* and Urdu dailies *Jang* and *Nawa-i-Waqt* had played an active role during the Pakistan movement. These newspapers, therefore, were traditionally close to the establishment in Pakistan and tended to tow the establishment line. Even if they had ever intended to take an independent line, they were effectively dissuaded from doing so by the closure of the *Civil and Military Gazette* and the takeover of the *Pakistan Times* in the early 1950's. Later a set of Press laws were contrived to keep the other papers in line. All these steps ensured that "newspaper owners, editors and journalists were not all convinced that it was worth risking palpable interests for abstract principles.... Ziaul Haq imposed pre-censorship and had the restive elements in the Press tried and convicted by Military Courts, a few even flogged. As he went along he also learnt subtler methods. He forged personal relations. Proximity to the throne was heady wine for some: it helped divide journalists, and it helped create a loyal phalanx."[17] By adopting a pro-establishment editorial policy, owners of these newspapers not only ensured their continuing control over their newspapers but were also bestowed with state patronage and power, pelf and privileges that come with such patronage. The survival of pro-establishment independent newspapers was also beneficial for the State, which could use the so-called independent Press for its own purposes.

While the pro-establishment newspapers had, in a manner of speaking, a run of the place until 1988, the entry of new players in the newspaper industry after restoration of multi-party Democracy gave these newspapers a run for their money. Not only were there many new Urdu newspapers, there was also a growth in the number of new English language newspapers. Among the pioneers was *The Muslim*, the permission for whose publication came during the Zia period. It came as a great surprise that a new and independent publication was allowed. But most of the other newspapers came into existence after 1988, when even the well established Urdu newspaper chains diversified and started publishing English newspapers. *The News International* of the *Jang* group of newspapers and *The Nation* from the stable of the *Nawa-i-Waqt* group are notable examples. Other independent newspapers like *The Frontier Post*, also started publication around this time.

Even though Democracy had returned to Pakistan, starting a newspaper was not easy. The permission for publishing a new newspaper was difficult to come by and prospective publishers needed either a lot of clout to get these permissions or else use other stratagems. The story of the English weekly *The Friday Times* is an illustration of how newspapers were registered even after the restoration of Democracy. The background of the weekly's Chief Editor, Najam Sethi as a leftist and maverick was enough to deny permission to *The Friday Times*. Therefore the applications for registration were made in the name of Jugnu Mohsin, Sethi's wife. According to Sethi, "Jugnu would go to meet with various officials and pretend she was a starry-eyed socialite who wanted to publish a gossipy social rag." She worked her way up the chain of officialdom until she reached Nawaz Sharif, who was the then Chief Minister of Punjab. "He laughed and said 'You're sure you won't write against me?' Jugnu laughed and said, 'of course not!'."[18]

With time, however, permissions for starting new newspapers were much easier to come by. But the manipulative power exercised by the State on the independent media has stayed intact. Even though the State has desisted from taking any drastic step like taking over a newspaper, it has employed other coercive measures to pressurize the newspapers into submission. The monthly news-magazine *Newsline* is an example of both the kind of pressures that the Government exerts on newspaper owners and the fight that many newsmen put up against such pressures. Many of the founders of *Newsline* had earlier worked for the *Monthly Herald* and had left that magazine on account of editorial differences with the owners, who under pressure from the Government had started interfering in the editorial policy of *the Herald*.

While the journalists at *Newsline* were able to follow an independent editorial policy, a number of other senior editors and journalists have become victims to the pressure tactics of the State on newspaper owners as well as the personal political agendas of the owners themselves. In 1993, the editor of the *Daily Muslim*, A.B.S. Jafri was unceremoniously sacked and his Editor-in-Chief, Altaf Gauhar resigned, victims to the bitter power struggle being waged between the then Prime Minister Nawaz Sharif and the duo of President Ghulam Ishaq Khan and Leader of Opposition, Benazir Bhutto. Since the owner was close to Benazir Bhutto, he felt that the editorial policy of his paper was tilted against her and in favour of Nawaz Sharif.[19]

There have also been instances where the Government has put pressure on newspaper owners to remove inconvenient journalists from their staff and replace them with favourites of the Government. In addition instructions have been issued and none too subtle threats made to newspaper editors and owners as to what could and what should not appear in their newspaper. The conversation between Senator Saifur Rehman and the owner of the *Jang* group of newspapers, Mir Shakilur Rehman, is a case in point.[20] In a writ petition filed in the Supreme Court of Pakistan in January 1999, Mir Shakilur Rehman accused the Government of forcing him to dismiss senior editors and journalists from his staff.[21] Although the Government later was forced to back off on this demand under intense international and domestic pressure, it started applying control upon newspapers and journalists in more subtle ways.

An article in the monthly *Newsline* exposed the kinds of pressure that were being put on the independent media by the Nawaz Sharif Government. "Surveillance by intelligence sleuths, threatening phone calls *et al* are now the order of the day. And in an unprecedented step, the Editor of *Islamabad News*, Maleeha Lodhi, has been banned from writing in the paper she has edited for the last three years...She was informed by the management that it had managed to resist the Government's demand to sack her by offering the assurance that she would not write under her own byline until she mended her relations with the Prime Minister.... Meanwhile, Nadeem Malik, senior economic correspondent of *News* is being continually harassed by intelligence sleuths and anonymous callers. The most serious incident occurred in January 1999 when unidentified people tried to break into his house. More recently, following a number of stories filed by him on the state of Pakistan's economy, he was blacklisted by the Finance Ministry and subjected to serious threatening phone calls. Last month, *News* reporter Amir Mir, who had written a series on Prime Minister Nawaz Sharif and Senator Saifur Rahman in *News* and *Newsline*, finally fled the country when Government pressure threatened his personal safety."[22]

A very senior journalist M. Ziauddin also exposed the not-so-subtle pressures being put on the Press in one of his columns in the *Dawn*. Ziauddin wrote: "On August 26, Hikmatullah Khattak, Director of the Intelligence Bureau (IB), visited the daily's bureau in Islamabad. He wanted to know the source of a story published in the newspaper earlier in the week. He was very polite and courteous in his manner and behaviour. In fact, he said he had told his colleagues in IB that since he knew me very well and considered me as his elder brother, I would be only too glad to co-operate." He especially expressed his abhorrence against the way

Sethi and Haqqani were treated by his colleagues. He insisted that he had met me two years ago, but I could not recall the meeting. This was unusual because normally when the Government needs to find out the source of a news report it adopts very subtle and highly discreet ways. So, if one were paranoid one would jump to the conclusion that perhaps the Government was not as much interested in the source of the news report as it was in sending a personal warning to the Bureau."[23]

This incident involving Ziauddin came not long after the publication of a most disturbing report that the Government had prepared a hit-list of journalists—practically a who's who of Pakistani journalism—critical of Government policies who would be targeted by a special media cell comprising officers from the Police, Intelligence Bureau and the Federal Investigation Agency. According to this report, the special cell would…abduct a 'defiant' journalist and subject him to physical torture at some 'safe house' and release him after 24 or 36 hours. In this way… the Government will not go through the legal process because it will not have to own the arrest….Another important job of the special cell will be to collect dirt against journalists, especially women journalists, to be used against them if they are found to be moving too close to the ruling elite's cupboards looking for skeletons. The special cell will also be responsible for dealing physical quickies against stubborn scribes… bizarre methods may be employed to punish newsmen by intimidating and terrorizing them in one way or the other. First, they can make some threatening calls at your residence, using filthy language. Then they can chase you. The next step can be the snatching of your car or motorcycle, maybe at gunpoint. You can also experience a dacoity at your home. You can also be arrested for being drunk. Your property and family can be damaged as well. So be careful…."[24]

Incidents like these prompted growing concern in the international community, so much so that donor countries had started to link aid with the treatment of the media by the Pakistani Government. A document prepared by the donors' community of Islamabad and circulated by World Bank reports 35 cases of Press harassment during the last six months. The report called for a "cessation of these attacks as a condition for continued support," and was sent to Finance Minister Ishaq Dar, who issued a Press release saying: "The Government believes that a free Press is a key element of economic and social development… and the

Constitution ensures the freedom of the Press."[25] But neither the harassment and intimidation of journalists and newspapers nor the protests by the international community of the Government's strong-arm tactics against the media is new. Almost all governments in the last decade of Democracy have resorted to such tactics against the independent media. Often the treatment meted out to inconvenient journalists is far more brutal and savage.

In 1995, human rights activist and journalist, Zafaryab Ahmad was arrested on charges of "crippling the economy of Pakistan by sabotaging its carpet industry in connivance with an Indian-sponsored organization."[26] He was also accused of "undermining the sovereignty of the country" because he had exposed the murder of a 12 year old child activist, Iqbal Masih, against bonded labour in the carpet industry. Zafaryab was lucky as he survived the case against him; but others have not been so lucky. Humayun Fur was one such journalist. In 1997, two weeks after he was kidnapped the Government admitted he was in their custody. Fur was tried by a Military Court on charges of spying for India, a favourite charge against targeted journalists, and was sentenced to 5 years rigorous imprisonment.[27] Three months after his sentence, Fur was released by the Army Chief on health grounds, but the old man's health had so deteriorated that he died within a few months after his release.

The cases of the abduction and subsequent arrest of famous journalists like Najam Sethi, Editor of *The Friday Times*, on charges of making a seditious and treasonous speech in India, senior columnist Hussain Haqqani, allegedly charged for corruption and tortured while in prison, and the arrest of the indefatigable Rehmat Shah Afridi, the owner-editor of *The Frontier Post* on charges of dealing in narcotics, are all too well-known to be repeated here. These people probably managed to survive because their cases became *cause celebre* in Pakistan and around the world. But a number of cases of harassment and intimidation of journalists escape notice because the journalists involved work outside the mainstream national media in smaller towns and cities. There are any number of cases in which journalists working in the vernacular Press in smaller towns and cities have been arrested on trumped up charges or even without being charged, kept in custody (legal or illegal), tortured and beaten or even killed.[28]

Over the years, however, the State has also devised other methods for keeping the Press under check. Often journalists are obliged by allotting them residential plots at concessional rates, keeping them on the pay-roll of intelligence agencies where discretionary funds available with these agencies are used to buy off journalists, giving lucrative contracts to journalists especially for hosting shows on PTV, absorbing journalists into the fold by granting them positions of power and pelf in Government or else inducting them into politics through the Senate. 'Lifafa' journalism (or handing out of envelopes containing money to journalists for getting stories planted or spiked in newspapers) is the term that is the contribution of Pakistan to the field of media studies. In 1994 a major scandal rocked the media world in Pakistan and brought to light the ugly face of 'lifafa' journalism.

According to the report that brought to light the scandal, a number of senior journalists were accused of taking undue favours from the Intelligence Bureau. These journalists were feted and hosted in the best of hotels, all their expenses were borne by the IB, and cars and drivers were placed at their disposal. The corruption of journalists by the IB was only part of the story. More concerning was the revelation that even newspapers were being funded by the IB, and the report alleged that *Khabrain*, an Urdu daily published from Lahore was financed by secret IB funds.[29] Unconfirmed reports, or rather rumours in journalistic circles in Pakistan also suggest that another Urdu daily, *Ausaf*, is funded by the infamous Inter Services Intelligence (ISI) Agency.

The *modus operandi* of corrupting journalists was remarkably similar to the *Frontier Post* report cited above. According to the report published in *the Nation* in 1994, most of the journalists named in the report were people who had opposed government policies. At first their telephones would be tapped to get some incriminating information about them. In case there was nothing incriminating from the bugged conversations, then the dirty tricks department of the IB would get to work to manufacture evidence against journalists writing critical articles against the Government. According to the report, "not only the extension of privileges but sometimes various plots were also made to depict some journalists as RAW agents...false evidence was created to name [the journalists] as Indian agents when they used to write critical articles against the Nawaz Government (1990-93)."[30]

Probably the most damning indictment of the role being played by the State in the media in Pakistan was made in an article by Khaled Ahmad in *The Friday Times*. In this article Ahmad draws a picture of the dynamic process through which the state tries to influence, divide and subvert the media in Pakistan. Rather than paraphrase Ahmad's article, it is better to quote excerpts directly from it. Ahmad wrote:

> "The right-wing journalists jailed by Bhutto had played *tertium gaudens* when Gen. Ayub Khan destroyed left-wing journalism by nationalizing newspapers. No lessons were however learned. Bhutto's action was revenged by supporting the martial law of General Zia and seeing the 'leftists' being whipped in public. Political alignment was so visible that it was difficult to distinguish between journalism and politics. Columnists...are known in the community for their political alignment. This alignment is firm because it is sometimes paid for. The senior ones write by instinct. Their column must appear at the opportune time, tackling the latest issue in favour of the Government. The pay-off could be in the shape of a regular 'honorarium' or other 'concessions.' Every time the Government changes lists of these 'concessionaries' which are printed out of secret files and fought over. Governments dole out residential and commercial plots of land that enrich the journalists to the tune of millions of rupees through the price differential in the market.
>
> "Editor-owners who have become rich over-night are often part of the inner sanctum of the Government. After the fall of Ms. Bhutto's last government, shocking revelations were made about journalists 'promoted' into wealth by Asif Zardari. The money runs into crores of rupees in cash, acres of residential land where houses worth crores of rupees are built, away from the scrutiny of the Income Tax Department which moves against a journalist only when the Government wants to 'correct' him.
>
> "Imagine yourself living in a far-off land. One owner is said to have sent abroad a million dollars from his foreign-exchange accounts days before the accounts were frozen by the Government. Another is said to have bought a ranch in the USA and owns a luxurious house there, where his family vacations regularly. In this far-off land, a kind of 'tension' of interests is maintained with the Government agencies. The journalist aligns himself with the militias passing off as

freedom-fighters and soldiers of revolution. In return for a good Press for the militias and their well-heeled clerical leaders, the newspaper is provided funds and given protection. The agencies, already entangled with the militias as 'handlers,' hover over this relationship. Then the agencies become the middlemen, arranging a truce with the Government. The deal is struck on specific areas of 'co-operation.' The paper savages the political opponents of the Government under the garb of 'ideology.' Government ads come flooding in. The police, fearful of the paper, begins to 'cooperate' with it. Investigations are shared. In some cases inside information is used to extract money from vulnerable citizens. The said journalist is easy with the militia leaders. He can be drinking Black Label when the country's most puritanical men of God are sitting in front of him in his well-appointed office. The state institutions soon become aware of this networking of power. When one institution is challenged by another, the journalist begins to be courted. The leaders of the State 'institutions' make him their guest.

"Thus the Editor becomes the bridge between the said institution and the militias who can challenge the State. How can the State take on the militias when they are being 'indirectly' used to curb the power of one institution by another? It is thus that the journalist becomes powerful. He has the money the Government makes over to him through ads and other 'concessions.' He has the money from the militia leaders. And he has all the money he can collect from the private sector where threatened 'revelations' become instruments of blackmail. The journalist pays off the militia leaders by making newspaper space available to them and by defending them when they fall foul of the Government. He pays off the Government by defaming the political opposition, printing damaging information prepared by government functionaries. The State agencies, embroiled in the complex network of the various power centres in the country, have to make compromises. They are forced to protect the journalist, saving him from the dragnet of the tax authorities. The said journalist functions in the penumbra of authority that is outside the ambit of municipal law. He participates in the politics of the country from a vantage point where he is never exposed to any punishment for acts of omission and commission. 'Branches' and 'bureaus' shadowing the opposition 'handle' the journalist in the realm of 'damage-control.' The flow of information is two-way. One influences the other. It is a symbiosis of the shadows.

"There may be a journalist who is secretly attached to an agency, drawing a secret salary for writing his columns. His writings are published not because they carry merit but because the 'branch' or 'bureau' he works for ensures publication. In fact he is 'adjusted' in newspapers in such a way that he draws a big salary from the newspaper as well. He is invariably an 'ideological' writer, subjecting everyone to the stringent demands of State ideology. It is to his advantage that the ideology supports only the militias. He is seen by the militias as their man because he never takes them on. If he did that it would be difficult for him to survive even under the umbrella of protection of the Government. In this far-off land, one columnist who is intimate with the Government made the mistake of taking on a militia. Soon, other columnists from his own coterie broke ranks with him and lampooned him till he had to beat a retreat. His own personal security was at risk. Not even the State agencies could ensure his safety. Why did his friends betray him in this stand-off? It happened because there is a baseline of conduct which cannot be violated. The militias form the leverage against the Government which forces the agencies to cut a deal with them. That is the power base from where the journalist derives his 'freedom.' The Government, challenged more effectively by the militias than anyone else in the opposition, then contents itself with the single return on its 'investment': the columnist's hostility towards its political opponents.

"Is it possible for a journalist who doesn't even own a newspaper and was a man of very few means five years ago to live in a five bedroom house spread over two kanals and drive a BMW car, take out declarations for new daily newspapers and recruit journalists promising them a salary package that comes to lakhs of rupees a month. Is it possible for a journalist whose newspaper is never seen on the stalls to live like a millionaire on the basis of his 'professional' earnings. The ideological divide is there because of the language. Nationalism and all its negative aspects emanate from the state-sponsored textbooks. Ideology also borrows heavily from the revolutionary militias who think the textbooks are not tough enough. But under the veneer of ideology there is a vast space of compromise where the governments helplessly cut deals in return for 'jobs' done on their political opponents. This is a space where the underworld of revolution and the State agencies consort with forces that may finally destroy the legitimacy of the elected government. This is the space where the journalist of our far-off mythical land plies his trade. There is nothing more damaging to freedom of the Press than division among the ranks of journalists. Governments can swoop down on the divided community, get a part of it to support its draconian actions, isolate the so-called rebels and bring them to heel through coercion. The basic (or base) human instinct of *tertium gaudens* (the rejoicing third party) came into play among the journalists."[31]

Despite the dismal scene painted above by Khaled Ahmad, the fact that there are people like him with the courage and conviction to highlight in such damning terms the State and the media, stands as testimony that there is no dearth of genuinely committed and intrepid journalists in Pakistan. Many of this genre of journalists also double up as activists to promote causes in which they believe sincerely. The role played by one such journalist, Imtiaz Alam, Editor current affairs, *The News*, in arranging a conference of parliamentarians of India and Pakistan in February 1999, in the face of all the hurdles and obstacles that were put in his path by the foreign policy establishment in Pakistan, is notable in this regard.[32] Journalists have also been active in organizing and taking out peace marches in Karachi at a time when the political establishment was determined to use the coercive power of the State to sort out what was essentially a political problem in the first place.[33]

With all the handicaps that the print media in Pakistan faces, it nevertheless takes its role as an information disseminator far more seriously than the print media in any other country in the region. For example, full texts of all court judgments of public interest are printed regardless of the space and newsprint used. All official Communiques, Statements, Bills and Laws are published in newspapers. As a result, the Pakistani newspapers serve as a vital medium for informing the public of the actual position, whether this be in case of a judgment or an official statement. This allows the reader to make his own assessment of a particular case or of a particular position that the Government may have adopted. Newspaper readers therefore do not need to depend on the intelligence or the discretion of the reporter for getting to know the actual position.

Op-ed pages in the newspapers, particularly in the English language Press, provide a wide variety of opinion to readers. It goes to the credit of most newspapers that in spite of the newspapers editorial policy, contrary opinion is generally not shunned. Also the fact that most newspapers have enlisted columnists who have acquired a degree of specialization in the subjects on which they write tends to make the op-ed pages not only eminently readable, but also extremely informative. Of course, if the reader happens to be an Indian, these articles and opinion will never fail to provoke. Indeed, the Pakistani Press has two blind-spots—Islam and India. Very seldom does one come across a piece which is able to transcend these two blind-spots.

These blind-spots are probably inherent in the character, structure and the ideology of the country. For a denominational country, formed and sustained on antipathy and antagonism towards India and Hindus, the blind-spots on Islam and India are perfectly natural. Pakistanis will be loath to even admit the existence of these blind-spots. The psychosis that pervades the Pakistani mindset is thus bound to be reflected in the writings in the media on Islam and India. In a sense, antagonism towards India has become part of the Islamic ideology, or whatever goes by that name, in Pakistan. For a Press, that despite the travails and tribulations has managed to stay vibrant and dynamic, such blind-spots are rather unfortunate.

References

1 *Herald*, November 1999.
2 Speech of the Chief Executive of Pakistan, Gen. Pervez Musharraf on 17 October 1999.
3 *News*, 6 November 1999.
4 *Dawn*, 20 September 1999.
5 *Ibid*.
6 *News*, 30 October 1999.

7 *News*, 28 July 1999.
8 *Op. cit.*
9 *News*, 25 July 1999.
10 *News*, 13 July 1999.
11 *Nation*, 29 September 1999.
12 *Frontier Post*, 11 February 1993.
13 *Muslim*, 30 March 1993.
14 *News*, 4 June 1999.
15 *Friday Times*, 18-24 June 1999.
16 *News*, 1 March 1999.
17 *Dawn*, 6 June 1999.
18 *New York Times*, 26 July 1999.
19 *Dawn*, 19 July 1993.
20 *Dawn*, 7 February 1999.
21 *News*, 28 January 1999.
22 *Newsline*, August 1999.
23 *Dawn*, 30 August 1999.
24 *Frontier Post*, 1 June 1999.
25 *Op. cit.*
26 *Frontier Post*, 6 June 1996.
27 *Dawn*, 10 September 1997.
28 *News on Sunday*, 22 August 1999.
29 *Nation*, 26 July 1994.
30 *Ibid.*
31 *Friday Times*, 18-24 June 1999.
32 *Herald*, April 1999.
33 *News*, 4 December 1994.

9

Censorship—Pros and Cons

*S. Prasad**

The day the Emergency ended, I congratulated a senior media person on the end of the ordeal. He turned to me with a wry smile and said, "Your Emergency has ended. What about ours?" My friend, who was working for a leading English daily, was only referring to a fact of life in newspapers. Censorship is hydra-headed, and can assume any form, covert or overt. It is going on all the time in news organisations, thriving on the need for selectivity and profitability. The shortage of space is usually a handy excuse.

Censorship is a historical process. The Romans, we are told, had an officer who kept account of the property of Roman citizens. He not merely imposed taxes, but also watched over their morals. From watching one's morals to public postures was a shortstep.

When the media assumed the mantle of a *Fourth Estate*, its power and sweep were an invitation to the politically ambitious for its exploitation to serve their own ends. Here was a chance to enter the people's mind as never before. A touch here, and an inflexion there, was the *modus operandi*, impercetibly at first and brazenly, if necessary, later. One cannot escape the feeling that the growth of the media contributed initially to the fashioning of censorship as an instrument of power. It also brought an increasing

---

* S. Prasad is a retired official of the Indian Information Service. He worked at the All India Radio, then as Information Officer, Government of India and Principal Information Officer at the UGC.

risk of exposure, as global communication overcame national frontiers. With a thousand eyes prying, it was difficult to be insulated.

Censorship, as a brand name, has already become institutionalised in the titles of our film certifying authorities. Do's and don'ts carry the seal of official approbation. It is not a question of names. It is the intent behind them that matters. Films are also a media form and their censorship has often become the subject of bitter controversy. Prurience and porn are described as a matter of perception. Beauty lies in the eyes of the beholder and so does ugliness, it is argued.

Censorship has not merely a negative content. It is both an act of omission and commission. Its finesse was evident abundantly during the Emergency, when sponsored stories overflowed with paeans of praise for the government's role. But there is always a risk of overplaying the propaganda hand. It was one of the factors that led to the undoing of the Emergency.

Voluntary censorship is different from the enforced form which becomes repugnant to human dignity. The pen is forced into submission under a penal threat which may include a fine, or incarceration or both.

The world of words is a favourite hunting field for the purveyors of censorship, for its opportunities of double *entendre*. The fight for the control of the mind is more exacting than any other struggle. That is why the media and the media-persons become important. They are both the hunters as also the hunted.

When censorship comes, dictatorship is not far behind. Perversion of truth takes the pride of place, and mediamen are forced to fall in line. It is a Hobson's choice; it was said of the Emergency by a political leader that journalists would crawl when they were asked to kneel. Of course, every crisis has its heroes and so had the Emergency when the dissidents were directly or indirectly persecuted. Many of them stuck to their guns and paid the penalty. Goebbels was a father figure in the artifice of propaganda. He believed in the dictum that a lie could replace the truth, if it was expounded repeatedly. Every dictator finds his own Goebbels as Hitler did. And he writes his own *Mein Kamf* like the latter.

Censorship is self-renewing, for it derives its strength from self-delusion. The interests of the individual become synonymous with the nation's. The state merges into the individual. It is self-defeating for the same reason, evident in the fall of the dictators. It is self-defeating for the same reason, evident in the fall of the dictators. It is difficult to sustain his (the dictator's) deification over a long period. But the malevolence of censorship is not unrelieved. It has been known to be used judiciously for channelising the people's strength into a national will, to meet national wants. The threat of self-delusion still remains.

In times of war, military censorship becomes a necessary exercise in the interests of security. Even in peacetime, defence matters are kept under some sort of wrap, for the same reason. But truth, like a buoy, has a way to surface despite censorship. Battered and bruised, but truth all the same.

In the initial stages of the last World War, it was said that while the Allies were achieving victories, it were the Germans who were marching forward. It showed up censorship in a poor light.

The British practised devious means to suppress the Press in India. One of these was the Press Act of 1910. Opposing the Act, Gandhiji said that the British were trying to destroy the barometer and still gauge the atmospheric pressure. Gandhiji writing in 1940, exhorted the people to become their own walking newspapers, carrying the news from mouth to mouth. "This no government can overtake or suppress," he said.

Censorship was made an official duty during the Emergency. Refusal to serve was punishable under the Government Servants Conduct Rules.

During my brief stint in the governmental set up, I found that damage control was possible from within while retaining plausibility. The difference between acceptable and non-acceptable versions was, sometimes, that between Tweedledum and Tweedldee. The margin could be bridged without offending either side.

There were some amusing experiences too, arising from the attitude of being more loyal than the king. In one such instance a colleague was called upon to examine a particular issue of the influential *Economic and Political Affairs* journal. The issue carried the famous line sketch of Gandhiji by Nandlal Bose, which showed the leader striding forward in his sandals, holding a staff. Inside was a story on Gandhiji. I stood behind my colleague admiring the beautiful sketch. Suddenly he said that he was not going to pass it. Surprised, I asked him for the reason. He pointed out that the picture showed Gandhiji walking away. I said that is how the sketch was and how could he turn it the other way. His argument was that it had been purposely done. The publishers could have found another cover picture. And that was that. I was still not convinced. But, sometime later, on second thoughts, I felt that perhaps my friend was right. If he was, we had witnessed a very clever piece of journalism.

Such cat-and-mouse games between the censors and the media were not unknown. In another example, where I was at the receiving end, an English daily in the capital had displayed on its front page the official spokesperson's version that everything was fine and normal in the city, following the imposition of Emergency. But the story was topped by a photograph, showing a group of policemen emerging from a lane. The photograph, by itself, was innocuous and bore my stamp of approval for its excellent composition. But its juxtaposition was damning for the story. I was called upon to explain my conduct. Fortunately, nothing happened as the original photograph could not be found, which bore my signature.

Working as a censor was virtually like keeping the cake and eating it too. We were called upon to sit in judgement on persons on whose support we were to depend on for our success as information people, once the Emergency was lifted. For, our gut feeling was that the Emergency was an aberration which would pass like a bad dream.

In sum, the art of fine tuning of public relations consists of selecting the right notes and rejecting the discordant ones. Call censorship by any other name, but it will fall in the latter category. We have the right to freedom of expression on the Statute book, but not access to information. This much-delayed measure had been accepted as a necessity in the Common Minimum Programme of the previous government but has now been pushed back by the winds of change that have taken place.

In preparation for the launching of the process, the Press Council of India had drawn up a draft bill which devoted an entire section to proposed restrictions on the right to information. It may be the antithesis of the buzz word of transparency. But its need has not yet been blanked out, what with the out-moded Official Secrets Act still holding sway.

The way out would lie in self-regulation which helps in the country's progress. But who would be the judge of this progress is a million-dollar question.

Section III

Religion, State and Media

10

Media and Religion: Convergence and Distinctions

*Upendra Vajpeyi**

Both religion and media are multidimensional. Their objectives and functions are independent of each other. Yet, during the course of their endless voyage, they do converge at some of the crossroads. At times, they run parallel to each other; on other occasions, they may be seen travelling together. In this complex relationship, their roles are generally identifiable separately. As a conduit to gain access to the *Unknown*, the *Unseen* and the *Ultimate*, popularly called "*God*," religion is believed to be an unassailable escort (today's black commando) to the other world. The divine commands for obedience in this world are also not man-made. They have percolated from the *Supreme* source through select persons. Resultantly, what could have remained a purely personal affiliation or involvement between *man* and *God*, has acquired a wide ranging social acceptability, covering innumerable regulations of human behaviour—all this, through a gradual process of known and unknown channels of communication over ages. *The Holy Vedas, Holy Bible, Holy Quran* and other scriptures are manifestations of the faith about eternal transmission of knowledge. The paradoxical feature of this communion between *Man* and *God* is that it has never been verifiable. In fact, based on undiluted faith, it is not supposed to be cross-checked because it is not questionable. And yet this communion or myth has not

* Upendra Vajpeyi is General Secretary, National Media Centre.

only survived, it has flourished beyond all imagination. The secret of its success lies considerably in its indisputability.

The character of media in this regard, is qualitatively different. Every information is subject to it being questioned. This is because the effectiveness of media will be directly proportionate to its credibility based on verifiable facts. The transmission of messages to be convincing have to be as transparent as humanly possible. It runs the risk of being disregarded or rejected if on cross-checking it is not found what it was claimed to be. Media's existence does not depend upon any mysterious power. Cross-checking its veracity wherever in doubt, is a cardinal duty of all those engaged in dissemination of information. This distinction in the approach of the two institutions—religion and media—does not take any responsibility for the claims made in the scriptures of any religion. It merely transmits the message, quoting the available scripture or the interpreter and then leaves it to the faithfuls to decide for themselves.

The second area of their alliance is the social discipline prescribed by each religion which may or may not be compatible with other religions. The norms of human behaviour supposedly drawn from unapproachable heavenly sources in different regions among different people are not identical, even if they may seem to possess certain similarities. One such similarity is that a person seeking to flout them would invite divine punishment to be determined by the conventional spokespersons of divine law on earth.

Thus, the heavenly voice received by some select persons, presumably chosen by *God* himself in various parts of the world, was gradually transmitted to potential believers by birth or by conviction, mostly, by birth, through inter-personal and other forms of communication, including printed word and (now) electronic media also (*Akashvani*). Man's efforts to dethrone *God* have at times marginally succeeded but it has been a losing battle. Irrespective of *His* being unseen, unknown, or unapproachable, *God* continues to be *Supreme*. The media can take credit for circulating *His* message, as and when received from *His* (often self-appointed) representatives. The media has also widely reported the recrowning of *God* in the areas where *He* had reclined in suspended animation for a brief period of history in East European countries.

As an illustration of benign alliance between religion and

media, it is maintained with cogent arguments that the unseen hand regulating human affairs through religious directions had a very major role to play in social evolution. To that extent, religion and media has together contributed to the processes of human development.

The third dimension of the alliance between religion and media presents itself when the malignant or distorted character of religion surfaces. Irrespective of the fact that they are protagonists of religion, it is against all canons of the faith they profess. History, including recent history, is full of evidence that religious militancy, most often owing its emergence from the same unknown, unseen and all powerful source, has manifested itself in a variety of convulsions which may be pre-planned or unforeseen. There has been vandalization of religion and religious beliefs with tacit support of the believers and repositories of that faith. Large scale deprivation, dehumanization and degeneration of all professed values have taken place. The terror has not ended. The role of media has not remained unquestioned in social disorder on these occasions.

What is then media's relationship with religion? Does it in all cases play a complementary role? Or, it seeks to contain the aberration of religion and religious practitioners as an independent watchdog? Is there an exclusive domain of religion acceptable to all? Does it harmonize human behaviour and foster kinship whatever be the physical barriers? Or, is it basically divisive and creates distance even when the people are living together? According to yet another view, religion has no permanent character. It plays both roles according to convenience or unforeseen compulsions?

Does media in such a situation, become an offspring of religion, or media has the capacity to convert religion? The answers to some of these questions will considerably determine whether media can stem the vulgarization and degeneration of human conduct in the name of religion which is believed all over to draw its authority from the *Omnipotent, Omniscient, Omnipresent God* who cannot do any wrong.

It may help us discover what are the points of religion and Media's convergence, where they bypass each other and how they happen to enter the conflict zone. It is worth analysing why media has, at times, colluded with religion's repulsive fervour. Also, how media picked up the courage to expose and contain the virulence of religion as perceived and practised by its agents. This leads us to the question: Are both religion and media not ultimately accountable to the community they supposedly seek to serve? Once this postulate is accepted, *Man* emerges as the principal focal point. And, why not? He is deemed to be the most precious creation of the *Almighty God*.

11

Media and Religion: A Post-Ayodhya Analysis

*Subir Ghosh**

The spontaneous growth of a tumultuous variety of life-patterns and beliefs has developed, through the ages, a rich and composite culture in India—exemplified by its music, arts, architecture, literature and even, religion. India's peculiar genius for synthesis has absorbed and assimilated throughout the course of its history, diverse religions and cultures while allowing each to retain its own distinctive character. It has given birth in the process to a 'mosaic of Indian culture,' an expression that found much favour with Nehru. The quintessential India is a great meeting place of humanity. In an inspired vision of this eternal India, Tagore had identified the country in his poem *Bharat Tirtha* as a pilgrimage for many religions, many cultures and many races. The Indian idea of unity is not uniformity but harmony. The vision of India, therefore, depends on how much of the country one has really discovered. If one discovers with one's prejudice certain periods of India's history to the exclusion of others, the resultant vision would be so much poorer, so much myopic.

As the pioneer of all progressive movements in our country, the Indian Press discovered the spirit of unity in diversity in the Indian milieu long before it became apparent to the rest of our society. It encouraged the growth of a national outlook amidst people with diverse religious beliefs and customs. In a memorable

* Subir Ghosh is at the Hindustan Paper Corporation Ltd., Calcutta.

ode, published in the *India Gazette* in the twenties of the nineteenth century, it was Henry Derozio, the leader of the Young Bengal Movement, who conjured up the vision of a united India. If, as some people argue, political and administrative integration of the country was forcibly imposed by the British, the far more difficult task of social and emotional integration was achieved through the relentless efforts of the Indian Press. During the day of national struggle, the Press had acted not merely as a mirror of national life but a mirror that inspired the viewer with the plurality of its culture.

Role of Newspapers

The significance of newspapers in a developing country stretches far beyond the reporting of current affairs. "A community needs news for the same reason that a man needs eyes. It has to see where it is going." Journalists serve not only as the eyes and ears of the people; they also determine the agenda of public discussion. media has the potential to help erase erroneous impressions and ease tensions; it can also create fears and needlessly perpetuate anxieties. It can shake people out of complacency or it could lull them into an unthinking and dangerous stupor. In today's complex and confusing scenario when secessionist forces and religious fundamentalists have launched a vitriolic campaign to demolish the mosaic of our ethnic and religious diversity, the average Indian looks upto the Press as the conscience-keeper of the nation to uphold the country's secular traditions and values.

Integration, as a function of communication—the Macbride Commission observed—means "the provision to all persons, groups and nations of access to the variety of messages which they need in order to know and understand each other and to appreciate each others' living conditions, viewpoints and aspirations." The citizens of the country must, at least, develop an awareness about their own social environment in order to be able to discover and realise the underlying thread of unity amidst diversity. Newspaper, sometimes described as the 'poor man's university,' face today the grave responsibility of assuming their traditional role as teachers to forge a closer bond of understanding among peoples of different faiths.

Dr. Radhakrishnan described secularism as 'religious neutrality.' Roughly translated as *dharma nirapekshata*, the concept implies equal unconcern for all religions. It seeks to limit the role of religious identities and values in public affairs, and claims to be rational and forward-looking rather than traditional in outlook. But though secularism intends to keep public policy free of religious considerations, in the Indian context it does not entirely prohibit religious groups from entering the public space. In other words, secularism in India is not necessarily a negation of all religions but rather a peaceful coexistence of all religions.

Nurtured in the secular environment of our national struggle for independence, the Indian Press has a healthy tradition of respecting the pluralistic nature of our societies. It adopted, almost always, a secular stance during the turbulent period of our freedom movement. It has, generally, resisted any attempt to iron out the distinctive identities of different religions and cultures in the name of unity or unification. The Indian Press has traditionally reflected and recognised the variety and harmony in national life, it has always tried to promote mutual tolerance and respect for all religions among the diverse groups of people. Above all it is particularly known for its rationality as regards sensitive issues like communal and ethnic disturbances.

New Polarisation Emerges in the Nineties

On the threshold of the nineties, however, it appears that a large section of the Press, almost all of a sudden, lost its balance and fairness while reporting communal, caste, ethnic and other confrontationist incidents. Praful Bidwai, a leading journalist, in an article "Media in Service of Communalism" published in a Mumbai journal *Communal Combat* (August 1997), deplored: "One of the saddest changes to have occurred in the Indian Media over the past 50 years is its communalisation or at least its opening up-to the communal influences as never before." A number of newspapers betrayed a dangerous slant in reporting the riots and other related issues, arising out of the Rama Janmabhoomi-Babari Masjid controversy. Unverified information, irresponsible guesswork and sometimes emotional writing calculated to incite violence, particularly in some of the Indian language newspapers—notably Hindi, Urdu, Gujarati and Marathi—have raised serious doubts about their social responsibility. In fact, in a Seminar in New Delhi in 1991, M.J. Akbar, a champion of Press freedom otherwise, pleaded for censorship because he strongly felt that the hate campaign, which some papers had built up, eventually led to communal violence in Meerut in the early nineties.

In the wake of the post-Ayodhya situation, a new kind of polarisation developed in the Indian Press on communal and regional lines between the "elitist" English papers, that are seen to be anti-*Hindutva*, and "sons-of-the-soil" regional papers which are believed to be in tune with the Hindu popular opinion. Suddenly, the language one wrote, determined one's political views. This is totally out of sync with the glorious tradition of the Indian Press. A free and objective Press can hardly flourish in a climate of distrust and suspicion.

However, a large section of the English newspapers retained their secular moorings in their options and approach. They strongly refuted the claim that the Muslim appeasement policy was making things difficult for the majority. Citing the Shah Bano case, it argued that a law condemning restrictions on the rights of the Muslim women cannot be held either to be an act of appeasement of Muslims or intended to hurt the interests of the Hindus; appeasement being defined as the provision of benefits at the expenses of other communities. Rajiv Gandhi's volte face in the Shah Bano case was not necessarily motivated by the desire to protect Muslim interests because it was again he who had gone to the other extreme to woo the Hindus by allowing the *shilanyas* ceremony at the disputed Ayodhya site. The *Statesman* asserted in an article that the Shah Bano case represented a submission to Islamic fundamentalism to preserve the Muslim vote bank of the Congress. The leftist Press also highlighted the failure of the Congress government to protect the Constitution as well as the ethos of the minority. It is perhaps due to the fierce resistance against the communal line in a large part of the Press that the *Sangh Parivar* is still defensive on the Babari Masjid issue. There have been attempts on their part to rationalise the act but no one could really assert that it was something one could feel proud of.

The malady, of course, afflicted the Press even during the fifties. In this respect, the observations of the First Press Commission (1954) about the role of Media in religion are extremely revealing. The Report noted: "A great deal of the scurrilous writing is often directed against communities or groups. Events preceding and following the partition of the country have left so many people with a feeling of grievance against one community or the other that newspapers have found it lucrative business to exploit these feelings. We have not been able to find many instances where the sober and responsible Press has come forward to condemn such writing intended to vilify communities."

The Second Press Commission (1982) felt that the duty of the Press "lies not merely in reporting incidents of communal violence in a manner that does not aggravate tensions or trigger retaliatory actions, but also in lending a helping hand in the long-term task of eradicating irrational prejudices which lead even ordinarily reasonable persons to be carried away by mass frenzy worked up by fanatics." The Commission had analysed newspaper coverage of four communal riots: in West Bengal in 1964, in Gujarat in 1969, in Aligarh in 1978 and in Jamshedpur in 1979. In all the four cases, it was found that the first day's sensationalised and communally slanted reports were followed by an intensification of communal conflict over a wider area.

The need for a balanced and discretionary evaluation of inflammable incidents and situations, sifting rumour and dis-information from facts, cannot but be underscored. The most horrific event can be narrated with restraint in order that tensions, at a time when passions may already be on the high, do not reach an ignition point. Writing in *Young India,* nearly seventy-five years ago, Gandhiji underlined the need for restraint:

> "Granting that a Hindu or a Musssalman utters a hasty word, it is no business of a Pressman, who wishes well to his country, immediately to advertise it. It would be criminal to exaggerate such blunders....No expression of opinion from anybody is needed to demonstrate the necessity of being accurate, of curbing our tongues, and checking our pens."

Without this basic commitment to the welfare of society, inherent in Gandhiji's observations the Press would be perceived as merely exercising power without responsibility, the prerogative of a section of society, people do not think very high of. Communalism of any kind, Hindu or Muslim, is anti-democratic and against the principles of a secular Press. Some newspapers treat communalism of the minorities arising out of fear psychosis as legitimate while that of the majority as illegitimate. Beneath the surface of *Hindutva* or Islam, there is, however, an identical narrow and parochial interest. In fact, shorn of the communal rhetorics, there is no difference between the two. Majority communalism, however, is more dangerous because it has greater chances of being transformed into fascism.

Communalism is not a religious but a political phenomenon. Communal riots mostly take place as a result of a clash between vested interests. The warring parties, fighting for their personal gain, may just only incidentally happen to be Hindu or Muslim. It is subsequently given a religious twist by interested parties through the help of a section of the Media. Indeed, while the causes of the spread of communalism vary from country to country, there is one common feature; the exploitative set-up of society, this has reached even the extent of perhaps influencing policies and national agenda. Man has created religion and it is his decision on how he manifests it: positively or negatively, cohesively or coercively, with sublimity or profanity, to make or to break. It is dangerous to allow feelings of religious and ethnic fundamentalism to take root in our society. It is specifically in this area that the Press can play its watchdog role to prevent religion from becoming an instrument of exploitation and disintegration.

The basic message of all great Hindu religious teachers throughout the ages has been tolerance and mutual respect for all. This has been expressed so spontaneously, among others, by Sri Ramakrishna Paramahansa in his gospels, "Routes are many but the goal is the same." Even the Veda says: *"Ekam Sat Viprah Bahudha Badanti*—Truth is one, the wise talk of it in a variety of ways." Intolerance which arises from the concept of a fanatical and dogmatic religion is alien to the basic concept of Hinduism. In fact, it is against the basic concept of all religions. Given the fragile condition of national unity, it is important that the Media remind us of the mutual love and respect for others' faith and provide society with the right guidance to restore its sanity.

Creation of Muslim Stereotypes Exploit Religious Sentiments

Creation of the Muslim stereotype in the Media has been one of the ways of spreading the poison of communalism. By concentrating at times upon stereotypical issues like the Muslim Personal Law, the Uniform Civil Code, the status of Muslim women, the Media only helped to create the illusion of presenting information. But it contributed little to enlightening the rest of the nation about the Muslim community. In the process, it served only the propaganda-oriented goals of the so-called Muslim leaders.

A monolithic and homogeneous Muslim is an artificial construct of the media and a constituency of some so-called secular parties.

The visuals that generally accompany articles on issues relating to Muslim women are that of a purdah-clad woman. The Media unwittingly constructs a cultural stereotype of a cloistered community for which nothing has changed over the years. In fact, such presentations tend to reduce the rich Muslim culture to a veil, a piece of cloth. Rarely are the protagonists of our films Muslims or Christians. While the hero's role is assigned to an Amit, Vijay or Raju, the Muslims and Christians are generally seen as denizens of the under-world. Occasionally however, Muslims appear as wise old mullahs or quwwali singers and Christians as benevolent priests or teachers.

It is easy to identify journals which brazenly exploit the religious sentiment and foment hatred for the sake of their selfish interests. In publications like *Saamna* of the Shiv Sena or *Panchjanya* of the Rashtriya Swayamsevak Sangh, militant, extreme and communal positions are taken. Often this extremism is wrapped in 'nationalism' while trying to fight the identified 'enemies,'—in this case, Muslims. Publications like *Dawat* and *Hindustan*, Urdu dailies from Bombay, provide the flip side, playing on and encouraging the siege and ghetto mentality of the minority community, constantly under pressure from the enemies which they have identified on their part.

These are all publications of communal and right-wing organizations which pursue the given line with a vengeance. Then there are publications which toe the same line although they are not party organs. Because they are not owned by avowedly communal organisations, the slanted reports they publish seem to carry a slightly greater degree of credibility. To that extent, they end up providing legitimacy to questionable forces. *Amar Ujala's* role in reporting on the Ayodhya episode, for instance, was part of this controversy.

The Press Council has hauled up several publications like *Aaj, Dainik Jagaran, Swatantra Bharat* and *Swatantra Chetna* over a period of time for their distorted and communal slant in reporting. The Urdu Press, by and large, was full of anger but not despair. Emotive in content and graphic in description, they too played on the sentiments of their readers in different ways. Very few in the Urdu Press however, rejected the notion of India as a secular democracy.

There were, however, many other voices crying for peace and sanity in an environment of suspicion and distrust. The Bangla Press, without any exception, condemned the blatant use of religion for political ends. It not only upheld the secular traditions of the oldest Press in the subcontinent but built up a strong public opinion against exploitation of religion for narrow political purposes. It is not without reason that till today religion does not sell in West Bengal as a political commodity. The *Prabhat Khabar* from Ranchi and the *Dainik Navjyoti* from Rajasthan have also called for sanity and balance in an atmosphere otherwise vitiated by provocative writings in the media. In such a situation, *Communal Combat*, a monthly brought out by conscientious journalists wishing to counter both majority and minority communalism provides a silver lining.

As the country continued to burn, some newspapers saw in this an opportunity to step up their sagging circulations. As Digant Oza, editor of the Gujarati *Loksatta-Janasatta*, observed: "For the proprietor-editor, newspapers are not a mission but a commission. They have become pro-*Hindutva* because of the number of copies being sold." Indeed, there appears to be some link between circulation and a paper's stand on Ayodhya. *Gujarat Samachar* in Surat crossed the one lakh mark after the riots to become the city's number one paper. *Navakal* is another paper which witnessed a dramatic rise of 50,000 copies in only two months, in the aftermath of the Ayodhya incidents. The front-page editorial of the *Navakal* after the mosque demolition was titled, *Revolution in Ayodhya.* In such torrid and turbulent times, when communal frenzy, at least temporarily, seemed to triumph over sanity and secularism, should not every professional journalist introspect about the ethics of building up circulation at the cost of social responsibility?

While it is not difficult to identify a blatantly communal statement, the problem often arises in reporting on the grey areas. One instance of this is reporting on a statement which may not, in itself, be communal but the intentions and the undertones of it are. Should a newspaper give space to L.K. Advani's concept of 'pseudo-secularism' which, shorn of its euphemistic political veneer, becomes blatant *anti-Muslimism* when translated by workers at the ground level? Should a correspondent be an inert carrier of what the Imam of Jama Masjid Syed Abdullah Bukhari or Syed Shahbuddin say, regardless of their possible impact at the grass-roots? Where does political reality end and politics of religion begin? The distinctions are increasingly becoming blurred. The role of the Press, Gandhiji told us seventy years ago: "consists not only in reflecting public opinion but instructing it and giving it proper orientation and guidance."

It is no longer a secret now that communal forces have infiltrated the Press to ensure that their viewpoint gets adequately reflected. Words which at one time figured only in party organs have been brought into the mainstream today through, for instance, street-level agitations. Suddenly, a whole new range of words have muscled their way into the political lexicon after establishing themselves in the party organs. By using terms like *pseudo-secularism*, or *minority appeasement*, there has been a calculated effort to make them popular and, therefore, legitimate and acceptable in Parliament and outside. The usage, without quotation marks of terms like 'sants,' 'sadhus,' 'mahants,' 'karsevaks,' 'karseva,' 'imams' and 'mullahs' not only legitimises them but even glorifies and sanctifies them. For the use of these words signify not merely a change in the vocabulary but also a definite shift in attitudes. A reporter covering these events gradually becomes a conduit of these views and terms.

Need for Objectivity in Reporting

The objectivity of a newspaper lies not in the high-sounding principles and theories enunciated by editors, executive editors and associates editors. Their 'objectivity' lies in the way they use every word and image that shapes popular consciousness. The city page of *The Times of India* on 10 December, 1992 (when the countdown for the holocaust to follow had already begun), in a prominent two-column report captioned: "2 Lakh Kar Sevaks Leave for Ayodhya from State," confidently and unequivocally stated: "Over 2,00,000 Kar Sevaks will leave Maharashtra to participate in Kar Seva in Ayodhya." Did the journalist count heads at the airport or the railway station? No, the Correspondent was merely being objective and accurate. The objectivity of the correspondent, however, gives out at the end of the report. The report mentions: "While over sixty thousand of them have already left, the remaining were expected to leave over the next two days. The information was given here by Reghunath Kulkarni, state BJP Secretary."

As a journalist, Gandhiji felt: "To be true to my faith, therefore,

I may not write idly. I may not write merely to excite passion. The reader can have no idea of the restraint I have to exercise from week to week in the choice of my topic and vocabulary. It is training for me. It enables me to peep into myself and to make discoveries of my weaknesses. Often, my vanity dictates smart expression or my anger a harsh adjective. It is a terrible ordeal but a fine exercise to remove these words." Written nearly seventy-five years ago, these words, to my mind, are far more relevant to our times. During the freedom struggle, 'nationalism' meant coming together for the singular purpose of an independent nation. As the country faces the threat of balkanisation today, the need of the hour is religious harmony. Just as during the independence movement, the Press had played a glorious role in achieving freedom, so can it now take on the role of a crusader for secularism. Some may consider this suggestion as naive Newspapers, like individuals, do not live in a vacuum. They point out "time is out of joint" and other venerable institutions like Parliament, Academia and Judiciary, to which society has traditionally looked upto for guidance, have already reached a state of abysmal decadence and degeneration. After all, the Press is a typical product of the society in which it functions. It will, as a result, invariably reflect the prevalent value systems of the contemporary society. It can seldom be more conscientious than the prevailing ethical values. Nobody should expect the Press to wear a chastity belt in a brothel.

Even while journalists may not be morally superior to the rest of society yet their basic task to transmit the aspirations and urges of the average citizen demands certain values and of course, integrity. No one today would like to share entirely the views of C.P. Scott, a former editor of the *The Guardian*: "Facts are sacred, comment is free" for the simple reason that no fact can be totally value-natural in today's complex society. But the thrust of his basic argument that it is the duty of the Press to check facts and to assess the context in which such facts exist has not lost its edge. If absolute objectivity is impossible to achieve, one should at least strive for fairness. Freedom of the Press carries with it an onerous obligation which is not diminished in times of stress and tension.

Appraisal

In the ultimate analysis the Press seeks to put everybody's house in order except its own. It is in this context that many have felt the need to enforce a code of conduct to restrain the Press when reporting sensitive issues. Most professional journalists would, at least, informally agree about the need for such principles as accuracy and fairness. But the crucial question is: Who is to, lay down such a guideline? Under a libertarian system, journalists must themselves determine, both collectively and individually, their own responsibilities and guard against the use of religion to foment social disorder. Any form of external control, however liberal, will always carry the danger of the cure being worse than the disease. If the Press is the watch dog of public interest today, its enlightened readers need to come forward and act as the watchdog of the Press to ensure that our Press, 'the Ark of the Covenant of democracy' does not become a tool in the hands of communal forces.

The Indian Press has always been a positive and ispensable ally in India's struggle for freedom and its consolidation. Its responsibility and tasks thus take on an added importance when in the name of religion vested interests seek to imperil not only peace and tranquility but India's stability even its entity, its soul, its spirit, its historically-evolved character. Every conscientious journalist must examine today the impact of reports of communal, caste and other confrontationist incidents, the manner in which the news is presented, occasionally also the editorial observations (or even, meaningfully, of their absence). The task, I am aware, is not at all easy. Especially when situations are difficult, when passions fly, when rumours, often malignantly planted, flow to poison the air, when communal or other frenzy banishes discrimination and wisdom from the scene, reporting of events, pure and serene and untouched by emotion of any kind is the most trying of tasks.

But whatever the gloom, this country has a resilience and an inner strength that disasters cannot defeat. Our media must do their historical duty in these distressful times. They must highlight again and again the essential oneness of all religion and point out that there is no religion greater than that of the religion of humanity. They must bring out the essential spirit of amity and harmony underlying the life-pattern of our people at the grass-roots. Prof. Hiren Mukherjee relates how he learnt from M. Mujeeb, a great Indian of our times, what he had seen at a Sufi shrine in Bihar, after an orgy of violence in 1947 that had sent Muslims out of the Dargah on the Ganga, a group of Hindu women at sunset performing perambulations and prostrations as if nothing had happened.

We look upto the media in these troubled times to spread the underlying message of synthesis and amity hidden beneath the surface of different religions in our country, as manifested through such incidents. We expect media, in these torrid and turbulent times, to fight against the vested interest which seeks to exploit religion for its selfish economic or political gain. We expect media to spread vigourously the underlying message of Swami Vivekananda: "Religions must be integrating and not look down with contempt upon one another because their particular ideals of God are different."

12

The Dangers of Being M.F. Hussain: Art, Intolerance and the Hindu Right

*Shohini Ghosh**

In October 1996, Bajrang Dal activists broke into the Herwitz Gallery near the famous Hussain-Doshi Gufa Art Complex in Ahmedabad and destroyed a number of rare Hussain paintings. Dal members pulled down the paintings, collected the tapestries lying in a corner and set them afire. As many as 23 tapestry items and 28 paintings, including some acclaimed masterpieces, were destroyed. In the process, the vandals also damaged glass panes, music systems and other articles in the gallery and walked away from the wreckage with Bajrang Dal stickers stamped all over the gallery. The destroyed paintings valued at Rs. 6 crores, were especially precious to Hussain and he had loaned them for the very first time.

The ostensible reason for the Bajrang Dal ire was that Hussain had painted the Goddess Saraswati in the 'nude' and thereby hurt "Hindu sentiments." The outrage from the Hindu Right that directly or indirectly supported the Dal's action attempted to create the impression that Hussain had come up with a new painting designed to hurt the sentiments of the Hindus. In the immediate aftermath, newspapers perpetuated the same myth by neglecting to check the details.

---

* Shohini Ghosh is Reader, Video and Television Production at the Mass Communication Research Centre, Jamia Millia Islamia, New Delhi.

However, the fact of the matter is critically significant. The so-called 'nude' Saraswati was painted way back in 1976 and had been reproduced in a relatively new BJP backed magazine in Bhopal called *Vichar Mimansa*. One Om Nagpal had written an article titled "Ye Kasai ya Chitrakar?" ("Is he a butcher or a painter?"). Accompanying the article was a photograph of the "nude' Saraswati that V.S. Vajpayee, the editor had discovered in Dhyaneshwar Nadkarni's book titled *Riding the Lightning*. It was a copy of this article that Pramod Navalkar had handed over to the Bombay Police Commissioner along with a letter.

With great haste, the Bombay Police treated the letter as a complaint and registered a case against Hussain on October 8 under Section 153-A (promoting enmity between different groups on grounds of religion, race, etc., and acting in a manner prejudicial to harmony) and Section 295-A (perpetrating deliberate and malicious acts intended to outrage religious feelings of any class by insulting its religion or religious beliefs.) These cases against Hussain are yet to be dropped.

In 1998, the Sangh Parivar returned once again to target Hussain. A Hussain lithograph titled "Sita Rescued" displayed at an exhibition curated by art critic Suneet Chopra at the Academy of Art and Literature, New Delhi, was deployed to create a controversy. The lithograph had been produced in 1984 and was part of a series that Hussain had created for the Ramlila programmes run by a Lohiaite socialist group. The controversy began when VHP artist Raghu Vyas drew attention to the lithograph. Ironically, Raghu Vyas had participated in pro-Hussain protests during the Saraswati incident. The attack on the exhibition was led by the belligerent B.L. Sharma "Prem" of the VHP and former MP from East Delhi. According to him the "painting" was offensive as both Hanuman and Sita had been portrayed in the "nude." Some other VHP protesters suggested that since Sita was perched on Hanuman's tail it carried a phalic resonance. B.L. Sharma's protest included physically assaulting painter Jatin Das and intimidating artists Aparna Caur and Ajit Caur. The exhibitors sought to quell the trouble by renaming the lithograph series "Epic Forms" and finally replaced it with another piece of work that Hussain had done for the Safdar Hashmi Memorial Trust. However, the threats continued with Sharma threatening to burn the place down.

Five weeks after the exhibition in New Delhi had closed

down, Hussain's home in Bombay was targeted by the Bajrang Dal on May 1, 1998. Bajrang Dal activists broke into Hussain's apartment at Cuffe Parade and began to ransack the place. As the police arrived the crowd dispersed. Finally only 26 people were arrested, to be released the next day after paying a fine of Rs. 1000 each. They were charged with unlawful assembly: for holding a demonstration without permission. Meanwhile, lawyer and Shiv Sena M.P. Adhik Shirodhkar advised that Hussain be charged under Section 295 (A) IPC for deliberately and maliciously outraging religious beliefs.

Political reaction to the incident was quick. The Left parties, Janata Dal and even the Congress (I) strongly condemned the incident. There was however, an interesting shift in the position of the BJP. During the Saraswati controversy, the BJP had expressed displeasure over the ransacking while maintaining that Hussain had hurt Hindu sentiments. This time around two significant changes had taken place. Kushabhau Thakre was the new BJP President and the party had just carried out the Nuclear tests at Pokhran. On May 16, 1998 Kushabhau Thakre told the Press that M.F. Hussain had no right to insult Gods of other faiths or their religious sentiments in the name of freedom of expression. Throughout the session Thakre refused to condemn the incident. Venkaiah Naidu, the party's General Secretary supported Thakre's statement saying that he advised Hussain not to create "such perverted works of art" (sic) and "incite communal passions by such paintings of Hindu Gods and Goddesses." He said, "Hussain was trying to create communal tension in the country and this would not be tolerated." The Sangh Parivar made it clear that Hussain had to stop his "perverted work or face the consequences."

A closer look at the controversy reveals that none of the Sena's allegations actually stand up to scrutiny. The primary allegation was that by painting Saraswati in the nude. Hussain had hurt Hindu sentiments. Invoking "culture" and "tradition" to communalize the issue, Ramesh Patel of the VHP said that "it was an uncivilized way of depicting a religious figure." Uma Bharti of BJP pushed the argument further by stating that "it is not only a question of Hindu sentiment but also that of women sentiment (sic). I would have protested if Hussain had painted Mariam or Khatija in the nude. Goddesses like Lakshmi and Saraswati are the ideal of the traditional Hindu woman....I think Hussain is a pervert and needs psychiatric treatment."[1]

The "nudity-against-Indian-culture" allegation was conclusively challenged by scholars and artists.[2] They pointed out that themes and conventions of nudity are integral to Indian iconography and painting and date back to the Indus Valley Civilization. For instance, the "Lajja Gauri" a term popularized by historians which loosely means "woman with no shame" was a popular folk and fertility deity dating back to the third century.[3] Moreover, the famous image of Saraswati of the twelfth century Hoysala period is dressed only in a belt of jewellery. It was further argued that clothing of deities was a relatively recent phenomenon and one that was started by the nineteenth century painter, Raja Ravi Varma. When the editor of *Vichar Mimansa* asked why he was not outraged by the "nude" Dilwara temple sculptures he said: "In those days it was very difficult to sculpt cloths in stone."[4]

It should be noted that the attack on Hussain, even though he happened to be a carefully chosen target, was not an isolated one. On April 26, about a hundred Shiv Sainiks barged into Centaur Hotel to disrupt a concert by Pakistani ghazal singer Ghulam Ali. The miscreants grabbed the microphone and shouted anti-Pakistan slogans. They also informed the audience that they would not permit any Pakistani artist to perform in India. In the face of Shiv Sena belligerence, Pakistani squash player Jansher Khan cancelled his trip to India. Between April and May 1998, the Shiv Sena stepped up its moral policing. The rock group Savage Garden and VJ Marc Robinson became targets. Marc had violated the Shiv Sena's code of conduct by kissing on stage and was finally forced into silence as even his employer, *Channel V* castigated him for jeopardizing business interests.

Cultural terrorism and street censorship have been Sena traditions. They have always countered dissent with either violence or intimidation. Nikhil Wagle, editor of *Mahanagar* had been physically attacked innumerable times for opposing Shiv Sena politics. The attacks on Wagle included two stabbings while the *Mahanagar* office was repeatedly ransacked. Manimala of *Navbharat Times* was seriously injured with a chopper when she protested against the harassment to *Mahanagar*. During the Bombay riots following the demolition of the Babri Masjid, Harun Rashid, editor of Urdu daily had his house looted and then set on fire. Rashid lost all his property including 3000 books and diaries that he had maintained since 1958 in order to write his autobiography. During and after the riots in Bombay the Sena conducted a witch hunt in the industry. All those who disapproved of the Sena's hate campaign were either harassed or persecuted. Film actors Dilip Kumar, A.K. Hangal and Shabana Azmi faced harassment and boycott; they were labelled traitors for having attended the Pakistan Day celebrations at the Pakistan High Commission.

The vicious politics of the Shiv Sena mouthpiece *Saamna* rests on the propagation that all Muslims are traitors of the nation, whose loyalties lie with Pakistan.[5] Both *Saamna* and its predecessor, the fortnightly *Marmik*, relentlessly propagate misinformation about minorities. On December 5, 1992 Thackeray wrote in his editorial: "The temple should not be constructed because the sentiments of the minorities would be affected. And who are these minorities? The Muslim traitors who partitioned this country and have not allowed us to breathe ever since."[6] Bal Thackeray's caricatures for the cover of *Marmik* represented Muslims as green monsters, green vultures or green serpents. That the Sena lexicon considers all Muslims to be anti-national and 'outsiders' is apparent in Bal Thackeray's response to the ransacking of Hussain's house "If Hussain can enter Hindustan, why can't we barge into his house?"

But what makes Hussain the Sangh Parivar's target for repeated attacks? I propose that Hussain, not the person but the persona, poses a threat to the Hindu Right's exclusive hold over cultural nationalism. Hussain is an uncomfortable, *albeit* inadvertent reminder, that Hindu traditions are not the exclusive domain of the Hindu Right. Moreover, Hussain is a reminder that so-called Hindu culture and traditions may actually not be so 'Hindu.' As Monica Juneja writes, "that which we today label 'Hindu' has in fact grown over centuries through constant interaction with cultures coming from the outside—Arabic, Persian, Greek—as well as myriad other traditions."[7] Nothing hurts the Sangh Parivar more than the realization that there is no 'Hindu' culture without Muslims.

In fact, the trajectory of Hussain's life and work is inextricably bound to India's multiple and syncretic cultural traditions. Maqbool Fida Hussain was born in a well to do working class family in Pundharpur, Maharashtra. He attended a local art college in Indore. When he was 17 he became an apprentice to a tailor and also trained to be a prayer leader. When he moved to Bombay he worked as an assistant to a billboard painter and lived in a slum. Thereafter, he became a furniture designer and a toy-maker.

Through all this he doggedly pursued painting. 1984 marked an important phase in Hussain's life when he first saw the Hindu sculptures of the Mathura School. Artist Anjali Ela Menon mentions how 20 years back, Hussain was so electrified by the *Ramayana* that he did 300 paintings on the epic. This feat, she goes on to point, has never been attempted by a Hindu painter.

It has been remarked that the vandals who attacked Hussain knew nothing about his work. This is probably true. Perhaps, it is equally true that they knew enough to realize that Hussain also embodies a tradition that exposes the lie of *Hindutva's* "Cultural nationalism." The *Hindutva* imagery of "Hindu culture" as homogenous, pure and original is threatened by any hint of diversity. In 1993, BJP and its allies had mounted a vicious campaign against the Safdar Hashmi Memorial Trust (SAHMAT) for a textual display of a Jataka story depicting Ram and Sita as siblings as part of an exhibition titled *Hum Sub Ayodhya.*[8] Once again, the familiar 'Hindu-sentiments-are hurt' argument was deployed to bring about six criminal charges against SAHMAT.[9] Thus an organization whose secular credentials had never been in doubt was designated as criminal by the state.

The notion that both culture and traditions are dynamic, changing, flexible, impermanent, porous and often contradictory destabilises the Hindu Right's notion of a centralized "cultural nationalism." The BJP bases its 'nationalist vision' on a "cultural heritage which is central to all regions, religions and languages, is a civilizational identity and constitutes the cultural nationalism of India which is the core of *Hindutva.*"[10] Any cultural praxis that counters this imagery of "cultural nationalism" is thereby seen to be inaccurate, wrong, distorted and harmful. Discrediting Hussain's work as "perverted" is a way to recuperate an authoritarian hold over the interpretation of culture and tradition. The inability, rather impossibility, of that attempt is *Hindutva's* failure and Hussain's victory.

Yet this victory is embedded in pain as it embodies secular-India's great betrayal to its syncretic, plural and secular traditions. Religious fundamentalism on both sides of the border have been threatened by multiplicity, plurality and diversity. The blurring of borders, the cultural mix, the impossibility of original claims, the occupation of multiple spaces have been historically resisted by all orders that seek to restrict, regiment, and control. The attack on Hussain is post-independent India's tragic failure to resist fundamentalist and authoritarian forces. Hussain is in fact a symbol of the Indian Muslim's painful journey through post-partition India. A figure who reflects the fictive Abul Mansur Kamaluddin in Qurratulain Hyder's *River of Fire*.[11]

A recurring figure born through different centuries, Kamal first arrives as the author of a travelogue titled the *Marvels and Strange Tales of Hindustan*. Born of Persian and Arab parentage, Kamal the 'foreigner' merges inextricably with the cross-currents of Hindustan's political and cultural history. Against the constant turbulence of feudal warfare Kamal falls in love with the Hindu Champavati, joins an order of Sufi mystics and inspired by the songs of Vaishnav women contemplates the Sufi notion of "*Fana-fi-allah*" through Radha's desire to be one with Krishna. Finally after travelling through innumerable cities and cultures, he marries a low caste Shudra woman Sujata Debi (re-named Amina Bibi) and fathers two sons called Jamal and Jalal. At the age of eighty-five, Kamal is accused of treachery by the soldiers of Sher Shah Suri, "Your architect son has gone to Delhi to join the Mughal government Traitor!" they say before they kill him. As death envelops him Kamal tries to think of a reason for this punishment. "What had he done to be treated thus?....This was his country, his children had been born here, his dead wife lay buried here. He had put all his energies into making these fields bloom, spent years beautifying the language these men were speaking. He had written songs and collected stories and he was going to continue living right here. No one had any right to call him an outsider or a traitor." Kamal dies but recurs over different periods in history and is finally compelled to migrate to Pakistan after the partition. The tragedy of Kamal is that he never ceases to be the 'outsider' even though he never feels like one.

The danger of being M.F. Hussain is that he is both in danger and perceived to be one. Yet Hussain's art is not a deliberate protest or a pre-meditated opposition to fundamentalism. It is an organic protest, as it were, of cultural heterogeneity itself. Yet, in this struggle for hegemony and resistance, the intervention of a secular and democratic polity has to be deliberate and determined. It must come with the understanding that the power to indict and silence is a majoritarian privilege. Perhaps also an authoritarian one. Rarely do speech, expression or representation that hurt minority groups get either indicted or silenced. The routine prevalence of Hindu communal speech is a clear instance. Sexist, heterosexist, classist and casteist speech and representations are other instances. To protect the metaphoric artist is, therefore, to not just protect the man but to protect the vibrancy of cultural heterogeneity itself.

More importantly, cultural diversity is precariously contingent upon free speech. This is because all cultural practices present sites of contestation and contradictions. Erasure is inimical to this process.

References

1 See "Agenda," *The Pioneer*, October 13, 1996.
2 See cover story titled "Communalism *vs.* Art" in *Frontline*, November 15, 1996.
3 For feminists the debate on nudity takes on a special significance as it is often used by the moral 'right' and conservatives as synonymous with degradation. 'Nudity' and 'vulgarity' have often been used to curtail women's right to sexual speech and expression and rights over their own bodies. Therefore, any deployment of 'nudity-as-degrading' arguments should be seen by feminists as suspect.
4 See *Frontline*, November 15, 1996.
5 Also see "The Challenge of Communalism: The *Saamna* Case" by Shohini Ghosh in *The Journal of Peace Studies*, February 1995.
6 This was one of the nine editorials that had been identified in a writ filed by J.B. D'Souza, former Chief Secretary of Maharashtra and Dilip Thakore a journalist, in April 1993. The writ sought to take the Maharashtra government to tasks for not initiating criminal proceedings against Bal Thackeray for his incendiary editorials during the riots. The Bombay High Court, however, not only dismissed the petition but in a long judgement sought to defend and justify the stance taken by *Saamna*.
7 See "Reclaiming the Public Sphere: Hussain's Portrayal of Saraswati and Draupadi," *Economic and Political Weekly*, Vol. XXXII, No. 4, January 25, 1997.
8 The text excerpted from the *Dasaratha Jataka* presented a version of the *Ramayana* that was at odds with the Sangh Parivar's view of the *Ramayana*. Activists of the Parivar vandalized the exhibition and launched a hate campaign against SAHMAT. The incident was discussed in Parliament for a week and soon SAHMAT was accused of indulging in "aggressive secularism". On August 21, 1993, SAHMAT was compelled to withdraw the said *Ram Katha* panel from the Teen Murti Museum where it was held at the time. On the same afternoon, the police confiscated the next panel.
9 In Faizabad, SAHMAT was charged under Sections 153; 153-A,

Section 125-A (deliberate and malicious acts intended to raise religious feelings of any class by insulting its religion or religious belief); Section 505 (statements conducive to public mischief) and Section 120-B (criminal conspiracy).

10 See the *BJP Election Manifesto*, 1998.

11 Originally written in Urdu as *Aag Ka Dariya* (1959) the noval has been translated by Haider herself as *River of Fire* (1998) published by *Kali for Women*.

13

Religion and the Film Media in India

*A.A. Khan Afridi**

Old traditions and religious sentiments, deeply ingrained in the Indian psyche, exercise considerable influence in our daily lives. It is also no surprise then that these traditions and sentiments have been widely reflected in the Indian film Media since its very inception.

India's first silent movie, Dadasaheb Phalke's *Raja Harishchandra* released in 1913, brought to every Indian home the religious history and traditions of the Hindus. Thereafter, Phalke's other films (more than 125), chief amongst which were *Bhamasur Mohini* (1913), *Satyavan Savitri* (1914) and *Lanka Dahan* (1917) were each distinctive in nature even while being based on Hindu mythology and traditions. While *Bhamasur Mohini* introduced for the first time a female artiste in Indian Cinema, *Lanka Dahan* and *Satyavan Savitri* had only one actor playing the role of both the hero and heroine. All these films had their own impacts on the religious psyche of the peoples.

During this early period of Indian Cinema, several religious themes and stories from mythology were also covered by the regional language films. Some of these were, in Gujarati, *Narsi Mehta* (1932); in Bengali, *Nal Damyanti* and *Jamai Sushthi* (1917); in

* Dr. Afridi is Programme Director, Central Institute of Educational Technology, National Council for Educational Research and Training, New Delhi.

Punjabi, *Heer Ranjha* (1932); in Telugu, *Bhisham Pratigya* (1920); in Kannada, *Bhakta Dharu* (1934) and *Mruch Katik* (1929); in Assamese, *Jog Mati* (1935); in Oriya, *Sita Viwaha* (1936); in Malayalam *Balan* (1938); in Bhojpuri, *Ganga Mayya Tohe Piyaree Charaibon* (1963); in Rajasthani, *Baba Rama Deva* (1964), etc. The fact that these films with themes from religion any mythology were made attests to the influence and popularity of the film Media.

Indian producers have also widely tackled the theme of the life and works of Indian saints—*Tulsi Das* (1934), *Bhagat Surdas*, *Bhagat Kabir* (1942), *Sant Tukaram* (1948), *Swami Vivekananda* (1996), etc. Muslim and other film makers have also looked at Muslim social issues, customs and religion in *Gul-e-Bakawli* (1939); *Alam Ara* which was the first Indian talkie produced in 1932; *Judgement of Allah* (1935); *Pardah Nashin* (1942); *Mere Garib Nawaz* (1973); *Shan-e-Illahi* (1995) etc.

Most of the Indian films produced have been widely screened in India and internationally. They have in recent years also been screened several times again—attesting to the high demand of such theme films among the masses.

Now as Television has overtaken Cinema, most of these above themes have received wide coverage in the serials. Well-known among these are Ramandand Sagar's, *Ramayana* and *Sri Krishna*, B.R. Chopra's *Mahabharat*, Dhiraj Kumar's *Om Namo Shivaya*, Sanjay Khan's *Jai Hanuman*, etc., which have been aired several times on popular demand. Similarly stories from Christianity, *Bible Ki Kahaniyan* and on Muslim social problems, customs and religion attained considerable popularity and success. All this is indicative of the influence of such themes amongst the Indian people. Dissemination of such themes is also educative for the young and the uninitiated.

Overall, films and TV have not only reflected the impact and influence of religion and custom in Indian social mores but has also acted as a medium of instruction for the unlettered and the uninitiated.

14

Nature of State, Media and Communications in India: A Theoretical Discourse

*Subodh Narayan Malakar**

To focus the corresponding relationship between the State, Media and Communications is a sensitive and volatile discourse as it reveals the truth of the nature of state and media's protection. The emerging state's characteristics in today's society is by no means separated from the laws of social development. Economic transaction being a guiding force of social development has shaped the state's nature in a more coercive form. It is due to this fact that economic determinism has become the necessary condition for the survival of a crisis-ridden state. Although, the role of economic determinism is not a new phenomenon in the stage of crisis-ridden capitalism, it appeared in history several times in many forms and resulted in a division and redivision of the world and thereby perpetuated wars and civic unrest.

Taking a lesson from history a capitalist state has operated with different regulative tactics. It has to stand by in the new circumstances of people's consciousness which has been transmitted into them (people) by the formation processes of history. Therefore, to match the new form of peoples consciousness,

* Dr. Malakar is Associate Professor, Centre for West Asian and African Studies, School of International Studies, Jawaharlal Nehru University, New Delhi.

as it is the product of the contradictions between the reality of life and the myth of state, has become an immediate task of the capitalist state. For it, the state needs the continuous transformation of information and opinion generating or producing technology.

As a matter of fact, the capitalist mode of communication is cut off from the social experiences of the mass of readers and listeners. It imposes on the masses the preoccupation and themes of the ruling class as if they are universal and ubiquitous, but this does not necessarily resolve the conflict dimension. Despite it's best effort to dismantle the ideological coherency and formation of opposite views, the contradiction increases in it's worst form as the State as a force does not stop the extraction of surplus value, rather it accelerates the process of accumulation of more surplus extraction which results in the further deterioration of the material existence of the people. This phenomenon is clearly visible in today's chaotic form of the states' affairs and rising mass awareness among the people against the state's validity. As much as the State is challenged through the people's consciousness, the production and reproduction of mass communications materials as well as the transformation and retransformation of communications structures becomes the need of the hour to maintain the existing State. In this context "mass communication is an arm of the ruling order of the strong agency of social control at least in the long run."[1] This marks a sharp break with liberation theory, which sees media as freeing people from ignorance and inherited superstitions and thus enabling them to govern themselves by reason and individual conscience.[2] 'Freedom of the Press' belongs to the catalogue of bourgeois liberal principles. Their proponents are in fact unable to apply their full sense when their interests are threatened, they revert to official censorship, as shown in Uruguay, Brazil and India (in 1975). Facing the menace of popular movements, the enlightened bourgeoisie and military dictatorship alike sing the same song. The other thing is the "engineering of consent' a term used for explaining the process of social control—as the significant feature of mass media. It has proved to be an adjunct of the industrial order (it is a cultural arm of industry)."[3] As the process of social control is strengthened the contradictions between people's minds and media projections increases.

The contemporary Indian State has been passing through various stages of state formation. It reflects the capitalist characteristics albeit carries the feudal reminiscences with it as the legacy. In the feudal age the instrument or the means of communication were different; it was in the form of literature, poetry recitation, drama, preaching, working history in the praise of masters, etc., which served the state forces or the King as the representative of state. This has been clearly visualised by the great poet Suryakant Tripathi Nirala in his famous poem given below:

राजे ने अपनी रखवाली की

राजे ने अपनी रखवाली की
किला बनाकर रहा
बड़ी-बड़ी फौजें रखीं ।
चापलूस कितने सामन्त आये ।
मतलब की लकड़ी पकड़े हुए ।
कितने ब्राह्मण आये
पोथियों में जनता को बांधे हुए ।
कवियों ने उसकी बहादुरी के गीत गाये,
लेखकों ने लेख लिखे,
ऐतिहासिकों ने इतिहासों के पन्ने भरे,
नाट्यकलाकारों ने कितने नाटक रचे,
रंगमंच पर खेले ।
जनता पर जादू चला राजे के समाज का ।
लोक-नारियों के लिए रानियां आदर्श हुई
धर्म का बढ़ावा रहा धोखे से भरा हुआ ।
लोहा बजा धर्म पर, सभ्यता के नाम पर ।
खून की नदी बही ।
आंख-कान मूंदकर जनता ने डुबकियां लीं ।
आंख खुली, राजे ने अपनी रखवाली की ।

• निराला

The poem clearly reflects the role of mass media in defence of the state master, 'the king' and how the king defends himself through the advocates of media personalities by breaking the unity of the people and creating false consciousness among the people. This process continued even while the instruments of media and Communications have taken a great leap forward in modernising; the process of transition from feudalism to capitalism has not changed the ownership system of property and the instrument of media and communications. And that is why it has proved to be the weapon of the ruling class. Challenges to such processes can be traced to the movement of people in various forms which history has not stopped. Certainly in Indian society media and communications has generated awareness among people in a sense, that they realise that the instrument of mass communication is a tool for exploiting class, caste, and communal forces.

Under the given premises the present study takes account of the meaning of media in a capitalist state as the theoretical discourse with the specific example of India. To substantiate the theoretical understanding, the study will focus on the historicity of the changing nature of the Indian state and the socio-political linkages, mass media, and the present day relations between the State and Media and its nexus to dismantle the process of idea formations in the minds of people against the state.

Meaning of Media in a Capitalist State—A Theoretical Understanding

In a capitalist state all activities and all products of human beings constitute as part of the world and logic of the market.[4] Even the language, whereby the meaning of this activity and these products, whatever they may be, is transmitted to the public is the language of the merchant, who is promoted to being the lord and master of all languages. The form of commerce is the general form of exchange. The activity and the products of communications form part of the dominant social relations. To establish this commercial form of communication and make it a natural activity, which is not suspected by the dominated (the 'receivers') as being an instrument of class domination, the media undergoes a process of fetishisation like every product and activity. Through this life style people are metamorphosed into things (factors of production) and things are given life. Thus, money 'works,' capital produces in the same way the media acts.'[5]

To guarantee its legitimacy, the capitalist mode of production needs a body of fetishes to confirm its rationality of social domination. The arrival of these fetishes on the scene is intimately bound up with the development of the production forces. Every fetish goes together with an entire rational corpus of mechanisms whose purpose is to obscure social relations of production in a given society. The fetish of communications conceals the repressive and manipulative power behind the dominant technology of dissemination (available new productive forces) and characterises it as a force for liberation and happiness. It is in this guise that it is presented to the dominated classes.[6]

Media structure is an important factor in organising a certain kind of opinion projection which suits, according to their class interests. While studying this problem in depth, two trends are generally visible. The history of media and communications should be traced to the mobility of cultural exchanges of the people which can be defined as the emergence of Media from the root which has natural characteristics to spread because it touches the reality of peoples lives. But it is not organised and structured. Secondly, an organised and structured form of media and communications appeared in the course of state formation to project and protect the interests of state forces which appear to maintain the existing ruling order.

Today the international and national bourgeoisies have made tremendous effort to strengthen the structured projection of media and communications. They all quickly introduce the new information technology to counter the people's mind through a network of *educated and elite forces.* Thus a form of technological determinism has come to the fore in structuring and restructuring of information technology. It has developed a technique of production and reproduction of new fetishes to grab the consciousness of the social environment. And to a great extent it has made possible the commercialisation of all kinds of media and communication which people of this country had been attached to. Thus the fragmentation in cultural and social values have been the consistent phenomenon today.[7]

Historicity of the Changing Nature of the Indian State and Media

Since the ancient period, the Indian State formation process is a reality. In the beginning media emerged from the cultural interactions, mobility of the people, and various activities such as printing or technological means of communication, but in the feudal stage the print written materials emerged. In the age of feudalism the State being an organised structure needed media to secure its stability. Since then state control over media has remained a persistent historicity with this long journey. Today, media is controlled by the ruling forces in contemporary capitalist society. It is not at all true that state controlled media was not challenged in the historical process of media development; it was as much a contradiction between social forces of production and owners of production or state forces. Buddhism in India combated the Vedic philosophy through its literature, talks, preaching and many forms of communication. Likewise, in the British period the peoples'-voice was raised forcefully and later after independence, peoples mind acted against the projected media. But the specific point is that state controlled media prevailed over the media that opposed it. The protest or opposing role of Media has appeared basically from the contradiction between peoples' mind and media's projection by the ruling class. media, which supported the people's cause maintained the movement syndrome rather with the structural proposition. The other factor expressed as the people's-oriented media has not made any technological breakthrough due to state control over the media structure. These forces are using the capitalist media to a limited scale. But the strongest element in support of people's voice media is rooted in the contradiction between mode of production relations and historically emerged productive forces. It is a fact that production is a social activity but ownership is an individual claim; thus the contradiction between the entire productive forces and ownership relations remains a reality. The ruling order has an advantage in visualising the contradictions in the beginning because they have an organised structure to locate it. To counter the opposition, the ruling class introduced a degenerating mode of media articulation and communication to overcome the contradiction but it proved only momentarily remedial. It created more and more problematic challenges, the challenges from the antagonistic socio-political forces of change remains constantly on the heads of the ruling order. And for that matter even while technology will be renewed for modernising the media and communications system, the challenges to the ruling order will be the same as those which arise from the people's conscience and understanding of the reality which helps in the formation of the objective truth.

Socio-Political Linkages and Indian Mass Media

Socio-political linkages are an important factor in determining the role of media activities in our country in particular and Third World in general. Media influenced and organised by the above has been playing a distinct role which has generally ignored the reality of media's link with the dominant class, caste, community and religious forces of the society. *Vice versa* we also ignore the media's role in the defence of the down-trodden class, caste and community of the society. This bifurcation in the role played by media depends on the very nature and composition of media structure in its above context.

Since the emergence of media structure in its above context, the economic factors appear decisive. Economic structure of any society determines the activity of the forces in the media behaviour.

The nature of the Indian State has varied in accordance with the development of its political economy. Since independence it has acquired a character that can be defined as the conglomotion of feudo-capitalist forces. Feudal forces have been utilised to fulfil the task for securing capitalism. Gradually a large number of the petty bourgeois forces emerged from the feudal section that had strong links with the feudal ethos and structure (like casteism and communalism) and later on in many other forms. But in the early stages feudal forces had resisted capitalism which they have now lost completely to capitalists interests. The fast eroding base of feudalism in India has forced the petty bourgeoisie to serve the interests of the nation and international capitalist media propaganda. Even though their caste and communal values have not been demolished, rather in some cases they are very conscious of such factors.

In various phases of history, some intellectuals or enlightened persons have declared themselves separate from the ruling class and caste values. In this our *Nirakar Brahm upasak sants, social reformers* and *revolutionaries* have also influenced the media and media has communicated their messages successfully. But today in the age of globalisation of economies, a process of declassification or decasteisation is losing the potential. The period is in transition and this process has to emerge in due course of history when the realisation will take place by experiencing the hard realities of life. Socio-economic and political linkages of media have been changing their dimensions due to the consistent change in the political economy of the state.

Nature of State and Media Structure in India

Though it is very difficult to determine the nature of the Indian State, broadly speaking it represents a combination of both capitalist and feudal forms where capitalism is the motive force while the feudal forces are losing their strength.

In the fast changing global scenario India has fallen in the micro-economic network of the international *bourgeoisie* and the Indian capitalists are losing its hold on the state. It has also lost its patriotic role against the new imperialist designs of multinationals as India has accepted the opening up of the economy and structural adjustment programme proposed by the World Bank and the international financial agencies like WTO and the IMF. Despite the contradictions among these three forces the international bourgeoisie has made it possible to guide the economic and state affairs of the country.

Thus capitalism is the motive force of the Indian State which is surrendering its national strength to the international monopoly classes by using the features of feudalism (casteism and communalism) to divide the people in the service of national and international ruling classes.

To maintain the state, the organisation and reorganisation of media and communications structure becomes a necessary course for the ruling forces. For that they have laid emphasis on the print and electronic media at large for "the engineering of consent"[8]—a term of the process of social control—as the significant features of the mass media. In the long-term and in a big way the development of media and mommunication infrastructures have been handed over to the national and international private financial companies. They are obnoxiously making a surplus and dismantling the truth. The social responsibility of journalists and media persons is virtually ignored and opportunism of caste and communalist projections have become the bargaining tendencies among them. Journalists contribute to the public's unrealistic expectations of the media and distort the projection of the media's actual power.[9] W.B. Yeats has rightly pointed out the media culture as it should be understood in the Indian context:

A statesman is an easy man
He tells his lies by rote
A journalist makes up his lies
And takes you by the throat;
So stay at home and drink your beer
And let the neighbours vote.[10]

While television has become the mass instrument of media and communications, the Indian society and masses have been intoxicated by the unreal projection of truth. Ruling classes have become successful to some extent to carry away the mental wavelength as they wish. Leonard has beautifully described the role of television that appears to be valid in Indian society too. He explains "Television is another kind of a car, as windshield on the worlds. We climb inside it, drive it, and it drives us, and we all go in the same direction, see the same thing."[11] Thus the Indian media structure is an instrument to create a false consciousness to keep out the masses from the real issues of the society and life.

Conclusion

The nature of state determines the role of media and communications. Media and communications ceing an arm of the ruling order has been challenged by the people's consciousness which is transmitted by the consciousness of history in due course of facing the reality of life. Even under restraint, media tackled by the state has played an important role in accelerating the understanding of people. The emphasis on the social responsibility of media must be emphasized. Nevertheless capitalism cannot allow it as it challenges the existing state structure.

References

1 Robert E. Krieger, *The Media and the People* (Huntington, New York, 1978), p. 37.
2 *Ibid.*, p. 37.
3 *Ibid.*, p. 38.
4 Armand Mattelart, *Mass Media, Ideologies and the Revolutionary Movements* (The Harvester Press, Sussex, Humanities Press, New Jersey, 1974, Translated in 1980), p. 7.
5 *Ibid.*
6 *Ibid.*

7 *Ibid.*

8 A. Joseph Klapper describes it so in *Media and the People* (Robert E. Krieger Publishing Company, Huntington, New York, 1978), p. 37.

9 *Ibid.*, p. 2.

10 *Ibid.*, p. 1.

11 *Ibid.*, p. 25.

Section IV

Social Impact of Media

15

Development of Electronic Media in the South Asian Countries

*Regina Mulay Parakh**

INTRODUCTION

There was a time when access to information was extremely difficult. In order to keep track of the developments in the neighbouring countries one had to depend on tertiary sources of information, which anyhow attached the stigma of being biased and selective. Today, we live in an age where man is trying to transcend both time and space. We have not only set foot on the moon, but are also carrying out voyages towards new galaxies.

The telecommunication network, the advent of satellite communication and establishment of internet systems have truly led to the collapse of geographical boundaries. The world community has turned into a global village with every one having the right to know. Communicating with others, not just for personal gains, but for mutual cooperation at economic, political and cultural levels has become the norm of the day.

The information crazy world has moved into a highly sophisticated electronic age; messages and information travel across the globe in fractions of electronic minutes. The rapid advance in communications technology in the past decades has given a substantially new dimension to the possibility for exchange

* Dr. Parakh is Research Fellow at the School of International Studies, Jawaharlal Nehru University, New Delhi.

of ideas and information. In fact, the intercontinental communications network has made the world really small.

The Third World countries in general, and the South Asian countries in particular, were and are still trying to cope with this information explosion. The societies of Asia, Africa and Latin America are still in various stages of development, and are undergoing transition from traditionalism to modernization/Westernization. The national development for the societies in transit involved three types of revolutions *viz.* economic, political and of communications. In fact, these three revolutionary processes got compressed in the Third World countries. The effect of this compression, compression of several centuries of development into a few decades, has created some contradictions, problems and unique opportunities, and may be considered both a curse and a blessing of *'backwardness.'* In the countries of Asia, Africa and Latin America the economic and political revolutions have run into a third kind of revolutionary process—the revolution of communications.

The already existing meagre infrastructures in communication, which were the legacy of the colonial era, rapidly underwent changes in the post-independence era. In South Asia, with the increase in literacy levels and national consciousness the process of national integration and development has received added impetus.

The South Asian region, quite unlike the other parts of the world, has upto a point a common history, shared experiences of freedom struggle and independence. If one takes a dispassionate, objective view of the region, one would find that the development of national infrastructures were more or less similar and at the same level of development during the period of the British Raj. It was only in the post-independence era that developmental inequalities became glaring. This is true not only of the economic, and the industrial sector, but also in the media world.

Mass media, particularly the print media, played an important role in the freedom movement of the British Indian Empire. Undivided India witnessed the development and expansion of newspaper journalism and the advent of some prestigious papers in the region. The present paper envisages to make a comparative study of the development of electronic media, a relatively new phenomenon, in South Asia, and analyse the role of media in building up a new 'third culture' in the region.

DEVELOPMENT OF THE ELECTRONIC MEDIA

The historical fact that most of the South Asian countries were part of the great Indian Empire, and have common cultural and linguistic linkages makes the development of electronic media very interesting. It is significant that:

> Commonalities in South Asia are mostly bilateral between India and each of the neighbouring countries separately and individually. There is a bit of India in every other country of South Asia. As against this, there is hardly anything of significance which is common between India's one neighbour and the other.[1]

Hence the expansion or non-expansion of electronic media in the region could be the result of following factors:

(*i*) Absence or very little developed media infrastructure during colonial rule.
(*ii*) Absence of trained personnel in Radio and TV.
(*iii*) Lack of economic back up—private or governmental.

Among the SAARC countries it was India and Pakistan that started TV telecasts on an experimental basis. While India in the late sixties and early seventies had black and white television programmes and not so sophisticated equipments, Pakistan was way ahead in both technology and production finesse.

Both radio and television broadcasts in all the countries began in the decade of the 1960s to late 1970s, with the exception of India and Pakistan which had radio stations during the colonial era. The following Table 15.1 indicates the establishment and control of electronic media in the seven countries of South Asia.

The resume shows that both Radio and Television are primarily owned and controlled by the governments in the different countries. The development of the media is directly correlated to the economic status and is a response to the societal demands. Whether in India, Pakistan or Bangladesh, the modernization of the media began in the late 1970s and early 1980s. It was the need to keep pace with the fast changing scenario that colour TV broadcasts and satellite TV networks began functioning in the region.

Table 15.1
Radio and Television Development in the SAARC Countries

Bangladesh		
Radio	:	The National Broadcasting Authority established in 1984, merged Radio and TV. Radio Bangladesh, under government control, was established in 1971.
Television	:	Government controlled since its establishment in 1971; it began colour transmission programmes in 1980.
Bhutan		
Radio	:	The Bhutan Broadcast Service was established in 1973. It became autonomous in 1992.
Television	:	Bhutan does not have Television services.
India		
Radio	:	Services started in 1927; came under government control in 1930. Post-independence it became All India Radio, which is government controlled.
Television	:	Established in 1959; first general service began in 1965. Began coloured transmission in 1981; satellite TV transmission by Star TV started in 1991.
Maldives		
Radio	:	Government controlled Voice of Maldives was established in 1962.
Television	:	Again government controlled, was established in 1978.
Nepal		
Radio	:	Services were started in 1951; government controlled.
Television	:	Established in 1986; TV Satellite transmission services and Time Network was established in 1994. It is government controlled.

(*Contd.*)

Pakistan

Radio	:	Pakistan Broadcasting Corporation was set up in 1947. It started Radio Pakistan and government controlled FM 100, a private owned music channel.
Television	:	Pakistan TV Corporation was established in 1964; it is government controlled. People's TV Network was established in 1990. Privately owned.

Sri Lanka

Radio	:	Sri Lanka Broadcasting Corporation was established in 1967. Government controlled. *Transworld Radio*, 1978, religious station.
Television	:	Started in 1979, government controlled. National TV Network established in 1982. Independent TV Networks, transfer to private ownership pending since 1996.

The advent of Star TV has opened up a whole new avenue in the South Asian region. It gives rise to a very fundamental question of how this collapse of international boundaries affect the socio-cultural milieu of the region. Constant exposure to Western cultural and societal problems, programmes, and aspirations go contrary to the cultural values of South Asian peoples. This would mean that new cultural values and norms would emerge and create a whole new 'third culture,' having a good or bad effect on both the cultures.

BUILDING A THIRD CULTURE

The concept of "third culture" building, or, creation of a mass culture is relatively recent and stems from the increased multi-ethnic and multi-cultural interactions. This 'third culture' phenomenon can be analysed from two angles:

(*a*) the emergence of "third culture" as a direct result of communication and interaction between two or more individuals,[2] and

(*b*) building of 'mass culture' due to the constant multimedia exposure to various cultural traits.

We shall first discuss the process of building of 'third culture' due to direct individual performance and then due to the role of mass media.

The process of "third culture" building is necessarily in two phases, first is the interpersonal communication at a limited level and second is at the wider spectrum involving external factors.

Model 1 as shown in *Diagramme I*[3] focuses on the limited scope of interaction. Foundation of the "third culture" is a fairly constant and consistent performance of individuals. *Model 1* indicates the interrelationships of the broadest possible categories connected with the individual's experiences. Once the perceptions or experiences have created needs, they are communicated to the other individual with a different cultural background, and this constant interaction leads to interdependence, thereby generating a third cultural factor, which stems from a certain level of adoption by individuals.

Model 2 as shown in *Diagramme II*[4] represents the complex processes of "third culture" building. The initial contact between individual 'one' of *Culture A* and 'individual two' of *Culture B* are independently affected by the other external factors like family, peer group, society, etc. Thus the interaction of these individuals along with their own complex cultures gives rise to the 'third cultural dimension,' which is a synthesis of both cultures.

Media and Third Culture Building

When one applies the above models of interpersonal interaction to mass media messages, one finds that the programmes telecast or broadcast by *Culture A*, and seen by the masses of *Culture B* over time creates an impact that leads to the creation of a new set of cultural norms. These cultural norms are evolved due to constant exposure to the *Culture A*.[5] This expansion or colonialism through media, has given rise to a kind of new media culture, where both at rural and urban levels certain value changes can be seen.

Thus, in summation it can be said that it becomes more than essential to build a national communications system, which could guard the onslaught of these structured and unstructured messages which have the potential of changing societal norms and value systems and adopt newer values which may not necessarily amalgamate with the existing social systems of the developing countries.

Diagramme I

Model 1

Third Culture Building Individual Performance Cycle

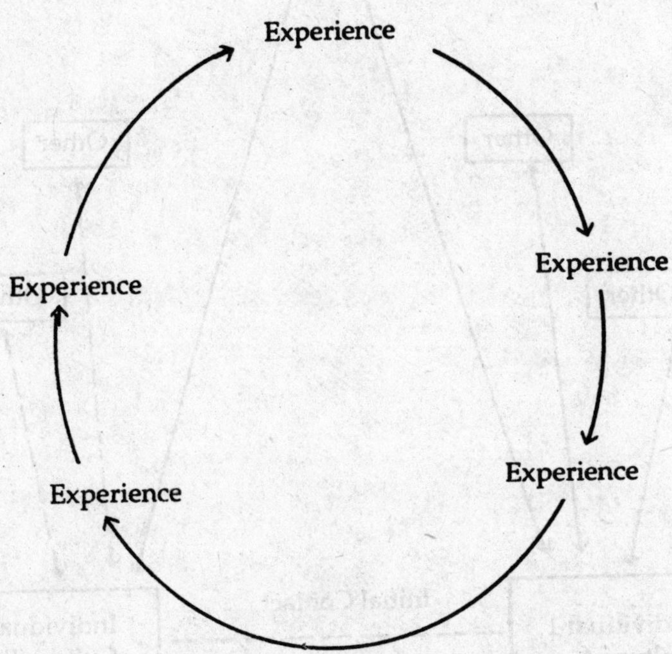

Source: Fred. L. Casmir, 'Third Culture Building' in *Communications Year Book*/16, 1993.

Diagramme II

Model 2

The Third Culture Building

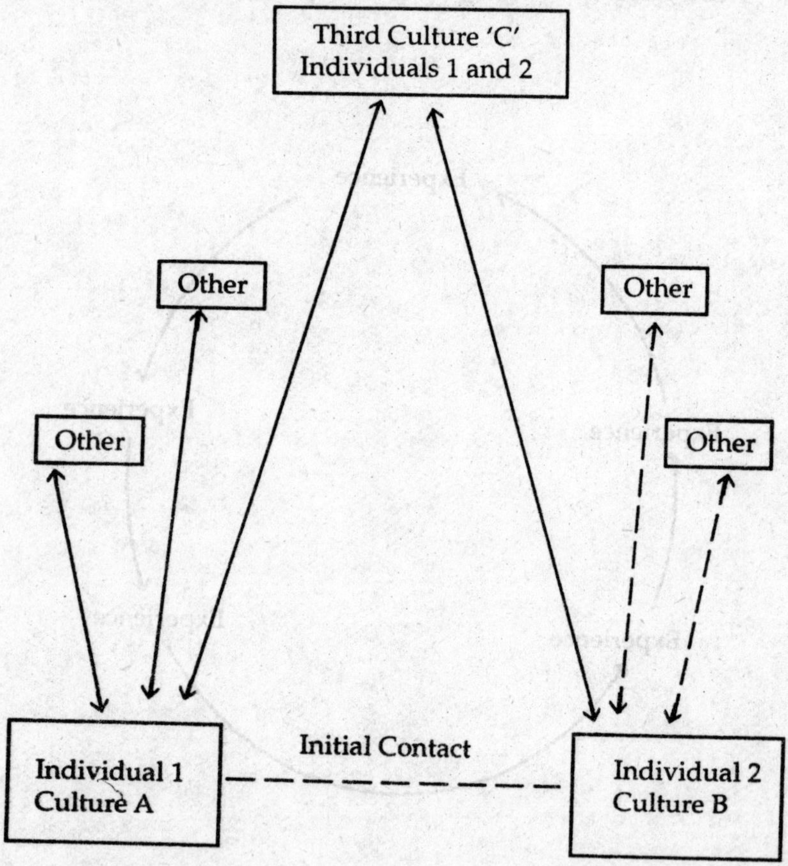

Source: Fred. L. Casmir, *Ibid*.

Diagramme III

Model 3

Media and Third-Culture Building

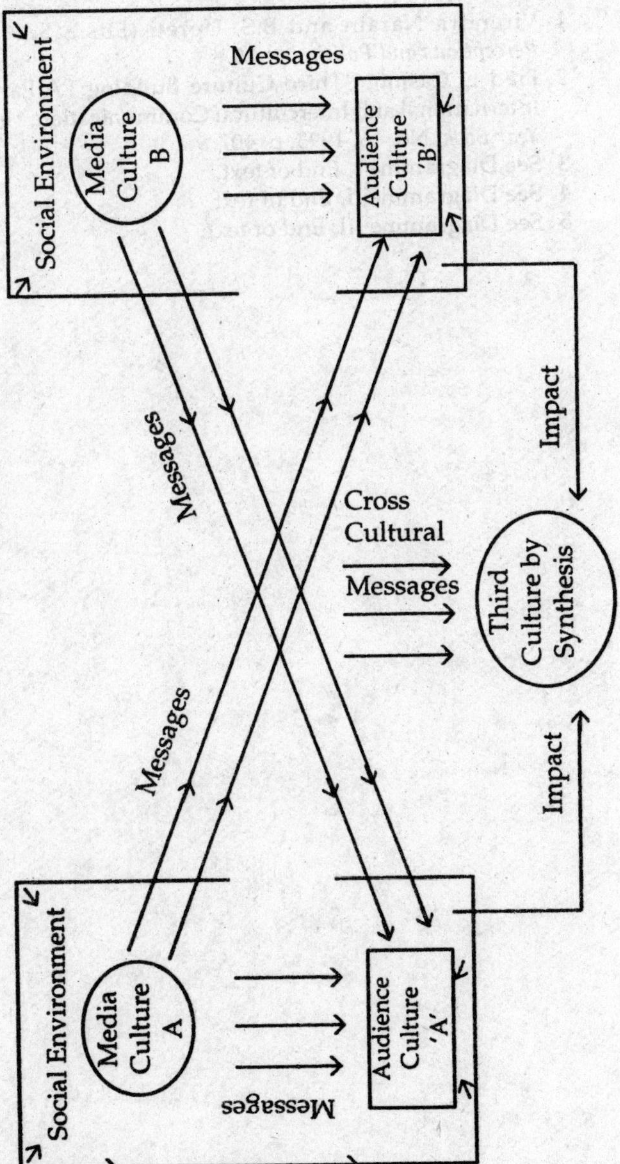

Notes

1 Virendra Narain and B.S. Upreti (Eds.), *SAARC: A Study of Perceptions and Politics*, p. 16.
2 Fred L. Casmir, "Third Culture Building: A Paradigm Shift for International and Intercultural Communication," in *Communication Year Book*, No. 16, 1993, p. 407.
3 See Diagramme I, End of text.
4 See Diagramme II, End of text.
5 See Diagramme III, End of text.

16

Social Impact of the Electronic Media

*Rajeev V. Bhatnagar**

Any analysis of the electronic media on society and social developments involves two different activities:

1. Freedom of thought and expression; a total freedom to think what we like.
2. The level to understand it, for this alone would enable evaluation and acceptance of another's point of view. Besides, to understand the thoughts of others, acceptance and tolerance would have to be inculcated.

India had until now a rich cultural civilization but as the society moved to the present scientific age the cultural heritage of the past seems to have been conveniently left behind. Our younger generation is responsible to a great extent for this downfall and thus without realising that in the mad rush to catch up with the West, a rich tradition of our forefathers was being left behind. We have in fact become quite unaware of our own rich civilisation and culture for which we had been known for so long. Several factors are responsible for this great fall.

Media is one of them. It has today taken a strong hold on society eliminating all moral values of peoples and man has come to be a puppet in its hands. Of its two parts—the electronic and

*Rajeev Bhatnagar is a freelance journalist based in Delhi.

the print media—it is the former through the radio, television, films, etc., that has a vicious grip of society. It has left far behind the first media not only because of the fast pace of modern life but also because of the lack of time available to most people. TV today has come to occupy the most important place in most peoples lives enabling easy and quick access to news and information from near and far. But the emergence of the private and foreign channels and the programmes beamed by them; without any holds barred have had not only an all encompassing influence but also an adverse impact on the moral values and traditions. Children and youth have been the worst affected. Being the most vulnerable elements in society the impact of sex, violence and such programmes on them is widespread. The rash of such atrocious incidents throughout the country is evidence of the overall and widespread impact on society all over the country. Today in fact media governs us.

We have moulded ourselves, and our thinking, according to the media. We have become narrow minded and I believe this is the reason that media has overpowered us in such a way that we and the media have become synonymous with each other. On the other hand, it should have been our hold, a strong hold on the media, instead of the media governing our lives. Actually, we lack full confidence in ourselves and continue to be dependent on others. We depend on others, no matter where this dependency takes us—whether backwards or forward. We find ourselves helpless at certain stages of life and then the media comes to our help and takes charge of our minds in such a way that we fail to realise when it has become an integral part of us and indispensable to one's existence.

Many new consumer products have entered the market through publicity in TV channels. Thus instead of sophisticated products, vulgar dreams, vulgar dresses, vulgar literature and video cassettes have gained wide circulation and have become a part of our lives. With such an impact on social life, our individual existence, thinking and actions have become a slave to the media. Such is the onslaught of the media, it has submerged our old and rich cultural heritage and involved us in a pattern of society that goes against the grain of our rich civilizational past. Now towards which downfall we are treading we ourselves do not know! I think this is what we call the social impact of media.

17

Media and Education

*Mohd. Miyan**

As technology grows its power and ability to either disrupt or heal increases. To heal we must move to new technologies, new social patterns, new types of consumer products and new ways of generating and spending wealth.

In a pioneering experiment at Brentwood School in California, one hundred small children in the first grade were introduced to computer terminals with screens and light pens. The machines were used to assist in teaching reading and arithmetic. Brentwood was an interesting choice as the first school to use computer assisted instruction because it is in a slum area, had an 80 per cent black enrolment and because the average IQ of the children participating in the reading experiment was measured at 89. The technique was very effective. The children loved playing with the terminals, and their teachers had to *peel them of the machines* to get them back to their other lessons.

At the same time IBM was setting up a network to provide computer-assisted instruction to its array of maintenance engineers. These engineers have periods of inactivity when no machine needs maintenance. They have a complex job and always the potential of learning to work with more elaborate machines. The engineers around the world are given access to terminals that would teach them new technology in their inactive movements. The scheme became a successful and important part of IBM's operation.

---

* Professor Mohd. Miyan is Head, Department of Educational Studies, Jamia Millia Islamia, New Delhi.

Telecommunications can deliver education in a variety of new ways, either with or without the help of computers. This has two benefits of great importance to society. First—the skills of the few, rare educators of superb quality can be made available to millions. This is an amplification factor that will greatly increase the levels of education in society. Second, small communities and remote areas far from sophisticated centres of learning can have access to excellent instruction. The village one-room school house could provide high quality education because it would combine the love and attention of a dedicated teacher with telecommunications access to the best instruction available.

Another interesting implication relates to teacher earnings. In comparison to other professions requiring qualifications equivalent to teachers, they remain a lowly paid personnel in the system. With this technological development and increased emphasis on the use of technology in imparting education, there will certainly be a betterment in the social and economic status of the teacher.

The future of educational technology thus lies in its ability to find a meaningful fusion between accumulated human knowledge and wisdom, emerging technologies and massive illiteracy and non-performance in education. Accumulated human knowledge refers to the understanding of how humans learn and continue to do so, technological developments that have significant meaning for communication and educational problems in the area of mass education.

How Do We Learn?

Over the decades, educational psychologists have made a significant contribution to the understanding of the processes of human learning. Skinners contribution to programming assumed classical significance. In designing self learning modules in print, computer aided instruction packages, audio or video programmes, task and content analysis and small frame structured presentations are common procedures. Programming has become the basis of all software designing. We know that if the subject matter is presented in small steps and proper sequence with intermittent evaluation, humans can learn on their own and at their own pace.

Interactive techniques are the hallmark of higher cognition which have been experimented again and again, and has provided new understanding for achieving better human learning. In the recent years, interactive technologies have also been developed. It is experimented and brought out that human interaction superimposed on interactive video is still the better alternative to interactive video alone.

Edward deBono's work on the other hand has indicated the possibility of training human minds in the process of thinking; and through lateral thinking the achievement of creative potential in humans. Computer scientists and psychologists have contributed the concept of algorithmic thinking; and taking a cue from the flowcharting exercises that it is possible to develop algorithmic thinking through a series of well designed exercises, and importantly even without the actual use of the computer.

More and more such contributions can be mentioned, but this may not be necessary. The intention here is to reiterate that human wisdom has in store the science and techniques of education in thinking, achieving mastery and means to achieve those; these are important since the primary concern of educational technology is optimization of human learning.

Developments in Technology

Developments in informatics, telematics, video technology and optical communications during the last two years have opened up radically new ways of transacting education within and beyond classrooms. Technology watchers and experts believe, there is much more in store than meets the eye. Time is not far when the computer telephone, television, radio and all other possible communications would become household communications, leave alone the technology of the organized sectors including education. I am not going into further details; now and more in the future, a computer can be a powerful tool in classroom communication. It can work as a sophisticated writing board or an electronic version of overhead projector, an electronic animator and a tool for solving problems. As pointed by experts, "to make possible a two way voice communication and a one way picture communication," all "that is needed is a personal computer, an usual OHP with an additional LCD panel or projection video." An ordinary telephone line would provide this linkage and in turn would sharply bring down the usual telephone costs. Rapid developments in technology would further enhance such possibilities.

The CD-ROM and now the laser disc have totally changed the concept of information storage and retrieval; and not merely that, with increasing adoption of interactive technologies, these would come close to being 'robot tutors.' The writing on the wall is clear that technological growth and development would continue unabated and in geometric proportions.

The developments in printing technology and research in the psychology of reading has also revolutionized the learning process. The design of reading materials with a variety of fonts is overgrowing in the hands of font designers, supported by desk top publishing systems and table top offset printers. These new generation high-tech low cost technology has brought text designs, illustrations and production at the door step of every institution. It is possible to imagine the teacher designing his/her own text and even students choosing their own fancy fonts and text layouts for study. Technological developments have in fact democratized the process and satellite communication has already made it possible to transport texts long distances without any risk of data loss.

The developments in printing technology, text design and production has increased efficiency in communication technologies and has already given birth to an open learning system which is the natural evolution to the next phase from classroom based education. It is important to note that technologies of the present and the future are not only supplementing the formal education of classrooms, but also trying to predict its capability as a stand-alone system.

The point that emerges from the technological developments of the past decade is that communications hold much promise for the future as,

(*i*) Computer, microprocessor technologies are fast becoming the central piece in communications.

(*ii*) The cost of such technology is fast coming down and would continue to do so in every country including the developing countries.

(*iii*) These technologies are losing independent identities, rather they are isolated from each other. Technologies like video, telephone, computer, projectors can be networked to create a new hybrid communication technology with enormous power and penetration. Thus networked technology is the scenario of the present.

(*iv*) Miniaturization would continue to be the order of the day. Computers are shrinking when their capacities are growing with replaceable hard disks, portable OHPs and episcopes, small laptop computers; the enormous capacity of CD-ROMs and video discs are too well-known to be described.

(*v*) Technology with more and more miniaturization and sophistication are becoming easier and easier to use. From the angle of skill these are within easy reach of many thereby breaking the age-old elitist character of this technology.

The important point is to note that both in terms of understanding how humans learn and the technology that could support human endeavours in learning is substantially rich.

Technology and Education

The education system is time and again criticized the world over by politicians, administrators and the users of the system. In the Third World countries there is massive illiteracy; large numbers of children remain out of the framework of education, there are drop outs that neutralize the effects of enrolment at the elementary grades of education, poor performance and gross under-achievement by large numbers of students at all levels. The problem in fact is common all over the world despite the shades of dark, grey and white, but larger and more severe are the problems of the Afro-Asian countries.

Most of these countries, India probably being the best example, have multiplied facilities in the form of setting up of schools within easy reach of children. The emphasis has been on supply, planning and around the age old concept-teacher is the only input required to run a school. Besides, the point that such an approach has disinterested even those who come to schools, the result is non-viable institutions, parental aloofness, teacher indifference and absenteeism, and the system's tolerance and tolerance by the society of all this half-hearted planning effort without any social accountability.

The curricular non-relevance and disinteresting monotonous process of transfer of knowledge enhances student drop-outs. The social divide between teachers, their values and communication styles and the students from the first generation learning homes also contribute to the phenomenon of drop-outs and under achievement.

The educational software, largely the textbooks, are yet dull and drab; even though some emphasis has been placed on the content of the textbooks, no serious effort has been made to look into their layout, illustrations, choice of papers and production; no comparison whatsoever with the reading material available from the market.

With the fast changes in technology and science, and growth of knowledge, professional and academic obsolescence is another major phenomenon. The issue of continuing education is becoming increasingly important and relevant; questions being asked is how frequent and in what kind of areas such training is needed and relevant? What are the new techniques of learning to learn fast and better?

Another major challenge in education is the preparation for future learning. Nowhere in the world, and today or tomorrow, it is possible to learn the skills of tomorrow. When we were in school and colleges, for example, we learnt many subjects, but did not realize that we have to learn the use of a pressure cooker to cook, or a computer to write, or a satellite to transmit a video or audio programme to other countries. We learnt all of them much after our formal education was over. But does education prepare for a life long learning capability? There are some projections by imaginative people but incorporating learning in the system still remains a remote possibility.

The problems in education, when elaborated, more and more paint indeed a gloomy picture. There seem to be two feasible assumptions to explain the situation. One, human wisdom is incapable of finding a mechanism to face the challenge of mass education, retention of students and above all to perform and bring out the best in them. Two, we have failed to master the knowledge and wisdom and press it into service for mankind. The stock of human wisdom briefly re-counted earlier does not testify the first assumption that we as humans do not know the techniques. This brings us clearly to the domains of managing education and educational technology—latter to serve the former.

Prospects

The future can be a value free description of developments of technology which I am afraid we cannot afford. The future has to be defined, defined in the interests of humanity. The future is in applying all that we know today and in store in future to educational developments; and applying it to mass education thereby shifting the focus of application of educational technology from higher and professional education. Later, it would be important for more than one reason that higher education stands on the foundations of mass education; more so, since world over developments in technology and human learning are federally supported and paid for by the common masses who have a natural right to the fruits of their own investments.

Defining mass education within formally defined boundaries of education appears to be too narrow a concept since education all over the world is not participated in by all. Regional disparities and disparities of sex, caste, rural and urban in educational participation of children in primary and upper primary grades also reveals wide gaps between the potentiality and actual participation. Thus formal education leaves out a large majority of illiterate adults and un-schooled children; and also it does not cover the need for continuing education. The issue is hence much larger. The issue is development which according to a good number of recent economic studies is indicated by levels of infant mortality, fertility rates, GNP, per capita earning, provision for health care programmes, literacy rates, educational participation, etc. Besides, macro level relational studies, there are a good number of micro level experiments which reveal that education, earning, health and development are inseparable from each other. Communication and absorption of health or vocational information gets across better and more efficiently with education, similarly, minimum nutritional levels are necessary for education to be fostered in individuals. The point that needs to be underscored is that education cannot be seen and treated as an independent and isolated school-based activity. The future of education would have to have a much larger connotation linking all aspects of life and living. This definition of the educational problem confronts us with the threatening figure of millions of adult illiterates and children yet to receive any kind of education and millions in school yet to perform.

Can this be achieved through the known obsolete institutional methods? Can educational technology through media play any role in this massive task of development? It is rich with potentiality but would it be chartered to perform this development role?

If educational technology is called upon to play a meaningful role, its developments and application would simultaneously define the future.

18

Media and Health Issues: A Study of HIV/AIDS Coverage

Anjali Gandhi and Niti Malhotra***

Media coverage of health issues has often dramatically raised awareness about them. They have resulted in heightened discussions and debate. As Jeffrey Chester of the Centre for Media Education puts it—in our mass mediated democracy, public health battles are fought not only in the clinics and the courts, but also on the ten p.m. news, the front pages, financial sections of newspapers and even on 24 hour radio talks. (Quoted by Wallack *et al.*, 1993).

Journalism, may be called the first draft of history. For that reason, the decade of the eighties may be remembered by the future generations for (among other events) the emergence of AIDS. This media fascination has endured into the nineties with AIDS becoming the media benchmark for evaluating the status of the world. (Brown, 1992) AIDS has thus been called the first *global health story* or alternately the first *international mass media disease.* Throughout the world, most people have learned more about AIDS from radio, television and the Press than from personal contacts with health professionals. Like no other health story before it, AIDS spans all cultures and societies,

* Prof. Gandhi is in the Department of Social Work, Jamia Millia Islamia, New Delhi.

** Niti Malhotra is a Research Scholar in the Department of Social Work, Jamia Millia Islamia, New Delhi.

in industrialised and developing countries alike. (Brown, Piotrow, T. Phyllis, Rita C. Meyer, and Bernard A. Zulu, 1990).

MEDIA SETS THE AGENDA FOR AIDS

Since the first HIV positive case was detected in the United States in 1981, it becomes relevant to study how the media agenda for AIDS evolved there over time. Rogers, Dearing and Chang (1991) followed the agenda setting process for AIDS from June 1981 through December 1988 and found that certain factors which may ordinarily have seemed to be important for media agenda setting did not actually influence the media agenda for AIDS in the United States. These included the actual number of AIDS cases and the reporting of important scientific findings such as HIV in the blood supply, heterosexual contact as a means of transmission and the identification of the HIV virus as the cause of AIDS. These factors may seem to be well suited to gain the media attention. The media in San Francisco did respond to these factors. But Rogers *et al.*, (1991), found that for three major television networks and the papers—*The New York Times*, *The Los Angeles Times*, and the *Washington Post*—coverage was slight. It was found that since the *New York Times* is a paper of record, other papers and television networks take their cue from it. Therefore, in effect, *The Times* sets the agenda for other media. According to Rogers *et al.*, personal and organisational variables at *The Times* limited the coverage of AIDS. For a long time *The Times* did not cover AIDS prominently because an editor of the paper thought that news stories about gays were not appropriate for the paper. Subsequently, other media also did not give importance to AIDS (Kinsella, 1989). It was only after the retirement of that editor and the breaking of stories like the seropositivity of Hollywood star Rock Hudson and Ryan White (this 13 year old boy was HIV positive and there was a controversy if he could attend school) that *The Times* vastly expanded its coverage of AIDS issues. Another reason for the poor coverage of AIDS in the US Press was that the US President did never mention AIDS at Press Conferences or include it in his speeches (Rogers *et al.*, 1998). Thus at the national level in the United States, there were two formidable barriers that kept AIDS off the media agenda. The disease had no familiar human face and it had not been acknowledged by the President. This position changed after the Rock Hudson and Ryan White stories. Rogers *et al.*, (1991) note,

"Hudson's familiarity with the American people, combined with the 'boy next door image' of Ryan White, were enough to personalise and humanise the issues of AIDS, something that prior media reports based on CDC statistics about the number of AIDS cases per month had not done" (p. 13). This is the same general scenario which was repeated and became the key category for the media agenda on AIDS in the United States. This was coverage of public figures with AIDS. The same cycle was repeated when Magic Johnson announced his HIV positive status in 1991 and in 1992 when Arthur Ashe announced his seropositivity. Furthermore, each new public figure focused attention on new aspects of the AIDS problem. With Johnson, the issue of heterosexual transmission from females to males and the recognition of young African—American males as a risk group was highlighted. And the case of Ashe, focused attention on the right to privacy and the role of the media. Thus, besides initial reports on AIDS because of the celebrity status of the people infected, many other stories were generated on issues closely related to AIDS. These were the spin-off stories of the main AIDS coverage.

How Journalists Have Covered It

It is often surmised that AIDS has retained its newsworthiness because it deals with the three basic elements of human existence: sex, life and death. And in an extension of that line of thought it is also believed somewhat cynically that journalists cover AIDS because it makes for a sensational copy. In a critique, Raymond Snoddy, himself a journalist, has severely criticised the British Press for irresponsible and biased coverage of AIDS which at best leads to homophobia and mininformation about the disease (Snoddy, 1992). Thus journalists have reported on AIDS within their own boundaries and prejudices. That is why AIDS became news as a problem of 'them' others—gay men, foreigners, drug users—and not as something that effected 'us.' Conversely it also explains how AIDS has possibly been the best example in recent memory to demonstrate that unless the mass media's core middle class constituency is perceived to be at risk, a disease does not constitute a story (Klaidman, 1990).

Quoting Ronald Milavsky: "News decision-makers are guided (*inter alia*) by assumptions about the needs, interests and values of the audience, (and that) most mass media try to attract and maintain the broad middle of the social landscape by keeping a mainstream tone and avoiding things that might drive audiences away—like bad taste" (p. 6). These assumptions Milavsky opines, took the *New York Times* despite being published in New York; which accounted for more than half of all the known cases of the time—a thousand AIDS cases—three years to give the epidemic prominent coverage (Milavsky, 1988, p. 7, cited by Klaidman).

The reporting of AIDS has often been criticised (Shilts, 1987 Panem, 1988; Watney, 1989, cited in Brown.). In fact there have always been complaints against the way science and health has been covered in the Press. As Jay Winsten has elaborated: "The Press attributes an unjustified degree of certainty to new findings;.... that the risks posed by putative health hazards are frequently exaggerated... that many medical news reports shamelessly exploit the emotions of desperately ill patients, their families, and the public at large; and that science news coverage often is plainly inaccurate due to errors of commission, omissions, or both" (Winsten, 1985, cited in Klaidman, p. 6). News coverage of AIDS, as it is criticised, concentrated on new information released by scientists, on human interest stories and on controversies rather than prevention messages. Very little space and time was devoted to a detailed analysis or to specific recommendations on how to avoid contracting HIV (Piotrow, Meyer and Zulu; Birchmeier, Richard and Hausser *et al.*, 1989; Lupton, 1991).

The unique positioning of AIDS as a bio-psychosocial phenomenon is also responsible for the unprecedented media interest in it. AIDS has raised many contentious issues and shaken us out of our comfortable definitions of gender equality, human rights, sexuality and nationality. But it is also acknowledged that every coverage of AIDS has broken earlier trends. Whereas syphilis, gonorrhea, and other sexually transmitted diseases remain even today relatively taboo as mass media topics, AIDS has been discussed extensively by the Press, radio and television. (Piotrow, Meyer and Zulu). In the US, AIDS was responsible for the first discussions of anal sex on television and, in many countries, for the first radio and television ads for condoms (Church and Geller, 1989, Liskin, Church and Piotrow).

Patterns and Content of Coverage

It is usually the content of coverage that has engaged the attention of most media analysts. There have been the recurrent and common themes in the reporting of the pandemic. Themes which have persisted over time and across cultures. Of these one of the most common has been that of the 'infected other' which also reflected the reaction of denial to the epidemic. In fact that is how the coverage of AIDS has evolved over time. Analysts in the United States and Europe have identified three broad phases (Cook, 1991; cited in Brown). Reporting in the early years of the epidemic was marked with ignorance, denial and moral panic. Thus, in the West AIDS was first labelled the 'gay plague' (Wellings, 1988). In many developing countries, the disease was perceived to be the outcome of the exotic and immoral Western lifestyle. In India, foreigners were accused of bringing in the virus. In Zimbabwe, journalists wrote more about AIDS in the United States than AIDS in Zimbabwe. (Pitts and Jackson, 1989) When it was established that AIDS was transmitted heterosexually as well, many journalists turned their attention to Africa and theories about a possible African origin for HIV received massive coverage. As a result, it conveyed the impression that the whole African continent was synonymous with the disease. This offended many Africans and triggered a spate of counterblame of the West (Sabatier *et al.*, 1988).

In the second phase, around 1987 and 1988 there has been an intensive coverage of AIDS when almost every event or scientific development was seen as news. From 1989 onwards, identified as the third phase, AIDS coverage has declined slightly yet continues to occupy more column space and air time than other health related stories. Reporting often centres around events like the international AIDS conferences and the World AIDS day.

Distinct from the extent of coverage, Rogers *et al.*, (1991), have identified four eras of AIDS coverage from 1981 to 1988 on the basis of the content or focus of coverage of AIDS. These were: the initial era, with little media attention (average of only four stories per month); the science era, focusing on reports of transmission by casual contact (average of 24 stories); the human era focusing on personal tragedies like that of Rock Hudson and Ryan White (average of 112 stories) and the political era with a special emphasis on testing and privacy issues (average of 168 stories). (Rogers *et al.*, 1991 cited in Wallack *et al.*, 1993).

Scapegoating has been the hallmark of AIDS reporting right from the time that AIDS found space in the newspaper columns. While the developing world rubbed its hands off it, calling it the 'white man's burden,' the West pointed at Africa as the origin of this dreadful disease. Then particular groups of people like homosexuals in the West, commercial sex workers and intravenous drug users were blamed. The disease thus came to be looked at as group specific rather than behaviour specific.

The Media has also drawn a distinction between the kinds of victims of HIV/AIDS. One are those identified as 'innocent victims' of HIV, like infants who have been infected through their mothers during pregnancy or childbirth, and recipients of HIV infected blood or blood products. The other category is that of those infected through sexual transmission, homosexually or heterosexually. These people are by implication perceived as guilty of causing their own affliction (Brown). AIDS has in that sense been an epidemic of prejudice. The prejudice has now shifted to include people with HIV/AIDS as efforts are made to alienate them and make them social outcastes.

Journalists have also consistently emphasised rare or bizarre ways that HIV could be transmitted (Brown). Although this is what a journalist would call 'newsy' and thus classify as a story it often ends up spreading misinformation. In the months of May-June 1998, many stories of a stalker trying to infect people with a needle in crowded places was highlighted in the Indian papers. But hardly any space was devoted to clearing the myths and confusions surrounding the transmission of the virus in this way. Such coverage thus leads to paranoia and fear among people and also increases hostility and alienation of people with HIV/AIDS.

Quantitative Analysis of Coverage

Within these recurring themes and phases of covering AIDS, the amount of coverage of AIDS has varied from month to month. Reporting has been cyclical. AIDS received saturation of coverage only intermittently usually coinciding with a prominent person being affected by the disease. As in the case of other subjects, the coverage of AIDS has been affected more by the agenda of the media rather than by actual trends. This is evident in the case of published research on AIDS which has increased sharply in the past decade. But generally news coverage of AIDS has been erratic.

In the same vein, the volume of reporting has also not matched the number of people being affected by the pandemic (Brown). However, it must be noted that this erratic or cyclical coverage of AIDS is not unique to AIDS. This is a common feature in media's response to many policy stories and is known as the 'issue attention cycle' (Berridge, 1991 cited by Brown).

INDIAN MEDIA RESPONSES

In India the first HIV positive case was detected in 1986. For what was then perceived as an impending AIDS disaster in India, the response of the Indian Media was 'quite inadequate' (Singhal and Ram, 1992). An exploratory content analysis study conducted by the Operations Research Group and/Singhal and Ram in 1989-90 revealed that the coverage of prominent urban news dailies was not only limited in quantity but also focused more on clinical diagnostic research on AIDS in Western countries. Scant attention was paid to the impending AIDS problem in India and its social implications. Very few independent reports on AIDS were found. The sources of most stories were international wire agencies, government releases or reports by Indian news agencies. Also most stories were superficial in content and located in the inside pages or supplements.

In an article published in 1992, Singhal and Ram concluded that the state run national television networks, Doordarshan and All India Radio, made only feeble and sporadic attempts in the shape of 'isolated' programmes which are 'highly dull in production quality and gain very low audience exposure.' The authors were very dissatisfied with the print coverage of AIDS as well, describing it as 'apathetic, superficial, and generally dismal.' They also stated that the coverage of AIDS in Indian newsmagazines was inadequate. Like the stories appearing in dailies, Singhal and Ram believed that the coverage in newsmagazines also comprised of stories which were 'reactive,' that is by way of responses or reactions to certain government AIDS policies and not 'proactive' that is setting the agenda of the Indian policy makers and the public about AIDS. The authors expressed satisfaction with the newsvideo magazine *Newstrack* on its reportage of AIDS but admitted that the magazine had only very limited urban circulation and a negligible rural circulation thereby rendering it quite ineffective in influencing policy makers.

The Women's Feature Service selected HIV/AIDS as one of the twelve indicators of population and development issues in its study monitoring the coverage of these issues in mainstream print media over a year. Four leading dailies namely *The Deccan Herald* (Bangalore), *The Telegraph* (Calcutta), *The Times of India* (Mumbai) and *The Tribune* (Chandigarh) were scanned from July 1, 1996 to June 30, 1997. The report concluded that issues relating to HIV/AIDS were conspicuous by their absence in the coverage of these dailies. Coverage was confined to news items and opinion pieces; editorials were generally missing. Even on events like the World AIDS Day, coverage was described as low to fair.

In another study conducted for the National AIDS Control Organisation (NACO) and UNAIDS, similar findings were obtained. News items appearing in 36 English-language dailies and periodicals and 19 Hindi language dailies in the Hindi belt during the month of June 1997 were analysed. A total of 232 items appeared which either dealt exclusively with HIV/AIDS or referred to it as part of another article. The coverage in the Hindi Press was far less (61 items) than the English Press (171 items). The frequency of coverage in regional English language dailies was significantly lower than the national dailies. This is significant since the awareness on HIV/AIDS is as it is higher in bigger cities from where national dailies are published and are largely distributed. Further, the content of the articles was largely dominated by the spread of HIV/AIDS and ongoing research for a cure for HIV/AIDS. Only 50 articles, that is less than one fourth of the coverage on HIV/AIDS in the month of June 1997, focused on the need to educate people on HIV/AIDS or actually tried to do so. It is also noteworthy that the trend of reporting has not changed since Singhal and Ram's study as the coverage is still reactive and not proactive. However it is significant that the Press is open enough to be critical of its coverage of HIV/AIDS *albeit* in a small way. In 14 items the role of the Press in reporting the Chochi Episode was criticised.

The Singhal-Ram study also revealed how a little irresponsible coverage by the Press can create an atmosphere of fear and suspicion. This was illustrated by what is now called the Chochi Episode. Chochi, a village in the Rohtak district of Haryana (about 65 Kms. from Delhi) became the centre of Media attention when a truck driver died there in the last week of April, 1997. He was suspected of having died of AIDS. The Rohtak Medical

College had refused to treat him and he was suspected of having received treatment from a village doctor or quack. It was feared that the quack had been using unsterilised needles and the infection may thus have been passed on. The incident received unprecedented media coverage. This resulted in panic among villagers, who were largely ignorant of the disease and the ways to protect themselves. In the days that followed, the village was almost ostracised with people from Choçhi being denied jobs and outsiders refusing to marry into the village. As with the Chochi coverage, in many other stories as well, identification of people with HIV/AIDS (PLWHA) has lead to their social boycott. The Press has thus, often breached the confidentiality of PLWHA. Interestingly, as the study reports, this is done with the collusion of the medical practitioner.

The study concluded that although the coverage of HIV/AIDS has shifted from the sensational to more informed reporting, the shift has been only marginal. The issue continues to get scant media attention.

PRESENT STUDY'S ANALYSIS

Even today, the coverage of HIV/AIDS continues to be the same in the Indian Press. A content analysis of seven English language national dailies and five English language financial papers was done to qualitatively assess the reporting of AIDS in the Press. The papers selected for the study were: *The Times of India, Hindustan Times, Indian Express, Pioneer, The Hindu, Statesman* and *Asian Age*. The business papers selected were *Economic Times, Financial Express, Business Standard, Business Line* and *The Business and Political Observer*. The reason for studying the business papers as well as because it has been observed that these papers often carry articles on social issues.

As previous studies have indicated the coverage of AIDS is largely concentrated around events like international conferences on AIDS and the World AIDS Day. The coverage of these papers was made from around the twelfth International AIDS Conference held in 1998 from 28 June to the 3 July and the World AIDS Day of 1 December.

The coverage of news of the Twelfth International AIDS Conference was almost negligible. Only one paper—*The Hindustan Times*—carried two articles on 5 and 7 July that reported the results of vaccine trials and treatment of AIDS as revealed by scientists at the Conference. There was no coverage of the Conference in the other papers. *The Times of India* in fact carried a fear generating story of how an HIV positive person ran away from his village when the villagers were informed of his seropositivity. In a refreshing change of coverage *The Business Standard* carried a critical piece on the achievements of the Conference.

The coverage of HIV/AIDS around the World AIDS Day was marginally better than of the International Conference, but this too was not very significant. Most papers carried reports on the walks, marches and events organised to mark the World AIDS Day. In a significantly different piece, *The Statesman* published an empathetic article on the plight of people with HIV/AIDS and carried a profile of an NGO committed to serving PLWHA. Apart from this exception, the coverage concentrated on the reports to mark the World AIDS Day. It seems that in some cases the reports were only used to fill the column space as they were carried on 3 December, even after the item had lost its 'news peg.' On the negative side, two papers carried fear generating articles on AIDS. *The Asian Age* carried a graph entitled AIDS in India showing a state-wise break-up of AIDS cases. It used a sign of a skull and bones on the graph. This type of a negative fear generating image was certainly avoidable. In the other case *The Times of India* carried a statistics heavy report on the alarming spread of AIDS in India on the World AIDS Day.

It is thus evident that the Indian Press continues to confine its coverage of HIV/AIDS to reports dealing with scientific findings, vaccine trials and the latest figures of AIDS cases. Even around events like the International Conference and the World AIDS Day, when the coverage was expected to be high, the reports concentrated largely on statistics regarding AIDS and reports of programmes and events around HIV/AIDS. Reporting was more when the event was attended by celebrities. Social, behavioural, emotional, familial, legal, ethical policy and human rights issues remained sidelined. It is noteworthy that not a single newspaper out of those studied deemed the issue important enough to carry a series of articles on the various aspects of the issue around these events. It needs to be pointed out that the present study was not confined to the specific dates of the Conference and the World AIDS Day alone but a week before and a week after the events.

Impact of Aids Coverage

Brown opines that assessing the impact of media coverage on nations, communities and individuals is fraught with complications. That is because, the author concludes, it is dangerous to conclude that a homogenous media works on an equally homogenous society. Another reason is that it is not easy to prove that specific coverage is causally linked with specific policy changes. Often journalists, like politicians or officials, can manipulate them to cover an issue from a particular angle, thus helping to set the political agenda (Berridge). But opinion is divided. Some researchers claim that when news coverage of AIDS touched a saturation level, it impacted policy. It is these coverage peaks, they claim, that have set AIDS on the agenda (Colby and Cook, 1991 cited in Brown; Rogers and Dearing, 1988). An analysis of the British Press, however, concludes differently (Berridge, 1993). Most media sociologists thus agree, that the media plays a part in setting the agenda by stimulating discussions. News media, they believe "may not be successful much of the time in telling people what to think, but it is stunningly successful much of the time in telling people what to think about." (Cohen, 1963, p. 13 emphasis in the original).

Apart from agenda setting, media coverage of AIDS has had an alarming impact on the economies of several countries. Using measures, *albeit* imperfect, (Brown, 1993) it has been shown that in countries like Kenya and Haiti, tourist inflow was seriously affected after adverse coverage in the Western Press about the AIDS epidemic in Africa (Press reports cited by Brown, 1993). As late as 1988, health ministers in some African countries were forced to spend time rebutting exaggerated reports by Western journalists instead of building up their own AIDS programme (Press reports cited by Brown, 1993).

It is easy to see the impact of the coverage of AIDS on the public particularly in the United States; the announcement of the HIV status of Rock Hudson and Magic Johnson were important milestones for health educators. A similar increase in reportage was evident in the case of Ryan White. People still refer to education about the AIDS epidemic before and after Hudson. Visible indicators show the spurt in the people's interest in AIDS. In just one county in California, for example, the weekly average number of HIV antibody tests increased from 62 to 152 after

Johnson's announcement. In fact more money was promised by the US Government for testing as a consequence (Contra Costa AIDS Programme, 1991). In another significant indicator, the Centre for Disease Control and Prevention (CDC) AIDS hotline received millions of calls from all over the country. These were far more than the Centre could handle. This single news event inspired more response than had all the CDC's public service advertisements on AIDS (Jorgensen, Nunnally and Dunmire, 1992).

Although the volume does indicate the impact of a story, it does not say much about the individual understanding of the story. (Brown) Some studies have attempted to do the same. A study by the Glasgow Media Group surveyed the understanding of AIDS in the media among different audience groups. It found that the audience was confused about the term body fluids and was unsure what it meant. This squeamishness by the editors could make people more vulnerable to AIDS (Brown).

CONCLUSION

There is no debate about the claim that the mass media plays a very significant role in bringing an issue to public attention. Just as Walter Lippmann (1922/1956) has described it: "Mass media is like the beam of a searchlight that moves restlessly about, bringing one episode and then another out of darkness into vision." This classic imagery of the media is as relevant today as it was in 1922 when it was first suggested. But it also suggests that the mass media has a brief attention span. And also that by withholding attention from an issue, the media can leave it in the dark. So whether or not an issue can be put on the public agenda and consequently on the policy agenda of a country, depends on how the media sets its agenda to cover the issue. This is because in most cases public agenda follows media agenda (Iyengar and Kinder, 1987). But whether or not this is successful in effecting a policy change depends to a great extent on how the media selects an issue, defines it, presents it and prepares the ground for discussion. It is here that media advocacy plays a crucial role. Media advocacy seeks to influence the selection of topics by the mass media and shape the debate about these topics. Media advocacy's purpose is to contribute to the development and implementation of social and policy initiatives that promote health and wellbeing and are based on principles of social justice. This purpose if implemented correctly, is a good portent not only for AIDS but also for any health or social issue.

Apart from media advocacy, there is an urgent need for sensitivity in the training of journalists and media executives so that issues of and surrounding HIV / AIDS are correctly and truly presented. Workshops like those organised by CAREC (Caribbean Epidemiology Centre), train and encourage reporters to maintain responsible reporting by discouraging them to use statistics to dramatise the HIV / AIDS situations on the ground that they could sometimes distort the social, economic and general health conditions of the people. CAREC has in this way, created a resource pool of responsible journalists reporting on HIV/AIDS in its 21 member countries. (Fitzpatrick, 1996). Such examples need to be duplicated all over the world to fully realise the critical role mass media can play in the field of HIV / AIDS.

References

Analysis of Press Coverage of HIV/AIDS in India (1997), A study conducted for the National AIDS Control Organisation (NACO) and the Joint United Nations Programme on HIV / AIDS (UNAIDS) by Shree Venkataraman, Coordinator, Unnati Features, Delhi, June-September 1997.

Bagarukayo, H. (1991), *KAP Study on AIDS Among School Pupils in Kabale District Uganda*, presented at the 7th International Conference on AIDS, Florence, Italy, June 1991.

Berridge, V. (1991), "AIDS, the Media and Health Policy," *Health Education Journal 50* (1991), 179-85.

Brown, P. (1992), "AIDS in the Media" in Mann, J.; Daniel J.M. Tarantola and Thomas W. Netter (*Eds.*) Harvard University Press, Cambridge, Massachussets and London, England, 1992.

Birchmeier, B.; Richard, J.E.; Hausser, D. *et al.*, (1989), *AIDS in Swiss Newspapers: Reporting of Preventive Events and Designing the Image of AIDS*, Paper presented at the 5th International Conference on AIDS, Montreal, Canada, June 1989.

Bosompra, K. (1989), "Dissemination of Health Information Among Rural Dwellers in Africa: A Ghanaian Experience," *Social Science and Medicine;* 29(9)(1989), 1133-40.

Church, C.A. and J. Geller, "Lights! Camera! Action! Promoting Family Planning with TV, Video and Film," *Population Reports* (Population Information Program, Johns Hopkins Centre for Communication Programs), Series J., No. 38 (1989).

Colby, D.C. and T.E. Cook (1991), "Epidemics and Agendas: The Politics of Nightly News Coverage of AIDS," *Journal of Health Politics, Policy and Law*, 16: 215-49 cited in Brown, 1992.

Cohen, B. (1963), *The Press and Foreign Policy*; Princeton, NJ, Princeton University Press.

"Contra Costa County AIDS Program" (1991), *Quarterly Report of HIV/AIDS Statistics*, Contra Costa County, CA.

Cook, T. (1991), "Notes for the Next Epidemic: Part One—Lessons from the News Coverage of AIDS," *Discussion Paper, D 12*, Harvard University, John F. Kennedy School of Government, (1991).

Convisser, J. (1991), "The Zaire Mass Media Project: A Model AIDS Prevention Project," in *PSI Special Reports* (Ed.) H. Crowley and B. Derr (Population Services International, 1991).

Fitzpatrick, L. (1996), *Sensitivity Training Workshops for Media Workers, AIDS/STD Health Promotion Exchange*, Royal Tropical Institute (KIT), The Netherlands, 1996, No. 4.

Jorgensen, C.; Nunnally, B. and Dunmire, R. (1992), "Forging Partnerships in Public Information: State and Federal Agencies Working Together in HIV Prevention Efforts," Paper presented at the 120th Annual Meeting of the American Public Health Association, cited in Wallack *et al.*, 1993.

Kinsella, J. (1989), *Covering the Plague: AIDS and the American Media*, New Brunswick, NJ, Rutgers University Press.

Klaidman, S. (1990), "Roles and Responsibilities of Journalists," in Atkin, C., and Lawrence Wallack (Eds.) *Mass Communication and Public Health: Complexities and Conflicts*, Sage, Newbury Park, 1990.

Kroger, F. (1991), *AIDS—Health, Communication's Greatest Challenge*, Case studies of effective health communication programs, presented at the 1991 Health Communication Day, Johns Hopkins University Centre for Communication Programs, Baltimore, Md., October 1991.

Liskin, L. Church, C.A., and Piotrow, P.T. (1989), *AIDS Education—A Beginning, Population Reports.* Population Information Program, Johns Hopkins Centre for Communication Programs, Series L., No. 8, 1989.

Lupton, D. (1991), "AIDS and the Popular Media: A New Perspective at Florence," *AIDS Care*, 3(4) (1991), 447-49.

Panem, S. (1988), *The AIDS Bureaucracy*, Cambridge, Massachussets, Harvard University Press.

Piotrow P.T.; J.G. Rimon II; K.E. Winnard *et al.*, "Mass Media Family Planning Promotion in Three Nigerian Cities," *Studies in Family Planning* 21(5) (1990), 265-74.

Pitts, M. and H. Jackson (1989), "AIDS and the Press: An Analysis of the Coverage of AIDS by Zimbabwean Newspapers", *AIDS Care* 1 (1989), 77-83.

Rogers, E. and Dearing, J. (1988), "Agenda-setting Research: Where Has it Been and Where is it Going?" in J.A. Anderson (Ed.), *Communication Yearbook*, Newbury Park, CA, Sage.

Rogers, E.; Dearing J. and Chang, S. (1991), "AIDS in the 1980s: The Agenda-setting Process for a Public Issue," *Journalism Monographs*, 126, 1-47.

Shilts, R. (1987), *And the Band Played On*, New York, St. Martin's Press, 1987; London, Penguin Books, 1988.

Sabatier, R. *et al.*, (1988), *Blaming Others: Prejudice, Race and Worldwide AIDS*, London and Washington, D.C., Panos Institute, 1988.

Singhal, A. and Anjali Ram (1992), *Can the Media Do More*? (Mimeo).

Snoddy, R. (1992), *The Good, the Bad and the Unacceptable*, Faber and Faber, London, 1992.

Watney, S. (1989), *Policing Desire: Pornography, AIDS, and the Media*, Minneapolis, University of Minnesota Press, 1989.

Wallack *et al.*, 1993, *Media Advocacy and Public Health: Power for Prevention*, Sage, Newbury Park, 1993.

Wellings, K. (1988), "Perceptions of Risk—Media Treatment of AIDS" in P. Aggleton and H. Homans (*Eds.*) *Social Aspects of AIDS*, Lewes, UK, Falmer Press, 1988.

WFS (1996-97), "Monitoring Coverage of Population and Development Issues in Mainstream Print Media 1996-97," *A Report from Women's Feature Service*, New Delhi.

The Hindustan Times, 5 July 1988, Vaccine to Prevent AIDS May Cause It.

The Hindustan Times, 7 July 1998, Why AIDS Treatment Fails Very Often.

The Times of India, 29 June 1998, Spectre of AIDS Haunts Villagers.

Business Standard, 7 July 1998, Condom Man Fails to Bridge AIDS Gap.

19

Impact of Media on Society

*Wajahat Alam**

Often when we discuss certain issues among ourselves, it seldom happens that when one person speaks from a certain angle the others keep quiet. In fact a debate soon starts, everyone voices their views. What is right and what is wrong becomes the focal point of debate. On the contrary when we watch television or read newspapers a live debate is not possible. Debates on television and newspapers are organised and published respectively but they are all stage-managed as the participants hold more or less the same point of view. The danger lies in that whatever is published in the newspaper or reported on television is considered to be the truth by the majority of the readers.

India, along with the rest of the countries of the Third World, lacks a solid democratic foundation and because of their deep-rooted backwardness whatever is brought out by the Media is not questioned but is considered the truth. During the British period and through the phase of the freedom struggle capitalists had not considered the publishing of newspapers as a profit making business and neither were the newspapers run professionally. They were generally representative of government views such as the *Civil and Military Gazette* (Lahore). Other papers published during this period were the *Statesman* and the *Times of India* from Calcutta, and the latter also from Bombay.

---

*Wajahat Alam is a freelance journalist writing on themes of social relevance.

Following Independence in 1947, the capitalist-run newspapers were converted into profitable enterprises as they realised that newspapers could be used not only to influence public opinion but also to dictate the government in matters of policy. It was then that newspapers brought out by the Birlas, Goenkas and other capitalists showed their respective political leanings. By being close to the government these corporate houses had made journalism into a high profile occupation, and as newspaper publishing and journalism came to be highly paid professions newspapers also no longer worked only for the betterment of society. Journalism meant being close to power.

Indian capitalists have always been enemies of Democracy. Not having confidence in themselves they have preferred to remain slaves of the American hegemony. For example, they write against Saddam and Iraq because Saddam challenged America's hegemony and because Iraq is a Muslim state. A close analysis of newspapers brought out by some of the top capitalists, show that they do not hesitate to malign the Scheduled Castes and Tribes. Also, their writings are anti-minority, anti-reservationist and opposed to positive change in society. Their stance is pro-Brahmin and they believe in caste wars and caste-discrimination. Generally, they also appear to be supportive of a divided society of haves and have nots.

The search for an alternative media has begun. But those reaching for the alternative also belong to the pro-Brahmin or trading community; neither do they believe in reservation for the Scheduled Castes and Tribes, nor do they want the upliftment of minorities and other backward communities (OBCs). The only differences between them and those who belong to the mainstream media is their belief that certain ills of society should be removed. Otherwise, as far as their basic thinking is concerned, there is not much of a difference. In fact, the Hindi Media by all means wants the hegemony of the Brahmin and trading community to remain intact and it is because of this that the Dalits, the minorities and the OBCs have a deep-hatred against the Hindi Press. I would like to illustrate this by giving an example. Soon after the demolition of the Babri Masjid, at a Dalit Convention held in Etawah (UP), a very simple and innocent looking man expressed regret over the 6 December, 1992 incident describing it as unfortunate but could not restrain himself expressing immense satisfaction at the beating of a journalist. As it transpired later, he was a Dalit youth.

Over the last few years there has been speculation that multinational companies start their own newspapers in India. This move was opposed by mainstream newspapers but has been welcomed by the alternative stream which had until now been a victim of their high-handedness. The Dalits generally have welcomed this idea believing that in journalism MNCs would be a better proposition and they would be able to challenge the Brahmin-Bania nexus.

The victims of *Hindutva* do not have a paper of their own. They have no option but to read newspapers which espouse the cause of the upper-castes. In 1997 a European research scholar, one who had studied Hindi journalism, published in great detail his findings in the *Economic and Political Weekly*. These revealed that there had been newspapers whose writings had a very positive impact on society; they did not encourage communalism or casteism. They believed in a united and strong India. But, after the demolition of the Babri Masjid and the Mandal Commission Report, when the circulation of *Punjab Kesri* suddenly increased because of its vitriolic writings, that dailies like *Aaj*, *Jagran*, *Nav Bharat* and *Amar Ujala* also changed their stance. In order to survive they resorted to sensational journalism. Their main agenda was communalism, being not only anti-Muslim but also anti-Scheduled Caste and anti-Mandal. *Punjab Kesri* changed the face of Hindi journalism and thinking. The writings of all Hindi newspapers thereafter underwent a sea change.

One does not know when the time will come when a newspaper in English or in Hindi which is sympathetic to the problems of the common man and deprived classes will be published and be able to stand up against the strong Brahmin and trading class lobby. Only a revolution by the Scheduled Castes, poor and the minorities would help the emergence of a new media as opposed to the present upper caste controls. Such a new media would have no place for communalism or casteism. Also the new media in India, and in the Third World in general, would have to safeguard its independence from Western domination for, that alone would help it to emerge as a strong entity.

Section V

Global Impact and Implications

20

Global Communications and Local Appropriation in the Third World: An Indian Experience

*Biswajit Das**

INTRODUCTION

Much is said about *Globalisation* nowadays. So much, in fact, that it has become almost obligatory to distance oneself from the notion, to see it as a fad and to insist on its having been overcome. It is my belief that the term *Globalisation* has a meaning, and that this meaning is linked to the fact that the society in which we live is a society of globalised communication. Further, the assumption underlying *Globalisation* is that we are facing a social upheaval, a revolution in fact, with consequences at least as far reaching as those of the Industrial Revolution.

With this paper I want to intervene in the current discussion about this revolution, a discussion which is normally coloured by a resigned determinism maintaining that the revolution will come about all by itself as an automatic consequence of the development of communications technology. As opposed to this, I want to politicise the discussion by insisting on the fact that the social

* Biswajit Das is Lecturer in the Department of Sociology, Jamia Millia Islamia, New Delhi.

revolution is not inextricably tied to the automatic growth and progress of technological development, but is dependent on a number of political choices. How these choices are made? What factors impinge on the process of making these choices? and finally, How these choices are internalised within a diversified regional, linguistic and cultural set up? are the central thrust of my paper.

An attempt would be made to analyse the global impact of media in a diversity of contexts in the Third World. The meaning of Third World and its relevance in the present day global social formations would be examined. Since comparative cross national media analysis in Third World societies is quite negligent, the paper would address problems of integration and rationalisation of the communications sector through the process of globalisation in India.

The present analysis is conducted at two levels: first, an attempt has been made to concentrate on the external problems faced by India within a larger context of Third World if any? Secondly, it addresses the internal difficulties which India faces as a result of globalisation and inadequate national policies.

GLOBAL COMMUNICATION AND THE THIRD WORLD

My starting point is that the term Third World persists in academic and political discourse when the conditions that produced it have disappeared. As long as global divisions configured by an opposition between capitalism and socialism (the first and the second worlds), the concept seemed to have a referential meaning. With the disappearance of socialist states, the structural conditions that endowed the Third World with meaning also disappeared. There is at the very least a numerical absurdity to speak of Third World when there is no longer a Second World. Under the circumstances, can there be any reason other than a failure to face upto a new world situation for the persistence of a concept. As Pletsch (1981) critiques the residual nature of the concept and locates its derivation in a conceptual structure informed by the juxtaposition of tradition and modernity, reconfigured by the Cold War opposition between Capitalism and Communism. The concept may represent something more than an ephemeral abstraction, if it serves as an autonomous source of alternative global visions, a question that is integral to the history of the concept, but is ignored in most of the recent critiques. As Gyan

Prakash (1990) comments that the modes of thinking that configure the Third World in such irreducible essences as religiosity, underdevelopment, poverty, nationhood and non-Westerness unsettles the calm presence that the essentialist categories—East and West, First World and Third World—inhabit in our thought. This disruption makes it possible to treat the Third World as a variety of shifting positions which have been discursively articulated in history. As a result, rather than appearing as a fixed and essential object, the Third World emerges as a series of historical positions, including those that enunciate essentialism. What is rejected here, it seems, is not the concept of Third World but the Third World as a fixed category, which also shifts attention from structures and structured conflicts to a politics of location and difference.

The Third World as a concept in turn appears as a discursive construct, constructed in different ways according to historical contexts and ideological dispositions. While the meaning and the location of Third World is yet to be settled, we are witnessing new emergent relationships due to recent global changes as restructuring (the new world order) or destructuring (the new world disorder) the world order. The question is does the disappearance of earlier forces lead to the emergence and reconfiguration of global relations in new ways? Further, however, unstable or stable such configurations may be, how do the earlier structures situate themselves in the new global relations?

The development of the global system is quite sporadic and uneven; it reflects fluctuations in economic activity and fundamental asymmetries in the distribution of power. The organisation of economic activity and concentrations of economic power have played no doubt a crucial role in the process of *Globalisation*. But all forms of power—economic, political, coercive and symbolic—have contributed to and been affected by this process. While retracing the process of *Globalisation*, one observes that these various forms of power overlap with one another in complex ways, sometimes reinforcing and sometimes conflicting with one another, creating a shifting interplay of forms of power.

The issues of *Globalisation* have a major political ingredient. It is not just that the concept of national culture and thus of nation state is central to the debate. When the issues are posed in policy terms, both in terms of the Third World and the New World information order, we observe political and cultural consequences along with the end of the Cold War, as these are bound to affect nations, states and the Third World. Since we live in a post-Cold War period and find ourselves without any political mentors and mental structures, that guided our thinking about global social relations till only yesterday, it equally makes us to realise the role and relevance of the Cold War framework that conditioned a great deal of our analysis of media, not least their role in international relations. It has also profoundly informed the normative criteria that we applied in identifying types of regime, and evaluating a given information order.

Information, communication and culture were increasingly to be found at the centre of international debates, and formed the basis of multiple confrontations. Since 1973, through organisations like UNESCO or the Non-aligned Movement, Third World countries have repeatedly denounced the unequal international flow of news—produced and distributed as it is by a limited number of Press Agencies belonging to the developed nations. The demand for a New World Information and Communications Order subsequently gave rise to a series of meetings and conferences. These meetings led up to the general conference of UNESCO in Belgrade in 1980 where the Macbride Report on the problems of communications was approved. Since that time, meetings of the non-aligned countries have continued to draw up a balance sheet of progress, noting for instance that new forms of alliance between the countries of the South have emerged, principally through the creation of national news agencies and regional networks of these agencies.

Initially centred on combating the imbalance of news flows, this debate on communications has progressively widened its scope under the pressure of non-aligned countries. International organisations of an essentially technical nature have also begun to feel the political effects of an increasingly global questioning of the geopolitical distribution of power in the field of information.

Recognition of this new phase in the political and cultural emancipation of the Third World should not, however, allow us to pass over the tensions within this movement. For are we really talking about a New Information Order or simply a new sharing out of the established order? The Third World consensus explodes as soon as we come to the central problems of a genuinely alternative form of communication. Who will produce this information? What subject matter will emerge from this transformation? What are the means of communication best adapted to these producers and to their content?

As the microelectronic revolution advances, much hope is placed on the possibilities for this revolution to bridge the gap between the information poor and the information rich countries. Interested sectors in the industrialised world advertise now that the rapid spread of information technologies might lead to an equally rapid decrease of the obstacles that hinder development in most of the Third World.

The reactions of the policy makers in the Third World tend to follow the same pattern. Thus imports of new goods are increasing at great velocity, as if this could be a remedy to the many information deficits that the Third World experiences now. What is painfully missing in Third World countries, however is a clear understanding of the value of information as a resource for economic development, and sufficient awareness of the need for clear information policies to guide their purchases and exchanges. Rather than adjusting technologies, the main problem for the Third World now is to adjust its own strategies to deal with information needs and priorities. Its relationship with the new technologies thus should be guided by a sharp appreciation of its necessities and possibilities.

Three points appear particularly worrying at this stage:

1. As the technological revolution moves fast towards an increasing convergence of all information flows and channels, Third World countries stick to a sectoral view of mass media, telecommunications and informatics.
2. Despite the many relationships that make contents and infrastructure inseparable, when it comes to international bargaining in communications the Third World takes into account mainly contents.
3. Its concerns over contents are restricted to the mass media only, thus neglecting the crucial flows of specialised information on which development depends most.

No significant action has been launched to undertake revision of such strategies. On the contrary, information now has a low priority on the agenda of the Third World and the inauguration of news networks feeds a feeling of accomplished task which makes future debates less likely. In this context, the new information technologies flow into the countries without much thought, more as part of a widespread modernisation wave than as an element in a strategy to change their position in the international system.

The literature addressed to the potential created by information technologies for self reliant, autonomous or sovereign development has located and exposed a significant barrier to effective national policy implementation. The messages promoted by the TNCs, offering information technology as the key to advancement of international cooperation, has become increasingly pervasive and persuasive. The administrative tradition in communications research has effectively evaded the contradictions in this offer. It has focused on hardware and software production and its effects, without analysis of institutional context and structural asymmetries. Furthermore, what sense are we now to make of the Third World as a term and as a reality? The nations which came together at Bandung in 1955 constituted themselves as Non-aligned, as something different from the two armed camps. Now that the Second World has disappeared as a coherent bloc, there is bound to be a redefinition of the Third World and not just from an external point of view, but internally as well, for there has been enormous and growing economic and political diversification amongst the Non-aligned states. It is such factors that have led some to begin the task of reclassifying the New World Order, on the basis of different criteria from those that went before.

While *Globalisation* calls for the development of a parallel concept of global citizenship and representative global political structures, at this time the only effective political structures we have are nation-states and our actual citizenship identities are national. Within this context globalisation represents a loss of power and the validation of cultural particularism, whether gendered, ethnic, linguistic, or religious is in part an expression of this felt powerlessness, a retreat deeper into the world of world colonisation.

Taking a close look at contemporary realities, it would seem that the pretence of *globalism* is not necessarily in step with the world as it is. The thrust of *globalism* is modern capitalism in favour of the internationalism of the world market place of ideas and commodities. Its agencies are the global corporations operating in most countries, locating wherever government interference is the least and profit opportunities are the most. Without telecommunications, transborder dataflows, electronic fund transfers, the global economy and corporation would have been inconceivable. *Globalism's* strategies of conquest are horizontal, vertical and spatial integration of the key world industries from oil transportation to telecommunications. Its mechanisms are the transfers of capital from the centres and peripheries orchestrated by the international agencies mobilising world capital, allocating it globally, and reducing the risk of private investors. *Globalism,* however has produced both majestic successes and grand failures. It has brought modern industrialisation to the remotest regions of the world, but it has also created growing gaps and antagonisms between rich and poor, humans and nature and centres and peripheries. In the peripheries, where the processes of development have taken place piecemeal and unevenly, the social system is torn between a modernizing elite and a traditional mass. Frequently, the two sectors of the population live in separate quarters, sometimes as if in separate countries and centuries.

The negative internalities of dualistic modernity thus outpace the positive externalities of growth and development. This used to be the primary characteristic of Third World societies, but increasingly the inner cities of the First and Second Worlds are plagued with such contradictions and ambiguities. Given the heterogeneity and complexity of the world, *Globalisation* attempts to develop global community through an interlocking system of smaller and more homogeneous communities.

Regionalism is one such trend. Regional formations such as the European Economic Community (EEC), Association of South-East Asian Nations (ASEAN), North American Free Trade Area (NAFTA) and others represent efforts by groups of relatively close countries to establish effective communities of interest, norms of laws and sanctions. There is a risk of course, that these budding regional blocs would turn to intense economic competition and possible political confrontation rather than cooperation. It can foster a new type of regional chauvanism or it can provide a protective shield for its members against the global hegemonic projects while opening upto the rest of the world for mutual cooperation and projects for mutual cooperation and benefit. Such regional formations, however, reflect the present dualistic structures of the world system divided between centres and peripheries.

While the world is fragmented in terms of regional, national and local social formations, it is still a long way from conducting financial business in a global currency or governing through a global government. What is generously termed the global economy would rather seem the economies of few OECD member states and newly industrialising countries. What is often referred to as global communication is virtually the transnational proliferation of mass marketed advertising and electronic entertainments by few mega companies.

Meanwhile, there is a strong disparity in terms of the volume and the directions of information flows and the possibilities for generating, distributing or accessing relevant information. Information flows across the globe are imbalanced; most of the world's information moves among the countries in the North, less between the North and the South, and very little amongst the countries of the South. Less than 10 per cent of all telephone, telex and telefax traffic and satellite channels are available in Southern countries. This does not mean that there would be no global reverberations in which all parts of the globe would become vulnerable to acts performed by some. However, it is still a far cry from a genuine understanding which would imply an acceptance and mutual recognition of socio-cultural differences and a perception of the local community.

The Indian experience does not necessarily conform to the images of the Third World, even if they share with other Asian and African countries many problems in their opposition to the industrialised countries. The expansion of the new communication technologies reveals both the existence of common questions in the different countries of the Third World and the increasingly large gaps between them. The differences in economic development within these countries, as well as divergences on a political level, often prevent them from finding common responses and constructing new solidarities. And yet, these new solidarities are essential if the mechanical repetition of the orientation of the present flow of communications, linked as it is to the movements of people and goods, is to be avoided. This orientation favours relations in the North-South direction, to the detriment of South-South exchanges.

INDIAN EXPERIENCE

The recent political decisions made in the sphere of communications have been more and more the subject of high level economic and commercial negotiations. But it also shows a characteristic disregard on the part of decision-makers for the cultural and educational dimensions of media. The communication policies of both the nation and the region as a whole are currently based on profit, market share, competition, economies of scale and rationalization. The move to a single market has gone hand in hand with an erosion of the cultural dimension upon which the recent Indian public service dimension has been based.

A cursory look at India's communication policy history illustrates that there are a number of ways in which the roles and the forms of power that state possessed and used affected communication channels, content and practices in meeting social, political, cultural and development goals. The communications policy prior to 1984 challenged market-oriented models of development directed towards integration with international trade, investment and finance. India's approach to development emphasised national self-reliance and the promotion of national industries or state agencies to develop technologies and services to meet India's developmental and economic needs. The consensus included economic development as a centrally important social task and the primacy of the Indian state in planning and directing development as well as of public sector undertakings as the commanding heights of the economy. Self-reliance and a strong independent nationalism as an element of identity became a cohering project for all Indians.

Policy discourse is still dominated by the rhetoric of concepts such as social justices, national sovereignty and freedom of expression. These are used invariably as sacred themes by all governments. Of late, there has been a distancing between the discourse and action through the rediscovery of the Indian communications sector and economy in early 1990s. Till the 1980s' Indian economy was rated as an underachiever of its growth, domestic regulation, lack of integration with international trade and investment and financial flows and characterised by a low density and service quality of interactive telecommunications opportunities that inhibited productive efficiency, modernisation and development. Indian communications is now presented as one of the big emerging markets for the next century.

India's information technology and software policies prior to 1984 were consistent with a model of state-led planned development. In the mid-1980s, a guided and guarded economic liberalisation took place that emphasised both a greater access to imports and the promotion of software exports while still closely regulating the domestic software and computer industries. The issues raised by information and computer services led to consideration of broader questions about the overall role of the state in electronic communication. It questions the objectives of the state and appropriate role for the state related to information technologies and services.

In assessing India's communication policy we need to distinguish two levels of debate. There is first, the question of whether the government's policy works on its own terms. Second, the question of what alternative policies might be feasible and desirable? This question has dominated recent debate, such as it has been, largely because those opposed to government policy most notably, have reduced the second question to a demand for a return to the *status quo ante,* a position that I hope to show is both untenable and undesirable. In judging the success of the government's policy in its own terms, the core question raised by its critics is whether in fact it has made good its claim to introduce sufficient competition to make the industry largely self-regulating or merely unleashed it as an uncontrollable private monopoly. While these issues are yet to be settled, the Indian communications policy has given due primacy to *Globalisation.*

The closer we move towards the implementation of the single communication market—the directive 'communications without frontier' has to be enacted by the government. The more numerous and complex the debates, questions and uncertainties arise: Will it be within the means of the Indian state to resist the globalisation of culture? and Can it preserve within the available resources its diversified communication industry?

It is difficult to know whether the state's policies have merely accelerated existing tendencies towards economic globalisation in the communications sector or whether they are the root cause of this evolution. But rather than reducing the problem to one of cause and effect, it is necessary to appreciate the extent to which India itself has been involved in the massive and irreversible industrialisation of the communications sector. This upheaval affects every aspect of the industry: it consists, on the one hand, of the vertical and horizontal integration of the production and distribution sectors, and of the industrialisation of programme production on the other.

The characteristics of technology, its production,

consumption, content accessibility and compatibility with domestic development plans must be critically examined. However, despite these evident setbacks for the public service sector, communications technology (television and telecommunication) remains, above all, an exceptional cultural vehicle, an economic dwarf and a cultural giant.

Concerning the first aspect integration of production and distribution, we have witnessed the emergence of large multinational, multimedia groups. A system of media oligopoly is in the process of installing itself; this has in turn spawned a merger mania with alliances forming and dissolving, a multitude of buyouts and fusions of all kinds. New foreign actors in the media sector are attracted by the unbridled possibilities for expansion. These phenomena in turn generate growing international competition and the transnationalization of a sector which had hitherto been managed and controlled almost totally by the state. Large multimedia groups have traversed their national frontiers in order to carve up the whole Indian landscape. As a consequence, any media group whatever its importance, becomes the target of the multinationals who are forever on the lookout for new markets.

The damaging effect of industrialisation will be particularly felt at the level of programmes to meet the ever growing demands of a multiplicity of outlets, it is necessary to produce more and more quickly, which in turn leads to a loss of quality and diversity in favour of easily consumable mass products. Televisions's news and current affair output is not immune from this market logic: information is increasingly becoming a commodity governed by commercial criteria. Moreover the Indian networks are increasingly turning to foreign imports for news programming as well.

In short, two interdependent and contradictory tendencies are following in the wake of the industrialisation of the Indian communications sector. Firstly the growing diversification in distribution possibilities is accompanied by a simplification and standardisation of programmes. Consequently, the question of a communications policy which will stimulate diversity and quality in programming, especially in news and information, is high on the agenda. Secondly, a fundamental contradiction exists between, on the one hand, the processes of transnational integration at the economic level and the tendency to supersede the national as the pertinent level of political decision-making and both national and regional aspirations on the other. This is the hub of the problem which Indian states must face upto.

Regional Scenario

The industrialisation and transnationalisation of the communications sector will pose very specific problems for regions within Indian states. For example, will the specificity of a regional culture be able to express itself in a sector which is increasingly provided for by the large transnational companies and where political and economic decisions are tightly centralised by the global technocracy.

The room for manoeuvrability of the regions and their respective communication industries will be effectively constrained on atleast two levels:

1. They have a limited market for their regional products and this in turn poses an obstacle for the profitability and survival of their small audiovisual industries; and
2. On the political front, the difficulty facing regional centres in affirming their cultural identity is compounded by a national policy which has weakened public service broadcasting and supported commercial television initiatives.

It is difficult to affirm cultural specificity and to protect a small audiovisual industry in the regional set up. This is the consequence once more of the destructive logic of economic planning and not, as some would have it, from the cultural incompetence of the small group of producers who run audiovisual industries.

The structural problems which the regions will encounter are linked to their marginal culture and linguistic status. Their markets are too restricted and, as a result the financial means available for regional production is meagre. The proximity of larger Indian regions with a wider language reach also constitutes an obstacle to the development of a competitive audiovisual industry for small states. Films or programmes which have been made in a minority language require an additional budget for dubbing or subtitling. Moreover, these products seldom meet with success on international television markets since the attention of buyers is more oriented to productions coming from the large, well established centres. Costs of promotion and distribution are, therefore, more important for small regions than for larger ones. Productions from small states are often not of an exportable nature because they are too culturally specific and hermetic to attract a large audience.

In the realm of popular fiction such as serials, soap opera and so on, small states once again find themselves at a disadvantage. Larger regions can often recover the costs of their fictional products in home markets after which they turn to outside markets, notably those of small regions, selling those programmes at very competitive prices compared to domestic products. This precarious situation in local production leads to another major problem: major talents at all levels of the audiovisual chain leave small regions to seek their fortunes in the larger artistic and financial centres.

Finally, let us note that, in comparison with the small regions, the large and developed regions have a more developed cable network and cable viewers have become rapidly accustomed to the presence of foreign channels and foreign programmes.

This situation has all the elements of a vicious circle and politicians of small regions are well aware that the comparatively weak audiovisual infrastructures of these regions necessitates a policy aimed at the expense of ameliorative efforts on behalf of public service broadcasting. A short-term economic policy has prevailed over a cultural policy based on the survival of audiovisual diversity. The second level of internal problems to which small regions are exposed is located in the audiovisual policy of governments themselves, and in particular in the alarming situations in which the majority of public service broadcasters now find themselves. Generally speaking, the industrialisation of the audiovisual sector will take a heavy toll on public service broadcasting which everywhere seems to have progressively lost its legitimacy. But what has changed in the attitude of politicians is that they now judge the public networks according to commercial criteria, *i.e.* in the market share they can wrest from private competition. Their reasoning is simple: if the public networks are not capable of attaining and maintaining the critical audience threshold, they are not competitive and must, therefore, disappear. The policy of devaluing public service and promoting the private chains is particularly dangerous for small regions, since they risk losing in the medium-term an audiovisual sector which has been the very basis of their communication system.

In terms of general trends, the audiovisual sector of small regions is being supported by the government according to purely economic and industrial principles. In the short-term, the effect is a positive one; the liberalisation of this sector will facilitate the breaking up of a public monopoly which tends to dictate its terms to the viewer. Competition will make this sector more dynamic and encourage the establishment of viable commercial alternatives.

Another paradox of national policy: the discourse which defends a local/regional audiovisual industry continually confuses cultural and economic arguments to the point of stretching its own credibility. In invoking the protection of its specific culture and audiovisual industry, it defends its own private chains. Deprived of legitimacy; its cultural vocation and its financial support—in many regions pubic service broadcasting does not receive its total income from the subsidy. Public service is no longer able to function as an alternative programme supplier to private chains. But instead of trying to carve out a specific role for themselves in this situation, public broadcasters have launched into vicious competition with private networks without the means to do so. Fierce competition inflates programme costs: targeting the same audience, broadcaster generally seek out the same type of programming. Similarity of programmes means efforts at differentiation focus on the image of the network. A significant proportion of budget is thus devoted to self promotion which in turn decreases the amount that can be spent on production itself and/or the purchase of original programming. Competition, then has the effect of levelling the differences between the public and private sectors.

So what are the likely consequences of a situation which has all the hallmarks of irrationality in both economic and cultural terms? First of all the lack of a clear definition of the role and function of public service broadcasting risks creating a situation in which two systems find themselves openly and directly in competition. Here the public networks are even more commercial in character than their private competitors. In India this kind of confrontation serves to discredit the public broadcasters. Why should a government subsidise a public service system if private channels, autonomously financed, can achieve the same objectives? We can understand how this kind of argument—advocating national services without public financing—has attracted the attention of the government.

In conclusion we can summarise the situation of the regions as follows: they will have a limited market and too meagre financial resources and possibilities of exploitation to be credible and profitable in a unified market. Harmful effects of the integration of the communication policy of Indian state will be reinforced by a short-term and defeatist policy at the regional level. If the problems of small regions are operative at both the transnational and national levels, solutions must be sought there as well: *i.e.* in the policies of the state and other transnational initiatives on the one hand, and in regional policy on the other.

While the discourse of the communications policy enthusiastically applauds the manifold variations on the theme of difference, pluralism, identify and cultural specificity, its realisation endorses the elimination or homogenisation of difference by an economically restrictive communication policy.

Efforts must be made for an investigation into the tastes and responses of the local viewer. How will the viewer respond to the increasing number of programmes on offer and to imported information? Why, when and in what circumstances does the viewer prefer domestic productions to imports and *vice versa*? Answers to these questions will determine the future and success of broadcasters in small regions since product diversification and multiplication have now become obstacles to securing audience loyalty. From a cultural point of view, the fragmentation of the public diminishes the capacity of the broadcaster to transmit to the public social cultural values common to a region or a nation.

References

1 Antonelli, C. 1992, *The Economics of Information Networks*, Amsterdam, North Holland.

2 Pletsch, Carl E., 1981, "The Three Worlds or the Division of Social Scientific Labour, Circa 1950-1975," *Comparative Studies in Society and History*, 23: pp. 565-90.

3 Chaturvedi, D.N.; Kelkar, V.L. and Darmadhav, K. 1991, "India's Information Economy: Role, Size and Scope," *Economic and Political Weekly*, Vol. XXVI, No. 37, September, pp. 2153-61.

4 Chowdary, T.H. 1994, "India's Telecoms: The New National Telecom Policy," *Asian Journal of Mass Communication*, Vol. 4, No. 2, Singapore, pp. 111-21.

5 Das, Biswajit 1997, "Citizenship in An Age of Globalised Communication" Paper presented in the International Seminar on "Culture, Communication and Power" organised by Centre for Human Sciences, French Cultural Centre, 21-23 April, Jamia Hamdard, New Delhi.

6 Das, Biswajit 1997, *Mass Communication in India at 50*, Manorama Publications.

7 Evans, P.B. 1992, "Indian Informatics in the 1980s: The Changing Character of State Involvement," *World Development*, 20(1), 1-18.

8 Finlay, Marike 1987, *Powermatics--A Discursive Critique of New Communication Technology*, Routledge and Kegan Paul, London.

9 Gyan Prakash, 1990, "Writing Post-Oriental Histories of the Third World: Perspectives from Indian Historiography," *Comparative Studies in Society and History*, 32.2, pp. 383-408.

10 Hamelink, Cess J. 1984, *Transnational Data Flows in the Information Age*, Lund: Studentlitteratur.

11 Hamelink, Cess J. 1994, *Trends in World Communication—On Disempowerment and Self-Empowerment*, South Bound, Third World Network, Malaysia.

12 Hamelink, Cess J. 1994, *The Politics of World Communication*, Sage Publications, London.

13 Lakha, S. 1994, "The New International Division of Labour and the Indian Computer Software Industry," *Modern South Asian Studies*, 28(2), 381-408.

14 Mattelairt A. and Schmucler, Hector 1985, *Communication and Information Technologies: Freedom of Choice for Latin America*? Ablex Publishing Corporation Norwood, New Jersey.

15 Mattelairt, A. 1979, *Multinational Corporations and the Control of Culture*, Harvester Press, Sussex.

16 Menon, V. 1989, "The Case of India" in Jussawalla *et. al.*, (Eds.) *Information, Technology and Global Interdependence*, Greenwood Press Inc. Connecticut.

17 Mody, Bella 1995, "State Consolidation Through Liberalisation of Telecommunications Services in India," *Journal of Communication*, 45(4), Autumn, pp. 107-23.

18 Mosco, Vincent 1989, *The Pay-per Society: Computers and Communications in the Information Age*, Norwood, NJ, Ablex.

19 Mosco, V. and Wasko, J. (Eds.) 1992, *Democratic Communications in an Information Age*, Toronto, Gramond.

20 Samarajiva, Rohan 1993, "Institutional Reform in Sri Lanka's Telecommunication System: Regulation, Corporatization and Competition," *Asian Journal of Communication*, Vol. 3, No. 1, pp. 37-63.

21 Schiller, Herbert I. 1986, *Information and the Crisis Economy*, Oxford University Press, New York.

22 Singh, Yogendra 1997, "Social Change: Rise of Popular culture" in *India at 50: Bliss of Hope and Burden of Reality,* (eds.) Narayanan, V.N. and Sabharwal, Jyoti, pp. 328-45, Sterling Publishers Private Limited, New Delhi.
23 Stubbs, R. and G.R.D. Underhill (Eds.) 1994, *Political Economy and the Changing Global Order*, Toronto, McClelland and Steart.
24 Sussman, G. and Lent, J.A. (Eds.) 1991, *Transnational Communications: Wiring the Third World*, Newbury Park, CA, Sage.

21

Telecommunications Infrastructures in Third World Countries

Moin uddin and M.T. Beg***

INTRODUCTION

Each of the past centuries has been witness to and been dominated by a single technology. While the Eighteenth Century witnessed the emergence of great mechanical systems accompanied by the Industrial Revolution, the Nineteenth Century was the age of the steam engine. During the Twentieth Century, the key technology which has dominated the lives and activities of all humanity is information gathering, processing and distribution. There has been uprecedented growth in the computer industry, networking, downsizing of computer operations, complex graphics, satellite channels, fibre optics, integration of services, intelligent and value added networks, mobile communications, etc., management of network global satellite communications and the Internet. The convergence of all these technologies and global standards,

* Prof. Moin uddin is Head of the Electrical Engineering Department in the Faculty of Engineering and Technology, Jamia Millia Islamia, New Delhi.

** M.T. Beg is Reader in the Department of Electronics and Communications in the Faculty of Engineering and Technology, Jamia Millia Islamia, New Delhi.

accounting rates, privatization, spectrum allocation and international connectivity are some important issues that require serious discussion and analysis.

Some of these issues and problems of telecommunications development specific to the Third World countries came to the fore in September 1997 at the Singapore Asia Telecom Conference. Some forty thousand trade visitors from 104 countries attended the meet. Realizing the importance of the Third World and the need for bringing to the peoples of the region the benefits of telecommunications, the participants at Singapore decided to accelerate development in the region. For the first time in the history of mankind the concepts of the global village and the global market place were recognised as a reality. The insignificance of social and physical distances between peoples was asserted. Delegates also recognised and advocated what Bill Gates had asserted, that the developing world would in future be the centre stage of maximum activity in this field. At present, the total number of lines provided in India is well over 10 million.

For a developing economy like India it is equally important that new policies and programmes be initiated and increased resources be allocated to bring about rapid growth in this sector for at present, even while it has a provision of over 10 million lines it ranks among the most poorly developed telecom sectors in the world with low penetration of 1.3 telephones per 100 population as of March 1996. This is low even when compared to other developing countries—Malaysia 14.7, Brazil 4.7 and China 2.3.

GROWTH OF TELECOMMUNICATIONS AND IMPACT ON ECONOMY

The telecommunications sector has undergone a massive transformation throughout the world during 1985-1995. Advances in the telecommunications technologies have brought about a revolution in the quality and range of services. Moreover, development and advances in the sphere of information technology, data communication, multimedia requirement and Internet are responsible for higher growth rates and the creation of a new social order.

Clearly, a country's ability to take advantage from this revolution depends upon its modernization programmes.

Countries that have access to information for their industrial structures through a modern telecommunication network will experience a higher growth rate. Large scale use of information and telecommunications technologies directly affects productivity, cost effectiveness and a high level of product differentiation leading to low levels of unit prices. It has been found that low tech industries in developing countries like Taiwan, Philippines and Singapore have used advanced telecommunication services to facilitate a tight link between local products and commercial distribution in American and European markets.

An advanced telecommunications system is equally important for service industries like banking, trading, retailing, transportation, maintenance, health and insurance, where information and real time communication are vital to the production process. A reduction in the cost of these services will directly effect the entire economic system since lower marketing costs means lower cost for manufacturing firms. The extensive use of telecommunications services by developing countries has also brought considerable efficiency in the financial market.

Investment Projections During 1996-2006

The demand for basic telecom services in India is expected to be of the order of 31 million lines by the year 2001 and 64 millions by 2006. The current basic services network of the Department of Telecommunications (DoT) has around 12.2 million subscribers with another 2.1 millions wait listed. Thus an additional 19 millions basic telephone lines would be required to be added in the next five years and another 33 millions in the subsequent five years to meet the expected demand. Department of Telecommunications and Mahanagar Telephone Nigam (MTNL) can put in an additional 10.3 million lines by 2001 and another 19 million lines by 2006 by maintaining a growth rate of 13 per cent through internal resources. The rest of the demand, which should be about 9 million lines by 2001 and an additional 14 million lines by 2006 is actually expected to be of the order of 2 million lines by 2001 and grow to 5 million lines by 2006.

The total funds required by the sector for the provision of basic and cellular mobile telecommunication services by 2006 will be of the order of Rs. 2000 billion. Of this sum, the Department of Telecommunications is expected to invest from internal generation Rs. 900 billion between 2002-2006. The contribution from the private sector is expected to be of the order of 11 billions. Funds would also be required for value added services such as paging, radio trunking, E-mail, VSATs, mobile satellite systems, etc., in addition to funds to set up infrastructure for manufacturing telecommunication equipment. The above requirements need restructuring of DoT, MTNL, Telecommunications Regulation Authority of India (TRAI) and a vision to implement a new telecom policy. The following table which indicates the growth rates of some countries in the telecommunications sector enables a better understanding of the underdeveloped status of telecommuni-cations infrastructure in the developing countries of the world.

Country	*Growth Rate*
Asia Pacific	27 per cent
Latin America	10 per cent
Arab States	09 per cent
India	13 per cent
Malaysia	23 per cent

An advanced telecommunications system would offer a developing country the perfect opportunity to leapfrog the need for development. In order to benefit from this situation, it would be essential to:

— Raise the penetration of and provide access to reliable voice communication connectivity to a larger cross section of the population.
— Satisfy the more demanding audio, video and data communication needs of the business community in all major business centres.
— Make provisions for easy upgradation of networks to meet future communication needs.

NEED FOR DEVELOPMENT OF RURAL TELECOMMUNICATIONS IN INDIA

About 74 per cent of India's population resides in rural areas where the demand for a telephone is yet to pick up. The present rural teledensity is around 2 per thousand compared to 34 for urban areas. To improve the situation, as part of the universal service obligation, the government has decided to provide telephone access to the entire rural population. A mapping of the total land area into 5 km. hexagons was made and it was first revised to set up a telephone line to each of the 360,000 panchayat villages, and later to at least one connection to each village in India by March, 1997. With only 184,890 villages covered by March 1995, about 70 per cent villages still remain uncovered. The need for a massive expansion of telecom services both in terms of switching and transmission requirements cannot but be underscored. This would necessitate an investment of the order of Rs. 30 billions. Department of Telecommunications expects to share this responsibility equally with private operators. Hence, provision of the Village Public Services tender document which was recently floated for privatisation of basic telecom services requires immediate implementation for upgradation of rural telecommunication services in the country.

CONCLUSIONS

The increase in the capacity of the computer and related equipment have encouraged users to think in terms of new applications. Multimedia is one such application. It demands more in terms of processing, storage and communications from the computer system. In addition there has been a tremendous growth in coding techniques, for applications support and system integration of technologies. The overall design and implementation of the inter-networking of telecommunication should be able to provide:

— Carrier technology
— Switching technology
— Protocol technology
— Sensor, coding, and compression technology
— Software technology
— Computation technology, and
— Systems integration technology

The survival and prosperity of India depends on our ability to adopt the new technology of the information age actively and not just welcome it passively. Traditional societies have come under pressure from this exposure and have to cope with changing cultures and life styles. Economic competition has become more intense as national boundaries become more and more irrelevant.

In this scenario an honest effort must be made to harness the new communication technologies to make life better and more meaningful for our people.

Table 21.1
Top 25 Countries in Terms of Total Number of Telephone Lines-1994

Country	*Lines Million*
USA	156.8
Japan	59.9
Germany	39.2
France	31.6
UK	28.4
China	27.2
Italy	24.5
Russia	24.1
Korea (Republic of)	17.7
Canada	16.8
Spain	14.7
Brazil	12.9
Turkey	12.2
India	9.8
Australia	8.6
Taiwan	8.5
Mexico	8.5
Netherlands	7.8
Ukraine	7.8
Sweden	6.0
Poland	5.0
Greece	5.0
Argentina	4.8
Belgium	4.5
Iran	4.3

Table 21.2
Telecom Network Growth in India

(Lines in Millions)

Year	*Working DELs*	*Waiting List*	*Exp Demand*	*Demand for New DELs*
1986	3.17	1.03	4.20	
1987	3.49	1.12	4.61	0.41
1988	3.80	1.29	5.09	0.48
1989	4.17	1.42	5.59	0.50
1990	4.59	1.71	6.30	0.71
1991	5.07	1.96	7.03	0.73
1992	5.81	2.29	8.10	1.07
1993	6.80	2.85	9.65	1.55
1994	8.03	2.50	10.53	0.88
1995	9.80	2.16	11.96	1.43
1996	1.98	2.28	14.26	2.30

Table 21.3
Annual Telecom Growth Rates in India

(Lines in Millions)

Year	*Percentage Annual Growth Rates*		*Teledensity*
	DELs	*Exp. DEM*	
1986	9.2	11.1	0.41
1987	10.1	11.1	0.45
1988	9.0	10.3	0.48
1989	9.6	9.8	0.51
1990	10.2	12.8	0.55
1991	10.6	11.6	0.6
1992	14.5	15.1	0.67
1993	17.0	18.2	0.77
1994	17.9	8.0	0.90
1995	22.0	13.4	1.10
1996	22.2	19.2	1.32

Table 21.4
Percentage Distribution of Telecom Services in Rural and Urban Areas (India)

1995	*Rural*	*Urban*
Population	74 per cent	26 per cent
Teledensity	0.2 per cent	3.4 per cent
No. of Exchanges	84.7 per cent	15.3 per cent
DELs	17.8 per cent	18.2 per cent

Table 21.5
Shift of Demand Over the Years from Metro to Non-Metro Areas in India

Metro Lines As % of All India Lines	*1989*	*1991*	*1993*	*1995*
DELs	33.7 per cent	31.9 per cent	31.2 per cent	29.3 per cent
Waitlist	36.5 per cent	32.8 per cent	25.5 per cent	14.8 per cent
Expressed Demand	39.3 per cent	33.8 per cent	31.3 per cent	27.7 per cent

Table 21.6
Growth Pattern of DoT (India)

(In Rs. Billion)

	1991-92	*1992-93*	*1993-94*	*1994-95*
Telephone Revenues	49.7	62.0	82.1	103.5
Net Income (Rs. Billion)	14.3	20.4	25.5	38.4
Capital Investment	34.0	46.1	55.8	69.9
Employees (Thousands)	373	385	395	405
Main Lines (Millions)	5.8	6.8	8.1	9.8
Metered Call Units	30.6	40.1	46.7	NA
Effective Trunk Calls	206	206	162	NA

22

Media and Environment—A Critical Study

*Sabiha Alam**

In moving environmental problems from the realms of scientific and academic concerns to issues of public debate and concrete policy, the role of the media is unquestionable. If issues like climate change, ozone depletion and loss of tropical forests, nuclear and industrial pollution, hazardous waste disposal, etc., loom large on the global political agenda and public consciousness, media coverage has played an important role. In fact most of us depend on the media to help make sense of the regular deluge of information about environmental hazards, technologies and initiatives. The role of the media as an agent of environmental education and agenda-setting is quite complex and has been a subject of debate ever since the advent of environmental journalism in the early 70s. Television has been the dominant medium through which environmental disasters and activism have been documented. Dramatic footage of the forest fires in Indonesia, smoke-spilling industrial units around the world, oil soaked sea birds struggling in the aftermath of the Gulf War oil spills confront us with disturbing regularity.

No matter how it is viewed, the environmental movement exists as one of the most important social movements of the 20th Century. Perhaps nowhere is the significance of the environment more noticeable than in the mass media. The complex role of the

*Dr. Sabiha Alam is a Lecturer in the Academy of Third World Studies, Jamia Millia Islamia, New Delhi.

media in politico-economic change and environmental degradation cannot be discussed without delving in the environment development debate and the rise of environmentalism in the Third World in some detail.

In the recent decades, two distinctive but interactive processes have severely affected the environment; the depletion of the natural resource base and the increasing appropriation of what is available for the benefit of a few. The rich pollute due to the wasteful overuse of resources and poor degrade the environment by surviving at its expense. At the same time the demand for control and rights over common resources has been the reason for growing discontent and conflict in many countries. The burgeoning world population has further heightened environmental concerns and has given it a new urgency. Over the past twenty years, the content and quality of the debate on environment has been completely transformed. By its volume alone, scientific evidence available on environmental problems commands the attention of governments and public alike.

Environmental degradation in the Third World is a result of several factors. Behind the rising prosperity in the region World lurked a lethal air in pollution from vehicles, industries and hearths causing severe and sometimes fatal respiratory problems. Throughout the developing countries such pollution kills hundreds of thousands of people. Work days lot to respiratory illness run into hundreds and the corresponding economic costs spiral into billions of dollars. What is true for air pollution is true for many other types of environmental emergent damages. Each year, diarrhoea diseases from contaminated water kill about million children and cause 900 million cases of illness, most of which basic sanitation could have prevented. Annual losses from soil erosion range from 0.5 per cent to 1.5 per cent of GNP in many countries, Green House gas emission will double within the span of a generation at the current growth rates. Large scale fertilizer and pesticide use to sustain increased agriculture is another important cause for Third World environmental problems. These problems were once viewed as the price of economic development. Over the last two decades, developing countries have become increasingly aware of the dangers inherent in unchecked and large-scale development projects. They have come to realise that development underscores the need for an institutional transformation that creates incentives for effort, innovation investment and other progressively complex exchanges that span increased distances and time. Improved information and communication is increasingly being recognised as a central factor in them. Development is much more than mere economic growth. It means the development of the society as a whole of and all its institutions economic, social and political.

For this purpose the Western models of development here found to be inadequate to counter challenges faced by Third World countries.

CONCERN FOR THE ENVIRONMENT IN HISTORICAL PERSPECTIVE

Concern for the environment is however not a twentieth century phenomenon. Plato had spoken about deforestation in Attica in the second century B.C. Ref. In India conservation was as much a matter of pragmatic management as spiritualism since the times of The Mahabharata. But through the centuries the matter here acquired alarming proportions. The need for the protection of the environment began to take the shape of a movement in the second half of the nineteenth century as a response to industrial expansion in Europe and America (MC Cornick 1989) concerns about conservation of land, preservation of animals and fish, industrial use of waterways and the public outcry over deaths in America in 1948 were as much part of public debate as it is today. The difference lies in the fact that these protests were local in nature—although similarities existed in the conflicts; the protesters were often middle class reformers, working with power groups within the community. Conflicts were reported in the media and usually a section of the public was informed about it.

The first efforts at international organisation of an environmental movement took place in the 20th Century (Boardman 1981), International environmental politics in fact is a post-war phenomena, took shape largely under the auspices of the United Nations. The United Nations Educational, Scientific and Cultural Organisation (UNESCO) established in 1945 and the International Union for Protection of Nature (IUPN) formed in 1948 played important roles in this process.

The early 60s marked the greatest change in the environmental movement and environmental politics. Rachel Carson's Silent Springs (1960) mobilized public opinion.

Environment moved from being an exclusive academic and scientific concern of conservation groups to the focus of a mass movement that had a profound affect in most parts of the industrialized world. Sharpening the focus on the environment was the growing concern about the potential dangers of a nuclear disaster. Much of it had to do with the influence and popularity of television. According to John Cracknell (1993) environmental stories are media generic. A series of environmental disasters between 1966 and 1972 gave a new dimension to the public concern about the environment. Among these was the coreck of the oil Tanker *Torrey Canyon* in 1967. 8,75,000 barrels of crude oil polluted hundreds of miles of the Cornish coastline. In 1969 an oil platform blowout off the coast of Santa Barbara, California polluted miles of the coastline. A well publicized disaster with direct human implications in Minimata in Japan, increased public sensitivity to environmental issues. Local residents were poisoned as a result of decades of mercury discharges into the ocean. 1,500 people became sick and more than 200 died. One of the reasons for the heightened impact of these disasters was the influence and popularity of television. The growth of television and the green movement across the world is a topic which has to be explored.

Throughout the 1970s a series of United Nations conferences also highlighted major problems that had become global issues—population (Bucharest, 1974), food (Rome 1974); the role and status of women (Mexico City 1975); human settlement (Vancouver 1976); water (Mar del Plata 1977); desertification (Nairobi 1977), primary health care (Alma Ata 1978); world development (New York City 1978) and several Law of the Sea conferences. Although not directly concerned with the environment, they made environmentalists aware of the broad spectrum of developmental problems. The main impacts for linking environment to development emerged in the 1970s with the first UN Conference on Environment and Development in Stockholm in 1972. The conference had been planned to address problems of pollution and resource depletion caused by unprecedented industrial growth in Europe, North America and Japan. It was here that issues like over population and over consumption were discussed and Third World concerns were raised regarding the negative consequences for their development prospects.

The industrialised countries were persuaded to broaden their environmental agenda to include issues of concern to the developing countries such as housing, food scarcity and clean drinking water in contrast to the developed countries concerns like pollution, population explosion, conservation of resources, etc., which were associated at that time with predictions of the collapse of the world economy due to the overexploitation of the world's resources. The most tangible outcome of the Stockholm Conference was, the creation of the UNEP (United Nations Environment Programme). In the decades since the Stockholm conference it has played a vital role as a co-ordinate and policy formulating body. Serious concerns about environmental issues were have been closely and hotly debated, with the media involved.

In the late seventies, the perceived threat to the global resource base seemed to be relegated, as a result of which extensive new oil finds being exploited to reduce the oil price hike by OPEC (Oil producing and Exporting Countries) thus effectively destroying the grouping as a crucial world force.

A second wave of environmentalism was triggered in the mid-eighties by events such as the Bhopal disaster, the Chernobyl nuclear explosion and the Exxon oil spill in Alaska. Global environmental problems such as ozone depletion, climate change, acid rain brought the issue of the environment surging back to global prominence. In addition tensions between development and environment re-emerged. The Brudtland Report of 1987 'Our Common Future' shifted concern over the environment/ development relationship from mainly a developed world focus to one which recognized its effects on local livelihood on all sections of the society. *Sustainable Development* became a familiar phrase and objective in all countries, because by then the most serious problems of non-sustainability and environmental degradation were evident in the Third World countries. The environment had became a Third World issue on global scale. It was within the context of this second wave of environmentalism that the UN General Assembly had called the 1992 Conference on environment and Development, (UNCED) or the Earth Summit held in Rio-DeJaneiro, Brazil. It was the result of nearly two years of preparation. More than 170 nations sent delegates were among those who attended the summit were more than 118 heads of State besides thousands of NGOs, many major industrial corporations and nearly 9,000 members of the media. The media importance of the Earth Summit is discussed hereunder.

Two distinct views were evident in Rio. The view from the

Third World indicated that global problems of climate change, sea-level rise and global warming, primarily because of carbon dioxide, sulphur oxide and CFC emissions in developed countries arising from their living patterns could only be resolved by better management of resource consumption in rich countries. It was also emphasized that this overconsumption was having serious effects on Third World countries and that substantial compensation was required to remedy losses of land and biological productivity. The sentiment was that an environmentally friendly planet was impossible in a world that contained significant inequalities.

By contrast the dominant view from the developed countries was that over-population and excessive deforestation in the Third World was equally important causes of environmental deterioration. Strong policies to curb population growth and over exploitation of resources were needed. It was agreed by most participants at Rio that there was no basic incompatibility between environment and development but the mode of development and its impact on resources needed to be managed in a balanced manner. It was accepted that future development could not proceed without environmental management but management required capital and skills that could be generated only as a result of development. The industrialized countries recognised the connection between environment and development in many of the conference documents and promised some monetary aid but refused to commit to specific steps to reduce their own industrial. They also pressed on the developing countries to protect their forests and wildlife. Recommended new models of development, of gender relationships and of environment and sustainable development demonstrate that in the past 50 years the developing countries have not benefited from economic and political ideologies and theories that were not rooted in their own experiences.

ENVIRONMENTALISM IN INDIA

It is within its broad global scenario that environmentation has taken shape in India. Environment or Media awareness of the need for the projection of the environmental protection of the Taj Mahal from the toxic fumes of the Mathura refinery, is barely 40 kms. away from it, was one of the earliest issues that has focused its attention. The Press Institute of India and the UNEP launched a programme of commissioning and circulating articles on environmental issues.

At the Stockholm Conference, India made its presence felt. The presence of the then Prime Minister, Indira Gandhi among other heads of State made the difference. She captured world attention with her famous comment that "poverty is the greatest polluter." Twenty years later, Indira Gandhi's emphasis on poverty alleviation as the prime concern was reiterated by India at the 1992 Earth Summit. India has maintained a high profile in global environmental issues and has been a strong supporter of the linkage strategy. It is also one of the countries that blocked the formulation of the Forestry Convention in what was perceived as the globalization of India's forest resources.

It was in the sixties that the direction and framework for development began to take shape in India the Five Year Plans set the tone for a mixed economy. Two severe droughts in the mid-sixties caused acute food scarcity with large-scale import of food grains. Self reliance in food production became the primary objective for development. With food shortage fuelling public unrest political changes became pronounced. Agrarian unrest increased continuously throughout the late sixties and problems of rural development moved to centre stage. It was in this period that development journalism began to emerge as an important subject. At the Stockholm Conference environmental problems had not received public attention. As with other spheres of the development process (building of infrastructure, transfer of technology etc.), the environmentalism adopted from the developed countries was coloured by Western concerns. To the masses struggling with food scarcity and problems of survival, environmental concerns seemed elitist. However this early form of environmentalism found acceptability among the urban elite.

Environment and its sustenance began to attract considerable attention by the mid-seventies mainly because of the oil crisis that threatened the base of industrial development that India was striving to attain. Indian environmentalism then took the form of a mass movement, the Chipko agitation, the Silent Valley and the campaign to protect the Taj Mahal from pollution. The movement had a profound impact through the mass media when a national dialogue about air and water pollution emerged. According to Schoenberg (1980) the sixties and seventies environment movement became a mass movement with a greater number of groups involved on a higher level of participation. Mass Communication was again the key. It is important to note that the environmental movement grow at roughly the same time that newspapers and magazines assumed a nature form as agents of social change. The protest movements like the Chipko and the Silent Valley went beyond the object of conservation to address the complex interaction between development and environment.

The Bhopal disaster in 1984 lent an urgency to the environmental movement. Increased academic research on the one hand and media attention on the other, helped to expand the environmental debate. For the first time, theories of development focused on 'basic needs' and the appropriateness for technological choices came in for critical scrutiny. This was also the period when the economic dimensions of the problems of pollution, deforestation, energy consumption and urbanization became the focus in debates of development (MOEF 1990).

Thus from a focus mainly on specific government policies and projects, environmental advocacy has matured from protests against environmental damage to a more holistic focus on the effect of development with environment.

By the time of the Earth Summit in 1992, the concept came to be a dominant factor in the environmental debate in India and environmental issues became subjects of the political economy. In recent years, the focus of the environmental debate has changed from environment planning and management to strong protest movements among people who are the victims of ill-planned and badly managed development programmes. For example, the Sardar Sarover Project was allowed to go forward without proper environmental or engineering appraisals (Rich 1991) at enormous cost in terms of displacement of local population and destruction of the ecosystem. The international movement against the Narmada Dam has become the celebrated symbol of the green cause, the anti-dam campaign has come to symbolize the struggle to alter the course of development.

Media coverage of environmental issues is shaped by the same constraints which govern news work in general: limited production period, limited story length and limited sources Clarke (1992) has grouped these constraints into two general categories: short-term logistical and technological constraints and long-term economic and occupational constraints which are rooted in the news process itself.

Short-term constraints force journalists to place environmental issues within an event orientation. Environmental issues sporadically drawn public attention in the form of some major disaster or international conference. This event orientation according to Dunwoody and Griffin (1997), absolves journalists from attending to the bigger environmental. Three major types of environmental issues can be identified: events (world environment day, the Rio Summit), disasters (oil spills, toxic fires, nuclear accidents) and legal/administrative happenings.

Symbolism is the trademark of milestone events where initiatives trend to be declared without establishing the institutional structures; a good Earth Summit held in Brazil on the twentieth anniversary of the Stockholm Conference. The conference below 118 Heads of the State, representatives of thousands of NGOs, major multinational corporations and nearly 9,000 members of the media and celebrities from the world of politics and entertainment. The symbolism of the occasion has not seen another parallel.

Environmental catastrophes are the lifeline of environmental news coverage. This is despite the fact that both the press and television have limited "carrying capacity" within a time frame and the environment related news wires/items have to compete with other political, economic and crime stories for limited space or airtime, the coverage even then focuses on loss of lives, damaged property, human interest stories like the child found alive after 3 days in rubble or stories of tremendous courage and sacrifice. Environmental fallouts and repercussions often become secondary concerns. Even centred reporting is characteristic of less dramatic and "non-immediate" issues like global warming, ozone depletion and coastal erosion. In order to fit these phenomenon journalists often place them into the 'event' form or as the recent outcome of an event rather than the result of larger developmental issues often ignoring the context within which they occur. For example the Ganga Action Plan is discussed more in terms of the tons of industrial sewage that the river receives. The lax law enforcing and legal instruments that fail to deliver environmental justice are seldom the topic of media attention.

Environmental news coverage also suffers because it does not fit easily into the structure of regular news production. The Indian Press is by and large urban-oriented. Newspapers are mostly concentrated in metropolitan cities and cater to the urban population and only nominally to readers in rural areas. Newspapers are being brought out in approximately 93 languages and dialects. The combined circulation of the Press is several million copies. But nearly 93 per cent of the total sale of daily newspapers is in large towns which account for only 10 per cent of the country's population.

The radio is by far the most extensive network which covers almost the entire country. However on an average there are only 4.4 radio/transistor sets per 100 persons, of the 60 million radio sets 80 per cent are in urban homes leaving only about 6 million sets with 525 million rural population.

In spite of the phenomenal exposure of television, the case of television, of satellite and cable television and of films is the same. On the whole the reach of the mass media is limited specially to those living below the poverty line which constitutes nearly 60 per cent of the total population. The national English news media tends to be organized according to fixed 'beats,' politics is their favourite subject, next comes crime or violence, investigative reporting and social and economic problems come next. This being so, editors and producers often know what to do with stories on the environment. Even those which cater to the rural areas suffer from inadequacies of editorial direction and management. The condition of the Indian language press and small newspapers is not very encouraging. The publisher usually is editor, reporter, clerk and advertisement collector, all rolled into one. To meet expenses, they undertake other printing jobs. The advertisement revenue comes from local businessmen. Though now slowly being equipped with computers and modern printing technology, it runs like a small cottage industry. It is in this struggle for existence that professionalism becomes the victim, along with objectivity. In these conditions small newspapers and local regional newsrooms are less likely to use beats. This has its own problems. General assignment reporters, despite their optimism that they can quickly acquire adequate knowledge about subjects in which they have no background or training are rarely capable of sophisticated reporting such as that demanded by many environmental stories.

When environmental journalism established itself (in 1969-70) in daily newspapers set up an ecology beat. At that time many of the relevant disciplines were very young, ecology was a minor branch of biology, and Indian sociology and social anthropology had barely taken root while the seeds of development journalism had barely been sown. Reporters were recruited from rural affairs, agriculture and science or from general assignments. This is one reason why while the volume of environmental coverage grew, the quality did not always keep pace. A final short-term constraint on environmental reporting is the role and influence of news editors. With one eye always fixed on circulation editors favour stories, which feature controversy and conflict. This many a times results in sensationalization. In addition most newspapers and magazines do not survive by virtue of their cover price but on the strength of advertising revenue. The major advertisers being multinational corporations who again are active in the environment and the Third World. These advertisers cannot afford critical newspaper coverage of their activities and their contribution to the environmental degradation of the developing countries.

In 1985 a public television station WNET lost its corporate funding from the Gulf + Western after the station showed "Hungry for Profit" which contained material critical of multinational corporate activities in the Third World. The Chief Executive of the Gulf + Western complained to WNET that the programme was "virulently anti-business" if not anti-American" and that by carrying the programme the station was clearly not a "friend" of the corporation (Edward 1999). As profit seeking corporations, the media are extremely vulnerable to business pressures of this kind. Reporters know this and on occasion may twist or deliberately overlook significant stories which involve environmental wrong-doing.

Long-term constraints of environmental journalism relate to the factors of "balance" and objectivity. These dual pillars of objective journalism arose during the nineteenth century as part of the sweeping intellectual movement towards scientific detachment and the separation of fact from value (Gitlin 1991), despite periodic lapses, objectivity and balance dominate the media profession. For environmental reporting objectivity implies that journalists take a neutral stance and distance themselves and their readers/viewers from the environmentalist struggle. The major shortcoming in this approach is that reporters are not sufficiently informed to evaluate the scientific objectivity. Alternatively reporters turn to the equal time/space technique whereby both the opponents are quoted with no attempts to resolve who is right. Being objective also means that environmental stories are not expressing the anti-establishment political leans rather opting instead for frames which emphasize conservation and civic responsibility, allowing formalities to subversively faster environmental protest; at the same time appearing to maintain political balance. Thus refraction of the environment through the journalistic prison reduces politically charged issues like global warning or industrial spills to move immediate and mundane domestic and leisure concerns like whether the summer holidays will be as pleasant in the bills as five years ago or the water in the lakes will be fit for swimming on the beaches of Madras.

The Role of the Media in International Environmental Negotiations

On December 2, 1984 tons of methyl isocyanide gas spilled from storage tanker of the Union Carbide factory in Bhopal killing more than 2,000 people overnight and maiming another 12,000. The response from different countries expressed in the media was angry, fearful and confused. Various quantitative estimates appeared about the magnitude of the disaster, reflecting the media's sources of information. The entire disaster had global dimensions. The press in other countries compared the accident to the Hiroshima nuclear tragedy. The media coverage of such environmental disasters is an important factor affecting the negotiations of the resulting disputes and the formation of co-ordinated and acceptable relief and rehabilitation in international policies. The media dominates the avenues of public information; it serves to inform the common man about environment. It also help frame social reality, public consciousness and re-enforce or demolishes existing myths. Media coverage/non-coverage of issues that sets the agenda for negotiations. If there has been a internationalization of the world environment movement since the eighties the media was an important agent, in the numerous efforts to bring governments to negotiating tables to work out legally binding international agreements to deal with transnational environmental problems the important role of the process cannot be denied. Two conventions—the Basel convention dealing with the trade in toxic wastes and the Montreal Protocol dealing with the protection of the ozone layer had media pressure as an important element. The linking of international aid and trade to environmental concerns has an important element of media in it. Although the media did not have a direct input into the negotiation process of the Montreal Protocol, through their continued pressure, they did affect the process and were also instrumental in their support of a technology transfer fund for developing countries. During the course of the negotiations, the Third World participants and all the NGOs increased their leverage through the media. As the negotiations progressed, media coverage increased since there was an increasing public interest in the issue of protecting the world's atmosphere.

The timing, content and tone of media coverage of environmental problems can serve to broaden international perspectives. But they can also cause conflict and evoke a parochial response. Thus the content and style of media coverage is critical to the understanding of international environmental negotiations. The active role of the media in the hazardous waste trade issue helped developing countries acquire a dominant role in the negotiation process. They were able to put the developed countries on the defensive by constantly putting forth the level of illegal wastes being transported from developed to developing countries. Television coverage also underlined the North-South dimension of the problem.

Transnational environmental disputes occur over several types of problems some are the outcome of major disasters such as the Chernobyl accident or oil spills. In such cases the media convey and interpret information of events that are of a broad and immediate public concern. Other disputes are over less dramatic long-term environmental problems. A common problem for most of the Third World countries is the pressure on them to service their international debt. As a result countries over exploit their natural resources (Myers 1980). The conflict between development and environmental protection or between the interests of the developed and developing countries. If the conservation of the tropical rainforests is a global problem, it is necessary to provide the countries technical and financial help that still have the rainforest.

Other disputes over long-term environmental problems requiring remedial action such as acid rain, the depletion of ozone—is more on the public agenda of the developed countries. On all these issues the media can create or limit public interest. In still other cases, the disputed issue involves a specific project—the location of a power plant or dam which may pose a problem for the future. The media can be instrumental in placing such issues on the public agenda. Defining environmental problems become a way of explaining failures of existing social and political relationships. Thus environmental issues are compounded with issue webs (Nelkin 1990). The web of issues influencing international negotiations over environmental problems can be diverse. They include economic and agricultural patterns, industrial domination, water and irrigation supply, levels of modernization. Many environmental problems touch on ethnic, political and ideological biases. For example, the Indian media reports environmental issues as conflicts between environment and development in a structurally unmanageable system whereas the American media tends to report on domestic environmental crisis as problems of corporate or government negligence in a structurally sound system. Thus accidents are blamed on aberrant individuals, sloppy corporate practices or informative decisions and euphemistically labelled "human error" (Nelkin 1990). Whereas in the case of the former the media has been instrumental in generating a serious debate on the deep-seated fundamental problems of industrial growth, development *vis-a-vis* population, bio-diversity and resource depletion in the case of the latter they have been unable to properly address problems in the organisation and regulation of industry, or the imbalance in the allocation of resources that are a cause of the neglect of public safety. However when American journalists reported on the Chernobyl accident they raised systematic questions about centralized control and implications for the Soviet Union. Political consideration shaped the interpretations of the press. Those interpretations can influence negotiating relationships according to the importance of environmental issues.

By their choice of metaphors and visual as well as verbal images they convey certain beliefs about the nature of environmental issues, investing them with social and political meaning. Selective use of adjectives can trivialize an event or render it important, marginalise some groups, empower others, define an issue as a problem or reduce it to a routine matter. Nevertheless the media does establish a framework of expectations that can help to set the goals and the agenda of negotiations. Once covered in the press, isolated events take on meaning as public issues.

The media coverage of the pollution caused by the fumes of the Mathura Oil Refinery to the Taj Mahal alerted the public to the dangers to historic monuments. Once established as a policy issue industrial pollution has been widely reported, not as an isolated event, but as part of a significant industrial problem. The media in fact made the problem visible and set out a context in which related events could be interpreted. The real power of the press comes from "its ability to surround facts by an environment of suggestion, which often subconsciously seeks its way into the mind of the reader and forms his premises for him' (Nelkin 1987).

International awareness of the dangers of nuclear tests came with the 1954 'Board' thermonuclear tests, but the extensive coverage of the Three Mile Island alerted people to the structural context and placed the issue of nuclear power safety on the public agenda. It also generated widespread public concern about the health effects of nuclear testing despite the overwhelming levels of secrecy that prevail in nuclear establishments. Due to extensive media coverage the nuclear debate has acquired international dimensions. This background suggests some ways in which the media can influence negotiations. The decade long debate on the issue of the CTBT in the Indian media is a case in point. The media is responsible for the judgemental biases that underline the position of negotiations and the relationships that develop in the negotiation process (Kalvin 1980).

Trans-border environmental problems are not new, nor are concerns about media communications, but both have assumed new dimensions. Environmental risks have been magnified by new technologies and by the scale of industrial development. At the same time, the impact of the media has also intensified by changes in communication capacity and scale understanding the relationship between media coverage of environmental problems and the process of international negotiation is thus increasingly important to the efforts to define and implement acceptable solutions (Nelkins 1991).

TOWARDS A COMMUNICATION POLICY ON ENVIRONMENT

Most of the media highlights of environmental problems is 'event' centred, important among them being World Environment Day (June 5), World Forestry Day (March 21), the Wild Life Week (October) or the commemorate day of the Bhopal Disaster (December 4). This is a time when there is a spate of articles on environment in the national and regional print media and electronic media, these programmes are rarely evaluated for their impact analysis or quality and content. Carefully planned, and sustained campaign on any subject of environmental management has not yet been attempted by the Indian media. The publicity surrounding the World Environment Day or any other event lacks focus and is sporadic. Similarly focus on environmental protest movements like the Silent Valley, the Narmada Movement or other forms of environmentalism have a quality of chance about them.

There is definitely need to provide the media authentic environmental information (projects, programmes, and scientific information). This does not however imply that the media must subsist on official agencies viewpoints at the cost of its own investigations and analysis, but when much of the basic information regarding natural resources, depletion or pollution is generated by government agencies, there is very little the media can do to communicate on such issues.

An effective media policy has to rest on the obvious considerations that need to be re-emphasized.

- That any attempt at checking the current sharp rate of erosion of environmental resources requires a careful understanding of many complex social, economic, technological and political factors.
- That such an understanding and the preventive, corrective, restrictive or extensive action that ensues can only be based upon a clean perception of overall societal and national interest.
- That such a perception requires most fundamentally, the availability of and access to authentic scientific and developmental information of relevance to environmental considerations.
- That such a perception requires most fundamentally the availability of and access to authentic, scientific and developmental information of relevance to environmental considerations.

The effort to convince has to be more intensive, for what appears right at the planning level is often upset by the reaction of unforeseen socio-economic forces. The mass media strategy for bringing about changes in concepts and attitudes towards the environment overlooks obstacles like poverty, illiteracy and complex socio-economic and cultural factors which exist in India. Most people cannot afford TV sets and few can read newspapers. Messages over the radio most often do not provide answers to problems in the local environmental context. Until the media act locally and until the producers of programmes can understand the ramifications and meaning of the minutest changes in the ecology mass media will remain peripheral to the case of environmental consciousness.

Role of the Media

Environmental journalism emerged as a concept nearby three decades ago as a part of broader canvas of development journalism at a time when science and technology was then making new strides, almost transforming not only economic and technical activities but also important aspects of private life. Initially environmental issues became newsworthy relative to other developments. It was the Stockholm Conference in 1972 which focused specific attention on environmental issues and the Indian media responded to the need. Problems of the common man were given due importance in the national media. But by the eighties environment coverage broke off from development. The emergence of specialized environmental journalism saw a shift towards activism and rhetorical excesses. Environment became a subject which needed no expertise. Thus 'fast food' ecology became a pathway to the perpetuation of myths.

After the energy crisis of the mid-seventies media coverage of the environment began to fall off. Moreover, media stories tended to be event related and problem specific. Simultaneously the media began to define environment largely in terms of anything nuclear (nuclear power, nuclear radiation, nuclear safety and nuclear weapons), in terms of pollution and in terms of conservation/protection. Global aspects of the environmental problems were very rarely highlighted.

As mentioned earlier during the eighties environmental journalism in India took up more of an activities role. In the development of environmental journalism the Indian language press gave an early lead. All the major environmental stories including the build-up of the Chipko Movement in the 1970s, appeared in the regional newspapers. They were then picked up by major Indian newspapers and only considerably later did the information reach the influential English dailies. Of late, an environmental issue appears almost simultaneously in local newspapers, regional dailies and the English news media. This succeeds in securing action from the government agencies, but the value of speedy reportage is undermined when it lacks informed and researched perspective.

References

1 Boardman, R. (1991), *International Organisation and the Conservation of Nature*, The MacMillan Press Ltd., London, p. 228.
2 Clarke, D. (1992), *Constraints of Television News Production*, M. Gernier (ed.) "Critical Studies of Canadian Mass Media," Toronto: Batterworth.
3 Dunwoody, S. & Griffin, R.L. (1993), Journalistic Strategies for Reporting Long-term Environmental Issues: A Case Study of Three Superfund Sites in a Hansen (ed.) *The Mass Media and Environmental Issues,* Leicester University Press.
4 Edwards David (1999), Can We Learn the Truth About the Environment from the Media? *The Ecologist Asia,* Vol. 7(2).
5 Gitlin, J. (1980), *The Whole World is Watching*, University of California Press.
6 Cracknell, J. (1993), Issue Arenas, Pressure Groups and Environmental Agendas in A. Hansen (ed.) *The Mass Media and Environmental Issues,* Leicester University Press.
7 Myers, N. (1986), Economics and Economy in the International Arena: The Phenomena of Linked Linkages, Ambio 15(5): 296-300.
8 Nelkins, D. (1987), "The Culture of Science Journalism Society," 24(6): 17-25.
9 Schnaiberg, A. (1980), *The Environment: From Surplus to Scarcity*, Oxford University Press.

Index